FRENCH AND INDIANS
IN THE HEART OF NORTH
AMERICA, 1630–1815

MAP 1. JACQUES NICOLAS BELLIN, "CARTE DE L'AMERIQUE SEPTENTRIONALE," 1743
SOURCE: LIBRARY AND ARCHIVES CANADA

FRENCH AND INDIANS IN THE HEART OF NORTH AMERICA, 1630–1815

Edited by Robert Englebert
and Guillaume Teasdale

Michigan State University Press   &   University of Manitoba Press

East Lansing   Winnipeg

Copyright © 2013 by Michigan State University

⊚ The paper used in this publication meets the minimum requirements of ANSI/NISO Z39.48-1992 (R 1997) (Permanence of Paper).

 Michigan State University Press
East Lansing, Michigan 48823-5245

Published in Canada by University of Manitoba Press, Winnipeg, Canada, R3T 2N2
www.uofmpress.ca

Printed and bound in the United States of America.

19 18 17 16 15 14 13   1 2 3 4 5 6 7 8 9 10

LIBRARY OF CONGRESS CATALOGING-IN-PUBLICATION DATA

French and Indians in the heart of North America, 1630–1815 / edited by Robert Englebert and Guillaume Teasdale.
    p.   cm.
    Consists mainly of papers concerning the history of French-Indian relations in the colonial Great Lakes region and Mississippi River Valley presented at the annual meeting of the French Colonial Historical Society in 2008.
    Includes bibliographical references and index.
    ISBN 978-1-60917-360-9 (ebook)—ISBN 978-1-61186-074-0 (pbk. : alk. paper)
    1. Middle West—History—Congresses.   2. Middle West—Ethnic relations—Congresses.   3. French—Mississippi River Valley—History—Congresses.   4. Indians of North America—Mississippi River Valley—History—Congresses.   5. French—Great Lakes Region (North America)—History—Congresses.   6. Indians of North America—Great Lakes Region (North America)—History—Congresses.   7. Mississippi River Valley—History—To 1803—Congresses.   8. Great Lakes Region (North America)—History—Congresses.   9. Canada—History—To 1763 (New France)—Congresses.   10. North America—History—Congresses.   I. Englebert, Robert.   II. Teasdale, Guillaume.   III. French Colonial Historical Society.

    F352.F85 2013
    977'.01—dc23   2012028341

LIBRARY AND ARCHIVES CANADA CATALOGUING IN PUBLICATION

French and Indians in the heart of North America, 1630–1815 / edited by Robert Englebert and Guillaume Teasdale.
    Based on papers presented at the annual meeting of the French Colonial Historical Society in 2008.
    Includes bibliographical references and index.
    ISBN 978-0-88755-760-6   1. French—Mississippi River Valley—History.   2. Indians of North America—Mississippi River Valley—History.   3. French—Great Lakes Region (North America)—History.   4. Indians of North America—Great Lakes Region (North America)—History.   5. Middle West—History.   6. Middle West—Ethnic relations.   7. Mississippi River Valley—History—To 1803.   8. Great Lakes Region (North America)—History.   9. Canada—History—To 1763 (New France).   10. North America—History.   I. Englebert, Robert, 1977–   II. Teasdale, Guillaume   III. French Colonial

Book design by Scribe Inc. (www.scribenet.com)
Cover design by Erin Kirk New

Cover map is courtesy of the David Rumsey Historical Map Collection.

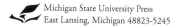 Michigan State University Press is a member of the Green Press Initiative and is committed to developing and encouraging ecologically responsible publishing practices. For more information about the Green Press Initiative and the use of recycled paper in book publishing, please visit www.greenpressinitiative.org.

Visit Michigan State University Press at
www.msupress.org

Contents

Acknowledgments   vii

Introduction by Robert Englebert and Guillaume Teasdale   xi

"*Faire la chaudière*": The Wendat Feast of Souls, 1636

     Kathryn Magee Labelle   1

Natives, Newcomers, and *Nicotiana*: Tobacco in the History of the
Great Lakes Region

     Christopher M. Parsons   21

The Terms of Encounter: Language and Contested Visions of French
Colonization in the Illinois Country, 1673–1702

     Robert Michael Morrissey   43

"Gascon Exaggerations": The Rise of Antoine Laumet dit de Lamothe,
Sieur de Cadillac, the Foundation of Colonial Detroit, and the
Origins of the Fox Wars

     Richard Weyhing   77

"Protection" and "Unequal Alliance": The French Conception of
Sovereignty over Indians in New France

     Gilles Havard   113

The French and the Natchez: A Failed Encounter

     Arnaud Balvay   139

From Subjects to Citizens: Two Pierres and the French Influence on the
Transformation of the Illinois Country

     John Reda   159

Blue Beads, Vermilion, and Scalpers: The Social Economy of the
1810–1812 Astorian Overland Expedition's French
Canadian Voyageurs

Nicole St-Onge   183

Contributors   217

Acknowledgments

When we first began this project, we envisioned a quick and relatively smooth process—famous last words. Such collections usually take longer than anticipated; however, we continue to believe that the works contained within these pages represent a wave of relatively new scholars who are pushing the boundaries of this bourgeoning field. As with any collaborative project, there are many people who provided invaluable assistance in bringing it to fruition. First and foremost, our sincerest gratitude to the contributors of this collection, whose hard work, dedication, and patience made this anthology possible. We would also like to thank Carolyn Podruchny, who provided invaluable counsel during the early preparation of the manuscript, and Jim Miller, Keith Carlson, and Gary Zellar, who all acted as sounding boards as the project approached completion. Finally, we would like to acknowledge the invaluable support of our spouses and families.

*To my parents and my wife, Heather, thank you
for your love, support, and encouragement.*

—ROBERT

*I would like to express my gratitude to my wife, Stacie,
and our two beautiful sons for their continuous support
during the preparation of this anthology.*

—GUILLAUME

Introduction

ROBERT ENGLEBERT AND
GUILLAUME TEASDALE

Scholarship concerning French-Indian relations in the heart of North America has seen a remarkable transformation over the past thirty years. From beyond the pale of historical inquiry, this area of study has gradually emerged as an important field for examining the complex relationships that defined a vast geographical area that for the purposes of this collection has been termed the heart of North America—the Great Lakes region, the Illinois Country, the Missouri River valley, and Upper and Lower Louisiana.[1] The history of French-Indian relations has perhaps most obviously been defined by the historiographical intersection of French colonial history and Indian history. Yet these two historical disciplines have often made for awkward bedfellows, complicated not only by differences between their respective historiographies but also by differences drawn along national historiographical lines.

FROM NATIONAL NARRATIVES TO FRENCH-INDIAN HISTORY

Initially tied to early national grand narratives, French-Indian relations in North America played out quite differently in the United States, Canada, and France. In the United States, French and Indians largely vanished from the historical narrative, masked by notions of Anglo-American exceptionalism and an expanding American frontier.[2] Conversely, in Canada, French-Indian relations became an undeniable aspect of a national grand narrative that grew out of a focus on the westward expansion of the fur trade.[3] And yet while French and Indians were seen as indispensable for understanding the fur trade, they were nonetheless depicted as remarkably predictable and essentialized characters, with little adaptability or motivation beyond subsistence. Constrained by the economic and geographical determinism of an expanding fur trade and the creation of the Canadian nation-state, any discussion of French-Indian relations in the heart of North America has been limited.[4] In France, the history of French-Indian relations was truly beyond the pale—at best a footnote, and at worst left out entirely in a fit of collective imperial amnesia following the traumatic loss of France's colonies in Africa and Southeast Asia.

Of course it is too simplistic to draw solid lines of distinction between different national treatments of French-Indian history. The division was never that stark, even if national grand narratives were, and continue to be, immensely influential.[5] While scholars may not have been able to entirely escape the trappings of national grand narratives, this did not mean that scholars operated in a state of complete isolation from one another. Looking back on his seminal piece of scholarship regarding French-Indian relations in New France, Cornelius Jaenen paid tribute to his early influences, which included American, Canadian, and European scholars. Moreover, he noted that "historical research and writing thrives on intellectual cross-fertilization, i.e., on conversations and exchanges between scholars in cognate fields."[6]

Ethnohistorical investigations of aboriginal societies brought historians, anthropologists, geographers, and archaeologists together in the 1950s and 1960s.[7] This new Indian history dovetailed with the efforts of historians working on French colonial history in the 1970s.[8] The American Society for Ethnohistory (1954), the North American Fur Trade Conference (1965), and the French Colonial Historical Society (1974) were but a few of the organizations and conferences that brought together scholars focusing on French-Indian relations from a number of different disciplines and nationalities.[9] Ultimately, the study of French-Indian relations in the heart of North America owes its early beginnings to this cross-fertilization, characterized by the free flow of scholarship across national borders as well as early attempts at interdisciplinarity.

BORDERS IN HISTORY

Despite the transmission of ideas across national borders, the treatment of French and Indians in North America continued to be hampered by anachronistic adherence to national and regional boundaries in historical research. In a recent essay that examined fur trade historiography, Bethel Saler and Carolyn Podruchny likened the situation to that of a "glass curtain," where academics saw to the other side, but did not cross over.[10] This is a nuanced and salient interpretation precisely because it speaks to the mutual influence of scholars from different nations, even if their studies remained geographically constrained by national borders. Joseph Zitomersky, an American working as a French colonial historian in France, has expressed amazement at the ubiquitous nature of contemporary geopolitics in history and the persistence of national borders in French colonial history.[11] This has been particularly visible in Canada. Allan Greer recently observed that "out of the vast domain claimed by France in North America, Canadian historians have long tended to focus on those portions currently under the Canadian flag."[12] Subsequently, the number of works on French-Indian relations in the heart of North America by English Canadian historians remains quite limited. For example, Kathryn Magee Labelle and Christopher M. Parsons, who authored chapters in this collection, are among a select group of English Canadian historians who have examined French-Indian encounters in the Great Lakes region during the New France era over the last half century.[13] Most work by English Canadian historians has focused on French policy, empire, and trade, with only a cursory discussion of French-Indian relations.[14] However, in the past ten years French-Indian interactions in the interior of the continent during the last decades of the eighteenth century and the first of the nineteenth have generated some interest among English Canadian historians.[15]

Surprisingly, in French Canada, New France historiography has virtually overlooked the history of the French presence in the heart of North America. This is particularly true in Quebec. As Greer remarked, "Francophone Quebec historians frequently limit their studies to an even narrower terrain [than their English Canadian counterparts], that is, to the St. Lawrence Valley between Montreal and the Gaspé Peninsula."[16] In the last two centuries, French Canadian historians have produced only a handful of studies on French-Indian relations in the heart of North America (including works both on the New France era and the post-British conquest decades).[17] Most of them are recent and were produced by historians outside of Quebec, including Nicole St-Onge, who contributed to this collection.[18]

Jean-Marie Fecteau has argued that post–World War II historical scholarship in Quebec has focused almost exclusively on the province of Quebec rather than on the broader history of French North America.[19] The major changes that took place in Quebec society during the 1960s undoubtedly help explain the lack of interest among French Canadian historians in topics that break beyond Quebec's provincial boundaries. French Canadians in Quebec reshaped their collective identity during the 1960s amid the Quiet Revolution, and created a new identity that no longer adhered to the long-standing tenets of a shared language and religion—French and Catholicism—with

French Canadians in other Canadian provinces or the United States. Rather, this new identity focused on a shared language exclusively within the geographical boundaries of their province. French Canadians who did not live in Quebec were altogether left out of this process.[20] This breakup of French Canadian identity led to a radical transformation of collective memory among Québécois.[21] The Quiet Revolution brought positive changes for Quebec society and contributed to spectacular growth in historical scholarship, mainly due to the rapid expansion of francophone academia. However, the inward focus on the province of Quebec meant that important parts of the historical French experience in North America remained beyond the pale of historical inquiry. The history of the French presence in the heart of North America, which had received limited attention until the 1960s, became even less relevant for the vast majority of Québécois over the last half century.[22] This was particularly true for the Illinois Country, which according to French scholar Cécile Vidal, Canadian scholars have largely ignored.[23] American historian Jay Gitlin has offered a somewhat harsher assessment of the way that larger French networks in the heart of North America have been studied: "Balkanized by local historians of the Midwest, ignored by French colonial historians interested primarily in imperial policymaking, and out of view of Canadian historians who tend to focus either on the colonial St. Lawrence Valley or modern Quebec, these French merchants from Detroit to New Orleans have not been seen as a coherent or a relevant group."[24]

In the United States, the study of the French in the heart of North America has seen a slow but steady trickle of scholarship.[25] In the 1980s, historical scholarship focusing on the French in the heart of North America was renewed by a number of scholars focusing on the Illinois Country.[26] A small but dedicated group of scholars have continued to publish studies on the French in the heart of North America, although not always with a focus on French-Indian relations.[27] Carl J. Ekberg has been particularly prolific in the field, examining French land settlement patterns, French and Indian relations, and Indian slavery. American historians have certainly been active in researching the history of the French in the heart of North America, but this literature can at times seem disjointed and disconnected from Canadian and French historiography. Some scholars, such as Ekberg and Margaret K. Brown, have gone back to the original French sources and have even published translations of texts.[28] And yet for many scholars, there is a heavy reliance on translated texts and manuscripts that can at times be problematic. Languages, be they French, English, or Indian, create obstacles to the desired interplay of historiographical influences across regional and national lines.[29] This is particularly true for the study of French and Indians in the heart of North America, where scholarship is published in French by French and French Canadian scholars, and published in English by English Canadian and American scholars. Of course there is some overlap. A few French and French Canadians write in English to reach a larger audience, and works are regularly translated from one language to the other, although it can take years before a translated copy becomes available. In a discipline where national grand narratives and national and regional boundaries work to dissuade the cross-fertilization of ideas and dialogue, languages often only help in putting up more walls.[30] Though many American studies make reference to Canada, Quebec, and the St. Lawrence valley, few give the extended attention necessary to contextualize these references, particularly for French history after 1763.[31] As Colin G. Calloway has so poignantly explained, "French presence and experiences in the West make little sense without considering events in Canada, notably, tracing Franco-Indian relations through Huronia."[32]

If bridging the gap between Canadian and American scholarship has its issues, then tying them to scholarship across the Atlantic would appear to be even more problematic. In France, the history of French-Indian relations in the heart of North America has received very limited attention, but for different reasons than in French Canada. During the first half of the nineteenth century, French historians had little interest in the French experience in North America. According to Joseph Zitomersky, this was largely due to the fact that France's colonial enterprise in North America—during the First French Empire—had occurred before the French Revolution, prior to the development of France's national identity.[33] In 1831, while in Canada, Alexis de Tocqueville wondered how France had forgotten almost everything about its former New France colony. He admitted that before visiting Lower Canada (Quebec), he himself, probably like most of his fellow French citizens, believed that its French population had culturally vanished shortly after the British conquest.[34] The rise of the Second French Empire during the following decades stirred up a new interest for the study of France's colonial past in North America.[35] However, as Gilles Havard and Cécile Vidal have noted, "with the traumas that accompanied the [Second] French empire's collapse [in the 1950s] came a long bout of collective amnesia," and France's former imperial presence in North America was forgotten again until the late 1980s.[36] Since then, Havard, who contributed to this collection, has played a significant role in promoting New France history in France through numerous publications on French-Indian relations in the heart of North America.[37] Arnaud Balvay, another contributor to this anthology, is also part of this growing movement in France that emphasizes the interactions between French and Indians from the Great Lakes region to the Mississippi River valley.[38] Though French scholars have made significant contributions to the history of French and Indians in the heart of North America over the last few years, only those works that have been translated into English seem to have captured a wider Anglophone audience.

FRENCH AND INDIANS IN THE HEART OF NORTH AMERICA AND THE EMERGENCE OF THE MIDDLE GROUND

Understanding the intricacies of the world that was created through native-newcomer interaction came to define the study of French and Indians in the heart of North America, and no one better represented this new scholarship than Jacqueline Peterson and Richard White. For Jacqueline Peterson, this was a world defined by miscegenation, which resulted in the Great Lakes métis and represented a precursor to the emergence of the Red River Métis in the Canadian Northwest.[39] Building on some of Peterson's work, White broadened out beyond those of mixed descent and focused on the inventive process of cultural encounters in the Great Lakes region, where French and Indians forged new ways of interacting with one another through creative misunderstandings and cultural accommodations.[40] He described this new world as a middle ground that grew out of a precarious balance of power between French and Algonquian, writing:

> The middle ground depended on the inability of both sides to gain their ends through force. The middle ground grew according to the need of people to find a means, other than force, to gain the cooperation or consent of foreigners. To succeed, those who operated on the middle ground had, of necessity, to attempt to understand the world and the reasoning of others and to assimilate enough of that reasoning to put it to their own purposes.[41]

Richard White's *The Middle Ground* was paradigm altering, bringing together the political and commercial focus that had been so prevalent in French colonial history, with the ethnohistorical emphasis on culture that had become a salient feature of the new Indian history. It highlighted the fact that French and Indians could not be studied in isolation in the heart of North America and gave a language to the process and outcome of encounters.[42] Jacqueline Peterson and Richard White helped set the foundation for the study of French and Indians in the heart of North America, and they inspired new scholars to expand upon and question their ideas and concepts.

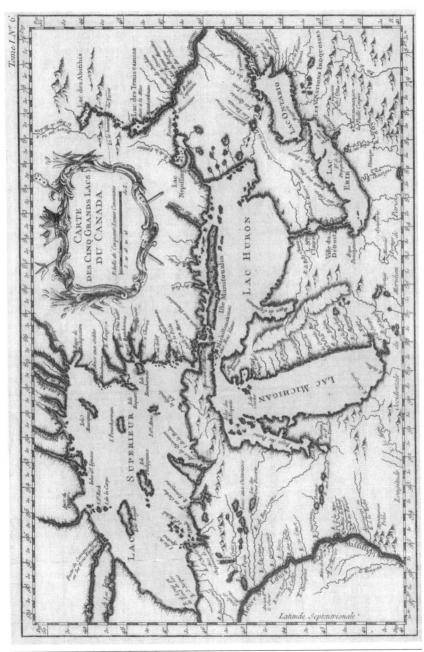

Map 2. Jacques Nicolas Bellin, "Carte des cinq grands lacs du Canada," 1764
Source: Library and Archives Canada

Scholars such as Kathleen DuVal and Alan Taylor tested the limits of the middle ground, both geographically and chronologically. DuVal's *The Native Ground* scrutinized the premise that Indians wanted to create middle grounds with Europeans through a historical examination of the Arkansas River valley. She argued that "in reality, only relatively weak people desired the kind of compromises inherent in a middle ground," and contended that larger and more cohesive Indian nations in the Arkansas River valley created a different environment where Indians were able to retain their sovereignty throughout the colonial period.[43] The result was not a middle ground, but rather a native ground, claimed by Indians, French, and later Anglo-Americans. DuVal's *The Native Ground* provides a stark contrast to Richard White's work and shows the geographical and cultural limitations of the middle ground concept. Just like DuVal, Alan Taylor played on White's well-recognized title for his book, *The Divided Ground*. Taylor's work focused on the post-Revolutionary period, when the Iroquois Six Nations of New York and Upper Canada faced an onslaught of Anglo-American settlers and a radical reorganization and redistribution of land.[44] Taylor's study exposes the chronological limitation of the middle ground by focusing on the post-Revolutionary period characterized by a strongly imbalanced power dynamic between Europeans and Indians. It also makes a clear distinction between the experience of the Iroquois Six Nations in the East and the Algonquian nations of the Great Lakes region, thereby setting and reinforcing the geographical boundaries of the middle ground.

In 2006, a special issue of the *William and Mary Quarterly* focused squarely on *The Middle Ground*, applauding its significant contribution while testing some of its primary assertions. For instance, Brett Rushforth's article, "Slavery, the Fox Wars, and the Limits of Alliance," demonstrated how France's Algonquian allies supplied the French with Fox slaves and then used the issue of French-held slaves in order to undermine French-Fox relations.[45] By examining a case where France's Algonquian allies were able to dictate the terms of alliance and force the French into uncomfortable accommodations, Rushforth's article calls for a reassessment of the power dynamics upon which Richard White's middle ground rests.

Another example is Heidi Bohaker's article from the same *William and Mary Quarterly* forum, where she used an ethnohistorical examination of Algonquian peoples as a way of deconstructing the essentializing notion of French-Indian alliance. Bohaker questioned the fractured state and dislocation of the Algonquian nations in the mid-seventeenth century and their motivation for an alliance with the French.[46] She argued that individual relationships drove the alliance process and that this has been mistakenly extended to all French and Algonquian.[47]

Bohaker's work speaks to the multiplicity of experiences involving French and Indians, and that not all encounters were uniform. Of course there is a tendency to oversimplify White's arguments, and Philip J. Deloria's contribution to that same forum warned of the inherent danger of reducing White's arguments and simply using the middle ground as a metaphor that is largely devoid of nuance and complexity.[48]

REVISITING FRENCH-INDIAN RELATIONS IN THE HEART OF NORTH AMERICA

This book is about trying to capture the complexity and nuance of French-Indian relations in the heart of North America from 1630 to 1815. In early 2008, a call for papers was made concerning the history of French-Indian relations in the colonial Great Lakes region and Mississippi River valley for the annual meeting of the French Colonial Historical Society. As a result, more than twenty scholars from the United States, Canada, and France met in Quebec City a few months later to present their research. Particularly exciting was the fact that these panels consisted of both established academics and a bourgeoning new group of young scholars. Throughout the meeting, there was also a growing awareness of the new directions in scholarship.

This collection of essays is very much about trying to capture that sentiment and present these new ideas to a wider audience. However, the eight chapters that make up this book are not just a collection of conference proceedings. The papers presented at the meeting and selected for this anthology have been considerably expanded and reworked. In addition, a number of new essays have been added to the collection since the conference. Together, they make a significant contribution to the history of French-Indian relations in the Great Lakes region, the Mississippi River valley (the Illinois Country, and Upper and Lower Louisiana), and the Missouri River valley— the heart of North America.

One of the aims of this collection is to examine the complexity and multiplicity of French-Indian encounters in the heart of North America that did not focus specifically on métissage and mixed-descent peoples. Part of the rationale for this decision was that there are a number of excellent studies addressing this aspect of French-Indian history. Influenced by

MAP 3. HEART OF NORTH AMERICA
SOURCE: E. WHITE

Peterson's emphasis on peoples of mixed French-Indian descent, and framed in the context of White's middle ground, scholars such as Tanis Thorne, Lucy Murphy, Susan Sleeper-Smith, and, more recently, Karen L. Marrero have made a compelling case for the salience of kinship connections and networks of a mixed-descent population in the heart of North America.[49] And yet the emphasis on unions between French men and Indian woman at times appears to overshadow the broader array of relations and encounters. In Jay Gitlin's recent book on French merchant families in the heart of

North America, he noted, "Although we may view cross-cultural partners and métis men and women as inhabitants of a literal middle ground, French and Indian places remained distinct. But they were connected by a variety of bridges—primarily economic and linguistic, but also religious and social. For me, the idea of bridges comes closer to capturing the essence of this French and Indian world."[50] This book can therefore be seen as an examination of the successes and failures of the bridge-building process that defined the French and Indian world.

In moving beyond the paradigms of the middle ground and métissage, this collection addresses a number of thematic areas in order to provide a broad assessment of the historical bridge-building process, including ritual interactions, transatlantic connections, diplomatic relations, and post–New France French-Indian relations. The first six chapters of this book focus on French-Indian relations in the heart of North America during the New France era. In *"Faire la chaudière,"* Kathryn Magee Labelle examines the significance of the Feast of Souls for early seventeenth-century Wendat who then lived near Georgian Bay, in present-day Ontario. She discusses their attempt to incorporate the French into this cultural practice in order to better cope with the difficulties of the time. The Jesuit refusal to have the bones of French buried alongside Wendat almost resulted in a complete breakdown of the French-Wendat alliance. Magee Labelle's article is a reminder that all too often encounters failed when creative misunderstandings did not materialize and lead to a middle ground. For Wendat, the ceremony was an inseparable combination of religious and diplomatic spheres, while for the Jesuits these spheres remained far more distinct. The result of this misunderstanding was degraded diplomatic ties between the French and Wendat.

Christopher M. Parsons's "Natives, Newcomers, and *Nicotiana*" offers a new interpretation of the custom of consuming tobacco in French-Indian encounters throughout the Great Lakes region during the seventeenth and eighteenth centuries. Parsons provides examples of how creative misunderstandings regarding the consumption of tobacco facilitated French-Indian encounters and led to a bridge between worlds. According to Parsons, French understandings of tobacco changed over time to focus on the act of smoking rather than the plant, whereas Indian understandings of tobacco were about the plant itself and using it in various sacrificial measures to connect with other-than-human beings. Despite these different understandings of tobacco, the plant was used effectively to create a bridge between French and Indian worlds. Both Magee Labelle and Parsons use an ethnohistorical approach that aims to improve our understanding of French-Indian contacts in the context of specific Indian rituals from the natives' perspective.

The contributions of Robert Michael Morrissey, Richard Weyhing, and Gilles Havard all delve into the transatlantic connections, ideas, and influences that came to bear on the French and Indian world in the heart of North America. In "The Terms of Encounter," Morrissey explores the early French missionary efforts in the Illinois Country during the last decades of the seventeenth century. His article sheds light on the tensions that existed between the Jesuits and other French Catholic orders regarding strategies to convert indigenous populations. These tensions reverberated throughout the French Atlantic world and became a defining aspect of French-Indian relations in the Illinois Country. Weyhing's "Gascon Exaggerations" also looks at French-Indian interactions in the heart of North America through a transatlantic perspective, and examines the circumstances under which Antoine Laumet dit de Lamothe, Sieur de Cadillac convinced French authorities to establish a new colony at Detroit and attempted to gather Indian nations there at the turn of the eighteenth century. Weyhing argues that French transatlantic ventures depended upon military entrepreneurs like Cadillac, even though his personal aspirations exacerbated existing conflicts between Indian nations and ultimately undermined French imperial interests. In "Protection and Unequal Alliance," Havard discusses the status of Indians in North America as conceived by the French monarchy throughout the New France era. Havard examines French discourses regarding Indians from the idea of Indians as French subjects under a policy of *francisation* to that of French protection of Indians under French-Indian alliance; such a transition increasingly placed Indians outside of French understandings of citizenry and more firmly in relationships of inequality and subjugation implicit in French notions of alliance.

In "The French and the Natchez," Arnaud Balvay addresses French-Indian diplomatic relations in the lower Mississippi valley during the first half of the eighteenth century. Balvay's article examines the events leading up to the Natchez Rebellion, portraying French-Natchez relations as a failed encounter. Carefully reviewing events, and various French rumors and speculations of Indian attack, Balvay argues that the French reacted violently out of a position of fear and weakness at the once-strong Natchez nation, which had been weakened from within by competing French and English factions.

The last two chapters of this book emphasize the continuity of French-Indian relations in the heart of North America after the end of the New France era. In "From Subjects to Citizens," John Reda examines the careers of Pierre Chouteau and Pierre Menard, two French colonials deeply involved in the fur trade who played determinant roles in the American transformation of the Illinois Country at the turn of the nineteenth century. Nicole

St-Onge's "Blue Beads, Vermilion, and Scalpers" contributes to our knowledge of the voyageurs' world by analyzing the socioeconomic behaviors of the French Canadians who took part in the Astoria overland expedition, which departed from Montreal in 1810 and aimed at crossing the entire continent via Michilimackinac and St. Louis to reach the Pacific Coast. St-Onge's systematic analysis of voyageur spending patterns reveals a far more calculated agenda than regularly depicted in the historical literature. Voyageurs thought strategically about their ambitions, their families, and their long-term goals, and not simply about encounters with Indian women. Reda and St-Onge place French merchants, Indian agents, and voyageurs at the center of the opening and early development of the American West and stretch our notions of French North America well beyond the end of New France.

The book as a whole brings together both new and established scholars from Canada, the United States, and France—a worthwhile goal in and of itself. And yet what this collection hopes to achieve is to rethink some of the underlying tenets of Richard White's middle ground concept and at the same time demonstrate the rich variety of French-Indian encounters that defined French and Indians in the heart of North America.

NOTES

1. The decision not to include studies of French-Indian relations in the St. Lawrence River valley in this collection was a conscious one. Given the heavy focus on French-Indian relations in the St. Lawrence River valley and adjoining regions, especially by Quebec anthropologists and historians (see, for instance, the many articles on this topic published in the journal *Recherches amérindiennes au Québec* over the last forty years, as well as works published in *Revue d'histoire de l'Amérique française*), it was decided that the essays in this collection would focus primarily on the heart of North America, broadly defined. However, it is both impractical and inappropriate to avoid the St. Lawrence completely, and whether it is Quebec City as an administrative center or Montreal as a fur trade center, the St. Lawrence River valley continues to loom large and shows up regularly in these essays.

2. Much has been written on the early influences of Francis Parkman and Frederick Jackson Turner on removing French and Indians from the American grand narrative. For early critiques of Parkman and Turner, see Francis Jennings, "A Vanishing Indian: Francis Parkman versus His Sources," *Pennsylvania Magazine of History and Biography* 87 (July 1963): 306–323; Robert

Shulman, "Parkman's Indians and American Violence," *Massachusetts Review* 12 (Spring 1971): 221–239; George Wilson Pierson, "American Historians and the Frontier Hypothesis in 1941 (I)," *Wisconsin Magazine of History* 26, no. 1 (1942): 36–60; George Wilson Pierson, "American Historians and the Frontier Hypothesis in 1941 (II)," *Wisconsin Magazine of History* 26, no. 2 (1942): 170–185; John Francis McDermott, ed., *The Frontier Re-examined* (Urbana: University of Illinois Press, 1967). One of the best books regarding the history of the frontier in relation to Indian history is Kerwin Lee Klein, *Frontiers of Historical Imagination: Narrating the European Conquest of Native America, 1890–1990* (Berkeley: University of California Press, 1997). For one of the more recent critiques of Parkman and Turner, see Jay Gitlin, *The Bourgeois Frontier: French Towns, French Traders & American Expansion* (New Haven, Conn.: Yale University Press, 2010), 3. Despite a large body of literature critiquing Parkman and Turner, notions of backward French and Indians, devoid of agency, continue to circulate. See Daniel Royot, *Divided Loyalties in a Doomed Empire: The French in the West from New France to the Lewis and Clark Expedition* (Newark: University of Delaware Press, 2007), 215. Royot cites Francis Parkman in his bibliography, but does not list Turner despite mentioning him on page 105.

3. Elizabeth Jameson and Jeremy Mouat, "Telling Differences: The Forty-Ninth Parallel and Historiographies of the West and Nation," *Pacific Historical Review* 75 (May 2006): 190; George F. G. Stanley, "Western Canada and the Frontier Thesis," *Report of the Annual Meeting of the Canadian Historical Association/Rapports annuels de la Société historique du Canada* 19, no. 1 (1940): 105–117; J. M. S. Careless, "Frontierism, Metropolitanism, and Canadian History," *Canadian Historical Review* 35, no. 1 (1954): 1–21; E. E. Rich, "Trade Habits and Economic Motivation among the Indians of North America," *Canadian Journal of Economics and Political Science/Revue canadienne d'économique et de science politique* 26 (February 1960): 35–53.

4. Harold A. Innis, *The Fur Trade in Canada,* revised ed. (Toronto: University of Toronto Press, 1999); Donald Creighton, *The Commercial Empire of the St. Lawrence, 1760–1850* (New Haven, Conn.: Yale University Press, 1937). Innis and later Creighton are generally credited with setting the foundation for the Canadian historical grand narrative. Both had elements of environmental determinism in their works, but Creighton's Laurentian Thesis took it to an extreme, largely removing human agency from the story of the St. Lawrence. Thus French, and to a great extent Indians, had a role in the part of the national grand narrative pertaining to the fur trade, but were noticeably absent from the modern story of Canada.

5. Klein, *Frontiers of Historical Imagination,* 5.

6. Cornelius J. Jaenen, "Friend and Foe Revisited," *French Colonial History* 12 (2011): 2. Jaenen specifically mentions Wilcomb Washburn, James Axtell, Bruce Trigger, James Ronda, Calvin Martin, Gordon Day, Louise Dechêne, Marcel Delafosse, and Gabriel Debien.

7. Perhaps one of the most detailed historiographical essays on Indian history is Philip J. Deloria, "Historiography," in *A Companion to American Indian History*, ed. Philip J. Deloria and Neal Salisbury (Oxford: Blackwell, 2004), 8. See also Roger L. Nichols, ed., *The American Indian Past and Present*, 6th ed. (Norman: University of Oklahoma Press, 2008).

8. For works that increasingly focused on the intersection of French colonial and Indian history in the 1970s and early 1980s, see C. E. Heidenreich, *Huronia: A History and Geography of the Huron Indians, 1600–1650* (Toronto: University of Toronto Press, 1971); Cornelius Jaenen, *Friend and Foe: Aspects of French Amerindian Cultural Contact in the Sixteenth and Seventeenth Centuries* (Toronto: University of Toronto Press, 1976); Olive P. Dickason, *The Myth of the Savage and the Beginnings of French Colonialism in the Americas* (Edmonton: University of Alberta Press, 1984); Bruce G. Trigger, *Natives and Newcomers: Canada's "Heroic Age" Reconsidered* (Montreal and Kingston: McGill-Queen's University Press, 1985).

9. Ethnohistory came from combining anthropology's ethnological methods with history's approaches to documentary records, which were initially understood as written sources (books and manuscripts), but now includes a wide array of evidence, including, but not limited to, oral accounts, paintings, and maps. The American Society for Ethnohistory was founded in 1954 and holds an annual conference and publishes the journal *Ethnohistory*. See chapter 2, "Ethnohistory: An Historian's Viewpoint," in James Axtell, *The European and the Indian: Essays in the Ethnohistory of Colonial North America* (Oxford: Oxford University Press, 1981), 3–15. The North American Fur Trade Conference began in 1965 in St. Paul, Minnesota. Taking place approximately every five years, it has been held in both the United States and Canada and has a history of publishing its proceedings. The French Colonial Historical Society was founded in 1974 and has been holding its annual conference in the United States, Canada, France, and other locations relevant to French colonial history around the world since 1975. It also publishes the journal *French Colonial History*.

10. Bethel Saler and Carolyn Podruchny, "Glass Curtains and Storied Landscapes: Fur Trade Historiography in Canada and the United States," in *Bridging National Borders in North America: Transnational and Comparative Histories*, ed. Andrew Graybill and Benjamin Johnson (Durham, N.C.: Duke University Press, 2010), 275–302.

11. Joseph Zitomersky, "Ville, état, implantation et société en Louisiane française: la variante 'mississipienne' du modèle colonial français en Amérique du Nord," in *Colonies, territoires, sociétés: l'enjeu français*, ed. Alain Saussol and Joseph Zitomersky (Paris: L'Harmattan, 1996), 23.

12. Allan Greer, "Comparisons: New France," in *Blackwell Companion to Colonial American History*, ed. Daniel Vickers (Oxford: Blackwell, 2003), 698.

13. In addition to their chapters in this collection, see also Kathryn Magee Labelle, "Dispersed but Not Destroyed: Leadership, Women and Power in the Wendat Diaspora, 1600–1701" (Ph.D. diss., Ohio State University, 2011); Christopher M. Parsons, "Plants and Peoples: French and Indigenous Botanical Knowledges in Colonial North America, 1600–1760" (Ph.D. diss., University of Toronto, 2011).

14. William J. Eccles, *France in America* (New York: Harper & Row, 1972); William J. Eccles, *The Canadian Frontier* (Albuquerque: University of New Mexico Press, 1983); William J. Eccles, "The Fur Trade and Eighteenth Century Imperialism," *William and Mary Quarterly*, 3rd series, 40 (July 1983): 341–362; Dale Miquelon, *New France, 1701–1744: A Supplement to Europe* (Toronto: McClelland and Stewart, 1987).

15. See, for instance, Heather Devine, *The People Who Own Themselves: Aboriginal Ethnogenesis in a Canadian Family, 1660–1900* (Calgary: University of Calgary Press, 2004); Carolyn Podruchny, *Making the Voyageur World: Travelers and Traders in the North American Fur Trade* (Lincoln: University of Nebraska Press, 2006).

16. Greer, "Comparisons," 698. See also Allan Greer, *La Nouvelle-France et le monde*, trans. Hélène Paré (Montreal: Éditions du Boréal, 2009), 62; Allan Greer, "National, Transnational, and Hypernational Historiographies: New France Meets Early American History," *Canadian Historical Review* 91 (December 2010): 709.

17. This is not to say that historians in Quebec have not examined the issue of French-Indian relations, but rather that most have given the heart of North America cursory treatment. For French-Indian relations within present-day Quebec, see the works of Denys Delâge and Alain Beaulieu. In particular, Denys Delâge, *Le Pays reversé: Amérindiens et Européens en Amérique du Nord-Est (1600–1664)* (Montreal: Éditions du Boréal Express, 1985); Denys Delâge, *Bitter Feast: Amerindians and Europeans in Northeastern North America, 1600–64*, trans. Jane Brierley (Vancouver: University of British Columbia Press, 1993); Alain Beaulieu, *Convertir les fils de Caïn: Jésuites et Amérindiens nomades en Nouvelle-France, 1632–1642* (Quebec: Nuit Blanche, 1994); Alain Beaulieu, *Les Autochtones du Québec* (Montreal: Fides, 1997). See also Catherine Desbarats, "The Cost of Early Canada's Native Alliances: Reality

and Scarcity's Rhetoric," *William and Mary Quarterly,* 3rd series, 52 (October 1995): 609–630.

18. Nicole St-Onge, "The Persistence of Travel and Trade: St. Lawrence River Valley French Engagés and the American Fur Company, 1818–1840," *Michigan Historical Review* 34 (Fall 2008): 17–37. In 2004, the Voyageur Contract Database Project was launched as one of several interrelated research projects undertaken by the Métis National Council Research Team, under the direction of Nicole St-Onge (director) and Robert Englebert (assistant director). Stemming from the early work of the late Alfred Fortier at St-Boniface Historical Society and hosted online with the help of Gilles Lesage through the Historical Society's website, the online database comprises approximately 35,000 contracts signed by Montreal notaries between 1714 and 1840, including thousands of contracts for voyageurs from the St. Lawrence valley who traveled to the heart of North America. The online version of the VCD is hosted by the *Centre du Patrimoine* (Saint-Boniface, M.B.) server: http://shsb.mb.ca/engagements_voyageurs.

   Guillaume Teasdale is another French Canadian historian working in Ontario who has examined the history of the French in the heart of North America (more specifically in the Great Lakes region) and their relations with Indians. See Guillaume Teasdale, "Les débuts de l'Église catholique américaine et le monde atlantique français: le cas de l'ancienne colonie française de Détroit," *Histoire & Missions chrétiennes* 17 (March 2011): 35–58; Guillaume Teasdale, "The French of Orchard Country: Territory, Landscape, and Ethnicity in the Detroit River Region, 1680s-1810s" (Ph.D. diss., York University, 2010); Guillaume Teasdale, "Des destinées distinctes: les Français de la région de la rivière Détroit et leurs voisins amérindiens, 1763–1815," *Recherches amérindiennes au Québec* 39, nos. 1–2 (2009): 23–45.

19. Jean-Marie Fecteau, "Deux ou trois choses que je sais d'elle . . . Une 'autre' histoire du Québec?," *Canadian Issues/Thèmes Canadiens: Quelle histoire pour quel avenir? Whose History for Whose Future?* (Fall 2008): 15. See also Thomas Wien, "Introduction: Nouvelle-France–Amérique française," in *De Québec à l'Amérique française: histoire et mémoire,* ed. Thomas Wien, Cécile Vidal, and Yves Frenette (Quebec: Presses de l'Université Laval, 2006), 4, 15.

20. On the breakup of French Canada into separate francophone identities within Canada and North America, see Marcel Martel, *Le deuil d'un pays imaginé: rêves, luttes et déroute du Canada français* (Ottawa: Presses de l'Université d'Ottawa, 1997) or *French Canada: An Account of its Creation and Break-Up, 1850–1967* (Ottawa: Canadian Historical Association, 1998). See also Yves Frenette, *Brève histoire des Canadiens français* (Montreal: Éditions du Boréal,

1998); Fernand Dumont, "Essor et déclin du Canada français," *Recherches sociographiques* 38, no. 3 (1997): 419–467.

21. Jocelyn Létourneau, *A History for the Future: Rewriting Memory and Identity in Quebec*, trans. Phyllis Aronoff and Howard Scott (Montreal and Kingston: McGill-Queen's University Press, 2004); Jocelyn Létourneau, *Passer à l'avenir: histoire, mémoire, identité dans le Québec d'aujourd'hui* (Montreal: Éditions du Boréal, 2000).

22. Few exceptions of works written by Québécois on the history of the French presence in the heart of North America include Rénald Lessard, Jacques Mathieu, and Lina Gouger, "Peuplement colonisateur au Pays des Illinois," in *Proceedings of the Annual Meeting of the French Colonial Historical Society, Ste. Genevieve 1986*, ed. Philip P. Boucher and Serge Courville (Lanham, Md.: University Press of America, 1988), 57–68; Michel Chaloult, *Les "Canadiens" de l'expédition Lewis et Clark, 1804–1806: la traversée d'un continent* (Sillery, Q.C.: Éditions du Septentrion, 2003); Denis Vaugeois, *America: l'expédition de Lewis et Clark et la naissance d'une nouvelle puissance, 1803–1853* (Sillery, Q.C.: Éditions du Septentrion, 2002); and Lina Gouger, "Le peuplement colonisateur de Détroit, 1701–1765" (Ph.D. diss., Université Laval, 2002). French journal accounts of expeditions in the heart of North America have also been published in Quebec. See Jean-Baptiste Trudeau, *Voyage sur le Haut-Missouri, 1794–1796*, ed. Fernand Grenier and Nilma Saint-Gelais (Sillery, Q.C.: Éditions du Septentrion, 2006); Charles-André Barthe, *Incursion dans le Détroit: journaille commansé le 29 octobre 1765 pour le voyage que je fais au mis a mis*, ed. France Martineau and Marcel Bénéteau (Quebec: Presses de l'Université Laval, 2010). However, it should be noted that the editors of the latter journey account do not work in Quebec, but in Ontario.

23. Cécile Vidal, "Le Pays des Illinois, six villages français au coeur de l'Amérique du Nord, 1699–1765," in Wien, Vidal, and Frenette, *De Québec à l'Amérique française*, 127.

24. Jay Gitlin, "Negotiating the Course of Empire: The French Bourgeois Frontier and the Emergence of Mid-America, 1763–1863" (Ph.D. diss., Yale University, 2002), 19.

25. For early works on the French in the heart of North America, see Nehemiah Matson, *French and Indians of the Illinois River* (Princeton, Ill.: Republican Job Printing Establishment, 1874); Clarence Edwin Carter, *Great Britain and the Illinois Country, 1763–1774* (Washington. D.C.: American Historical Association, 1910); Louise Phelps Kellogg, *The French Régime in Wisconsin and the Northwest* (Madison: State Historical Society of Wisconsin, 1925); Clarence W. Alvord, *The Illinois Country 1673–1818*, vol. 1 of *The Sesquicentennial History of Illinois* (1920; repr., Urbana: University of Illinois Press,

1987); J. M. Carrière, "Life and Customs in the French Villages of the Old Illinois Country, 1736–1939," *Canadian Historical Association, Historical Reports* (1939): 34–47; Natalia Maree Belting, *Kaskaskia under the French Regime* (Urbana: University of Illinois Press, 1948).

26. A helpful historiographical essay on the Illinois Country is Vidal, "Le Pays des Illinois." In it Vidal details the rise in the 1980s of Margaret K. Brown, Carl Ekberg, and Winstanley Briggs. See Winstanley Briggs, "The Forgotten Colony: Le Pays des Illinois" (Ph.D. diss., University of Chicago, 1985); Margaret K. Brown, "La colonisation française de l'Illinois: une réevaluation," *Revue d'histoire de l'Amérique française* 39 (Spring 1986): 583–591; Carl J. Ekberg, *Colonial Ste. Genevieve: An Adventure on the Mississippi Frontier* (Gerald, Mo.: Patrice Press, 1985).

27. Joseph L. Peyser, *Jacques Legardeur de Saint-Pierre: Officer, Gentleman, Entrepreneur* (East Lansing: Michigan State University Press, 1996); Roger M. Carpenter, *Renewed, the Destroyed, and the Remade: The Three Thought Worlds of the Iroquois and the Huron, 1609–1650* (East Lansing: Michigan State University Press, 2004); Susan C. Boyle, "Did She Generally Decide? Women in Ste. Genevieve, 1750–1805," *William and Mary Quarterly*, 3rd series, 44 (October 1987): 775–789; Winstanley Briggs, "Slavery in French Colonial Illinois," *Chicago History* 18, no. 4 (1989–1990): 61–81; Winstanley Briggs, "Le Pays des Illinois," *William and Mary Quarterly*, 3rd series, 47 (January 1990): 30–56; Margaret K. Brown and Lawrie C. Dean, *The French Colony in the Mid-Mississippi Valley* (Carbondale, Ill.: Kestrel Books, 1995); Margaret K. Brown, *History as They Lived It: A Social History of Prairie du Rocher, Illinois* (Tucson, Az.: Patrice Press, 2005); Colin G. Calloway, *The Scratch of a Pen: 1763 and the Transformation of North America* (New York: Oxford University Press, 2006); Shirley Christian, *Before Lewis and Clark: The Story of the Chouteaus, the French Dynasty That Ruled America's Frontier* (New York: Farrar, Straus and Giroux, 2004); William E. Foley and David Rice, *The First Chouteaus: River Barons of Early St. Louis* (Urbana: University of Illinois Press, 1983); William E. Foley, *The Genesis of Missouri* (Columbia: University of Missouri Press, 1989); Jay Gitlin, "Old Wine in New Bottles: French Merchants and the Emergence of the American Midwest, 1795–1835," in *Proceedings of the Thirteenth and Fourteenth Meetings of the French Colonial Historical Society*, ed. Philip Boucher (Lanham, Md.: University Press of America, 1990); Gitlin, *Bourgeois Frontier*; Robert Michael Morrissey, "Bottomlands and Borderlands: Empires and Identities in the Illinois Country, 1673–1785" (Ph.D. diss., Yale University, 2006); Clairborne A. Skinner, *The Upper Country: French Enterprise in the Colonial Great Lakes* (Baltimore: Johns Hopkins University Press, 2008); J. Frederick Fausz, *Founding St. Louis: First*

City of the New West (Charleston, S.C.: History Press, 2011); Patricia Cleary, *The World, the Flesh, and the Devil: A History of Colonial St. Louis* (Columbia: University of Missouri Press, 2011). Carl J. Ekberg has been especially prolific, publishing numerous books and articles on French land settlement patterns, French and Indian relations, and Indian slavery. In addition to his first major work, *Colonial Ste. Genevieve*, see Carl J. Ekberg, "Black Slavery in Illinois, 1720–1765," *Western Illinois Regional Studies* 12, no. 1 (1989): 5–19; Carl J. Ekberg, "Marie Rouensa-8cate8a and the Foundations of French Illinois," *Illinois Historical Journal* 84, no. 3 (1991): 146–160; Carl J. Ekberg, *French Roots in the Illinois Country: The Mississippi Frontier in Colonial Times* (Urbana: University of Illinois Press, 1998); Carl J. Ekberg, *François Vallé and His World: Upper Louisiana before Lewis and Clark* (Columbia: University of Missouri Press, 2002); Carl J. Ekberg, *Stealing Indian Women: Native Slavery in the Illinois Country* (Urbana: University of Illinois Press, 2007).

28. Margaret K. Brown worked extensively cataloging and indexing the Kaskaskia manuscripts. For a number of translated documents and journals, see Margaret K. Brown and Lawrie C. Dean, *The Village of Chartres in Colonial Illinois, 1720–1765* (New Orleans: Polyanthos, 1977); Nicolas de Finiels, *An Account of Upper Louisiana*, trans. Carl J. Ekberg, ed. Carl J. Ekberg and William Foley (Columbia: University of Missouri Press, 1989); Joseph L. Peyser and José Antonio Brandao, *Edge of Empire: Documents of Michilimackinac, 1671–1716*, trans. Joseph L. Peyser, ed. José António Brandão (East Lansing: Michigan State University Press, 2008); Joseph L. Peyser, *On the Eve of the Conquest: The Chevalier de Raymond's Critique of New France in 1754*, trans. Joseph Peyser (East Lansing: Michigan State University Press and Mackinac State Historic Parks, 1998).

29. For an interesting view on the effects of language, see Catherine Desbarats, "Following *The Middle Ground*," *William and Mary Quarterly*, 3rd series, 63 (January 2006): 93. Desbarats mentions that scholars, too, often have written these histories with little attention paid to Indian languages.

30. Desbarats, "Following *The Middle Ground*," 93.

31. Robert Englebert, "Merchant Representatives and the French River World, 1763–1803," *Michigan Historical Review* 34 (Spring 2008): 63–82.

32. Colin G. Calloway, *One Vast Winter Count: The Native American West before Lewis and Clark* (Lincoln: University of Nebraska Press, 2003), 14.

33. Joseph Zitomersky, "In the Middle and on the Margin: Greater French Louisiana in History and in Professional Historical Memory," *Alizés* (La Réunion, France: Université de la Réunion, 2001), 217–218.

34. Alexis de Tocqueville, *Œuvres complètes* (Paris: Gallimard, 1951–2003), 14:129.

35. Historian François-Edme Rameau de Saint-Père and archivist Pierre Margry are good examples of French individuals who, during the second half of the nineteenth century, developed a fascination for the history of French colonization in North America, including in regions such as the Great Lakes and Mississippi River valley. See, for instance, François-Edme Rameau de Saint-Père, *Note historiques sur la colonie canadienne du Détroit: lecture prononcée par Mr. Rameau à Windsor sur le Détroit, comté d'Essex, C.W. le lundi 1er avril 1861* (Montreal: J. B. Rolland & fils libraires-éditeurs, 1861); François-Edme Rameau de Saint-Père, *La France aux colonies, études sur le développement de la race française hors de l'Europe*, 2 vols. (Paris: A. Jouby libraire-éditeur, 1859), 1; Pierre Margry, ed., *Découvertes et établissements des Français dans l'Ouest et dans le Sud de l'Amérique septentrionale*, 6 vols. (Paris: D. Jouaust, 1879–1888).

36. Gilles Havard and Cécile Vidal, "Making New France New Again," *Common-Place* 7, no. 4 (2007), http://www.common-place.org/vol-07/no-04/harvard/. See also Gilles Havard, "L'historiographie de la Nouvelle-France en France au cours du XXᵉ siècle: nostalgie, oubli et renouveau," in Wien, Vidal, and Frenette, *De Québec à l'Amérique française*, 95–124. This new interest in the late 1980s is in part attributable to the publication by Philippe Jacquin of *Les Indiens blancs: Français et Indiens en Amérique du Nord, XVIe-XVIIIe siècles* (Paris: Payot, 1987).

37. See Gilles Havard, *Histoire des coureurs de bois* (Paris: Flammarion, forthcoming); Gilles Havard, *Empire et métissages: Indiens et Français dans le Pays d'en Haut, 1660–1715* (Sillery, Q.C., and Paris: Éditions du Septentrion and Presses de l'Université de Paris-Sorbonne, 2003); Gilles Havard, *The Great Peace of Montreal of 1701: French-Native Diplomacy in the Seventeenth Century*, trans. Phyllis Aronoff and Howard Scott (Montreal and Kingston: McGill-Queen's University Press, 2001); Gilles Havard, *La Grande Paix de Montréal de 1701: les voies de la diplomatie franco-amérindienne* (Montreal: Recherches amérindiennes au Québec, 1992). See also Gilles Havard and Cécile Vidal, *Histoire de l'Amérique française*, 3rd ed. (Paris: Flammarion, 2008).

38. Arnaud Balvay, *La Révolte des Natchez* (Paris: Éditions du Félin, 2008); Arnaud Balvay, *L'épée et la plume: Amérindiens et soldats des troupes de la Marine en Louisiane et au Pays d'en haut, 1683–1763* (Quebec: Presses de l'Université Laval, 2006). Other French historians who have made significant contributions to the historiography of French-Indian relations in the heart of North America over the last fifteen years include Cécile Vidal, Guillaume Aubert, and Saliha Belmessous. See, for instance, Vidal, "Le Pays des Illinois"; Cécile Vidal, "Les implantations françaises au pays des Illinois au XVIIIᵉ siècle, 1699–1765" (Ph.D. diss., École des hautes études en sciences sociales, Paris,

1995); Guillaume Aubert, "'The Blood of France': Race and Purity of Blood in the French Atlantic World," *William and Mary Quarterly*, 3rd series, 61 (July 2004): 439–478; Guillaume Aubert, "'Français, nègres et sauvages': Constructing Race in Colonial Louisiana" (Ph.D. diss., Tulane University, 2002); Saliha Belmessous, "Assimilation and Racialism in Seventeenth- and Eighteenth-Century French Colonial Policy," *American Historical Review* 110 (April 2005): 322–349; Saliha Belmessous, "D'un préjugé culturel à un préjugé racial: la politique indigène de la France au Canada" (Ph.D. diss., École des hautes études en sciences sociales, Paris, 1999). See also Tangi Villerbu, "Pouvoir, religion et société en des temps indécis: Vincennes, 1763–1795," *Revue d'histoire de l'Amérique française* 62 (Fall 2008): 185–214; Stéphanie Chaffray, "Corps, territoire et paysage à travers les images et les textes viatiques en Nouvelle-France (1701–1756)," *Revue d'histoire de l'Amérique française* 59 (Fall 2005): 7–52; Charles J. Balesi, *The Time of the French in the Heart of North America, 1673–1818*, 3rd ed. (Chicago: Alliance Française, 2000).

39. Jacqueline Peterson, "Prelude to Red River: A Social Portrait of the Great Lakes Métis," *Ethnohistory* 25 (Winter 1978): 41–67. Peterson examined the Great Lakes region, but was part of an emerging group of scholars focusing on the métis in the Canadian Northwest. See Sylvia Van Kirk, *"Many Tender Ties": Women in Fur-Trade Society, 1670–1870* (Winnipeg: Watson & Dwyer, 1980); Jennifer S. H. Brown, *Strangers in Blood: Fur Trade Families in Indian Country* (Vancouver: University of British Columbia Press, 1980). Jacqueline Peterson and Jennifer S. H. Brown, eds., *The New Peoples: Being and Becoming Métis in North America* (Winnipeg: University of Manitoba Press, 1985), provides a who's who of métis scholarship in the mid-1980s.

40. Richard White, *The Middle Ground: Indians, Empires, and Republics in the Great Lakes Region, 1650–1815* (New York: Cambridge University Press, 1991), 50–51; Richard White, "Creative Misunderstandings and New Understandings," *William and Mary Quarterly*, 3rd series, 63 (January 2006): 9–14.

41. White, *Middle Ground*, 52.

42. White extended the work of Cornelius Jaenen geographically to the Great Lakes and Illinois Country, and chronologically to include the eighteenth and nineteenth centuries. He also used Jaenen's work to help define his middle ground concept. See Cornelius Jaenen, "'Les Sauvages Ameriquains': Persistence into the 18th Century of Traditional French Concepts and Constructs for Comprehending Amerindians," *Ethnohistory* 29 (Winter 1982): 43–56.

43. Kathleen DuVal, *The Native Ground: Indians and Colonists in the Heart of the Continent* (Philadelphia: University of Pennsylvania Press, 2006), 4–5.

44. Alan Taylor, *The Divided Ground: Indians, Settlers, and the Northern Borderland of the American Revolution* (New York: Vintage Books, 2006).

45. Brett Rushforth, "Slavery, the Fox Wars, and the Limits of Alliance," *William and Mary Quarterly*, 3rd series, 63 (January 2006): 53–80. "Fox" in the context presented here refers to the Meskwaki, who were given the name Fox by the English.

46. The middle ground is based on the premise that the Great Lakes were part of a shatter zone, where the destruction of Huronia in 1649 and the continuing hostilities between the Five Nations Iroquois and the Algonquian of the Great Lakes weakened the Algonquian nations and made alliance with the French attractive.

47. Heidi Bohaker, "*Nindoodemag*: The Significance of Algonquian Kinship Networks in the Eastern Great Lakes Region, 1600–1701," *William and Mary Quarterly*, 3rd series, 63 (January 2006): 50.

48. Philip J. Deloria, "What Is the Middle Ground, Anyway?" *William and Mary Quarterly*, 3rd series, 63 (January 2006): 15–22.

49. Tanis Thorne, *The Many Hands of My Relations: French and Indians on the Lower Missouri* (Columbia: University of Missouri Press, 1996); Lucy Eldersveld Murphy, *Gathering of Rivers: Indians, Métis and Mining in the Western Great Lakes, 1737–1832* (Lincoln: University of Nebraska Press, 2000); Susan Sleeper-Smith, *Indian Women and French Men: Rethinking Cultural Encounter in the Western Great Lakes* (Amherst: University of Massachusetts Press, 2001); Karen L. Marrero, "Founding Families: Power and Authority of Mixed French and Native Lineages in Eighteenth-Century Detroit" (Ph.D. diss., Yale University, 2011). See also Devine, *People Who Own Themselves*.

50. Gitlin, *Bourgeois Frontier*, 10.

"*Faire la chaudière*"
The Wendat Feast of Souls, 1636

KATHRYN MAGEE LABELLE

THE SEVENTEENTH-CENTURY WENDAT CONFEDERACY WAS A COALITION that included the Bear Nation (Attignawantan), the Nation of the Rock (Arendarhonon), the People of the Cord (Attigneenongnahac), the People of the Deer (Tahontaenrat), and perhaps a fifth group, the People of the Marsh (Ataronchronon). The confederacy inhabited the Great Lakes region along the shores of Georgian Bay (otherwise known as "Wendake"), in present-day Ontario.[1]

Writing on the importance of feasts in Wendat society, seventeenth-century Jesuit Jérôme Lalement observed they were "the oil of their ointments . . . the honey of their medicines, the preparations for their hardships, a star for their guidance . . . the spring of their activities . . . in short, the general instrument or condition without which nothing is done."[2] To be sure, feasts played a pivotal role in all aspects of Wendat affairs. They were a ritualized celebration that often worked within multifaceted levels of spiritual, cultural, political, and economic frameworks. The most significant of the Wendat Confederacy's feasts was the Feast of Souls.[3] Modern scholars have affirmed the importance of this ceremony for over a century. Writing in 1899, the historian Francis Parkman acknowledged that the Feast of Souls was the "most solemn and important ceremony" of the confederacy.[4] More recently, Bruce Trigger asserts that "[by] far the most important of all [Wendat] ceremonies was the Feast of the [Souls]."[5] Wendat traditionalist and scholar Georges Sioui supports this trend by indicating that the feast "was certainly one of the most remarkable and most pivotal features of [the Wendat] civilization."[6] For Sioui, the feast was central to the stability and security of the confederacy, as it became one of the main ways Wendat reinforced traditions and relationships.[7]

Despite a consistent line of argument that the feast was an important aspect of Wendat society, literature on the subject is limited to a small number of common observations within more general works on Wendat religion, economy, and trade.[8] In most cases, these accounts include a factual narrative of the chronological events involved in the Feast of Souls supplemented with a short analysis of the ceremony itself.[9] The use of the feast as a means to connect allies is also highlighted within these accounts. Trigger, for instance, emphasizes this last aspect by concluding:

> The most important element [of the Feast of Souls] remained the great affection that each [Wendat] had for the remains of his dead relatives. By joining in a common tribute to the dead, whose memory each family loved and honoured, the [Wendat] were exercising a powerful force for promoting goodwill among the disparate segments of each village, each tribe, and the confederacy as a whole.[10]

In the same way, Sioui interprets the feast as a celebration of "the people's unity and their desire to live in peace and to extend the bonds of symbolic kinship to the greatest possible number."[11] The extent of the unity discussed by Trigger and Sioui is far-reaching. Although located within one host village, the feast promoted a sense of unanimity that stretched beyond the local community. The function was, as Allan Greer contends, "a ceremony that united (in theory) [*all*] the [Wendat] people."[12] In addition, the inclusion of "other [friendly] tribes" outside the confederacy has not gone unnoticed. The importance of this, Trigger claims, is that only "very close allies appear to have been asked to mingle the bones of their dead with those of the [Wendat]."[13] Thus it would seem that the nature of the Wendat's most important ceremony was based on a desire to create unity and solidarity among their family, friends, and neighbors.

This chapter aims to contribute to our understanding of the Feast of Souls by highlighting an attempt by the Wendat to incorporate the French into their Feast of Souls in 1636. Through this approach, the feast of 1636 becomes a means to interpret Wendat foreign relations, domestic policies, as well as political and spiritual divisions in the 1630s. Notwithstanding the important religious and economic aspects of this ceremony, its diplomatic significance deserves more attention.[14] Alliance building and maintaining had always been a major component of Wendat strategy and identity, and continued to influence their geopolitical networks during the first decades of European-native encounters. The fashion in which Wendat formed alliances helps to contextualize these encounters, delivering a concrete example of the ways in which the feast functioned, and strengthening the assertion made by Sioui that the feast was "pivotal," if not critical, to Wendat society during this period. Ultimately, I argue that through an examination of the rhetoric surrounding the Feast of Souls in 1636 and its manifestation, invitations to the French were not just friendly gestures, but official requests to solidify a Wendat-French alliance.

YANDATSA, EHEN (THE OLD FEAST)

The Feast of Souls, in its most basic sense, was an ossuary burial ritual practiced by the Wendat Confederacy.[15] It took place every eight to ten years as a result of a village's decision to move location or in reaction to social insecurities within the region.[16] Preparations for the feast were made well in advance. To begin, the master of the feast, who was usually a leader within the host village, would call a meeting of all the headmen of the villages within the confederacy. Plans were then made to hold a Feast of Souls within the next year, and invitations were sent throughout the confederacy, as well as to non-Wendat allies (such as the Algonquian). The number of participants for a feast varied but could include thousands of people.[17]

When it came time for the ceremony to take place, participants traveling to the host village gathered the bones of those people who had died since the last feast and wrapped them in beaver robes. The women carried these bundles on their backs as they proceeded in the direction of the feast. As they made their way, other invited participants joined them. Upon arrival at the host village, the women cleaned the bones of their deceased relations, while the robes that had carried the corpses from their temporary resting place to the feast were placed in the fire. The cleaned bones were then rewrapped in fine beaver skins. Subsequently, relatives and friends of the deceased distributed wampum beads in honor of the dead and decorated the sacs of bones with necklaces and ornaments. The sacs were then carried into the village ceremonially, and a feast took place as a memorial for each soul being buried. The packaged bones were then hung at the door of the person charged with providing a feast in honor of that deceased person.[18]

The ossuary pit itself has been described as quite large, with a depth of about ten feet.[19] This was big enough to hold all the bones, gifts, articles, and robes that were to be buried. Around the pit were high scaffolds. In some instances, the bags containing the souls were hung along the scaffolding the night before the burial, while other times the sacs were carried to the platform at the time of burial. The pit was lined with beaver skins and robes.[20]

The burial itself required that all bones be placed within the ossuary pit at daybreak. There were five or six people in the pit in charge of mixing the bones. Gifts, furniture, ornaments, kettles, corn, as well as other goods were also placed in the pit. Once everything had been deposited, mats and bark were placed on top of the bones, along with sand, poles, and wooden stakes. The rest of the day was taken up by gift giving, songs, and feasts. Combined, these activities marked a symbolic confirmation or renewal of alliances within the confederacy, as well as with neighboring peoples. Just as the bones were physically united within the same ossuary pit, the living relatives of the deceased were united in a similar synchronic state of kinship.[21] Overall, the entire ceremony could last up to ten days.[22]

PUT THE KETTLE ON

In 1624, French Recollect Gabriel Sagard had the opportunity to attend a Feast of Souls as an observer. Sagard took notes on his experience, making particular reference to the "other savage tribes" or Algonquian nations that participated in the feast in addition to his Wendat hosts.[23] Just over ten years later, in 1636, French missionaries were once again present at a Feast of Souls. This time, however, there was less of an emphasis on the incorporation of Algonquian allies, as the major source of discussion concerned the incorporation of French participants. Several factors led to the Wendat desire for French involvement in the Wendat Feast of Souls of 1636.

Almost immediately after the establishment of the trading post at Quebec in 1608, the Wendat and French began what would become a long history of close interaction. Beginning with early encounters between Wendat traders and French explorers, a number of agreements were made creating a loosely defined alliance based on economic reciprocity and military support.[24] Soon after, French missionaries began to make the trip to Wendake. As early as 1626, Jesuits had established permanent residence within the borders of Wendat territory. According to one missionary, the Jesuit presence was strategic in that by "fixing the Centre of their Missions in a Country [Wendake] that was also the Centre of Canada, they would easily be able to bring the light of the Gospel to all parts of [North America]."[25] Thus Jesuits such as Jean de Brébeuf and Anne de Noüe and Recollect Joseph de la Roche Daillon made it their purpose to Christianize the Wendat and to live with them.[26] This situation created a new and complex social dynamic within Wendake. At times the cultural differences resulted in frustration and conflict among the Wendat.[27] Despite these obstacles, however, the Wendat continued to allow the Catholic missionaries to stay. Scholars have explained this decision as a case of circumstance and dependency. Trigger, for instance, asserts that

> the [Wendat] headmen were convinced that these priests had the backing of the French traders and the officials and could only be expelled at the cost of giving up the French alliance. To make things worse, there was no alternative to trading with the French. European goods could no longer be done without and the Iroquois, who were the principal enemies of the [Wendat], lay between them and the Dutch.[28]

Despite the missionaries' cultural differences and the complications resulting from their presence, the French were a familiar feature of the Wendat Confederacy by the 1630s.[29]

The French possession of guns also enticed the Wendat to confirm an alliance. Unlike the Iroquois, the Wendat were not able to acquire guns in significant numbers.[30] This was due to the fact that the French, who were the primary European trading partners of the Wendat, refused to trade guns for furs.[31] This was not always the case in Euro-Amerindian relations. For instance, the Iroquois formed a trading partnership with the Dutch, who traded guns freely for pelts.[32] Nonetheless, French missionaries gave guns to actual or potential converts, thus leaving some room for hope that the French would change their policy and begin to trade weapons. The degree to which the Wendat perceived the French firearms to be important was reflected in a headman's discussion with the missionaries on the matter. This headman is said to have stated: "On this account the whole Country [Wendake] turns its eyes upon you; we shall esteem ourselves quite beyond fear, if we have you [the French] with us; you have firearms, the mere report of which is capable of inspiring dread in the enemy, and putting him to flight."[33]

The acquisition of firearms, or at least an affiliation with those who possessed firearms, was paramount if the Wendat were to remain on equal footing with their competition, namely the Iroquois. Even if the French still refused to trade guns directly to the Wendat, an official alliance between the two would have linked the Wendat more strategically with the French and their weapons. According to the headman's view of the situation, the actual *acquisition* of firearms was not as necessary as the *perception* that the Wendat had access to guns through the French. The Wendat belief that there were significant military gains to be made through the French and their possession of guns cultivated a closer relationship with the French.

Another factor influencing the Wendat's decision to incorporate the

French into their Feast of Souls was the highly tense and uncertain atmosphere in Wendake. Throughout the 1630s the Wendat and their allies were continuously faced with Iroquois ambushes and battles. These conflicts were particularly frequent throughout the year leading up to the Feast of Souls ceremony. Rumors circulated during the summer of 1635 that the Iroquois were planning an all-out attack on the whole of Wendake.[34] The timing of these rumors created particularly high amounts of anxiety throughout the confederacy because it was during these summer months that Wendat men were absent from their villages in the pursuit of trade.[35] It was customary that upon hearing the warning calls of the Wendat men charged with keeping watch for Iroquois attacks, women and children would begin to pack their belongings and prepare to flee. In the summer of 1635, warning cries rang throughout the villages both day and night. If an attack did take place and the village was well fortified, the women and children were to remain and await the assault. This, however, rarely happened. Due to the small number of men, a lack of firearms, and the overpowering number of their enemies, the villagers almost immediately tried to escape the confines of their home and go into hiding. In reality, only the older members of the village, too weak to flee, remained within their longhouses. These were the intense conditions surrounding the summer of 1635.[36]

Notwithstanding a momentary truce with the Seneca, the Wendat remained subject to threats of an Iroquois attack in 1636.[37] During the winter of 1636, threats were so prevalent that even the Jesuits, who had guns and a means for protecting themselves, began to pack their bags.[38] This time around, escape was much more complicated than the previous summer. Jesuit Paul Le Jeune's recollection of a winter flight highlights the differences between the seasons and their effect on securing oneself during times of war. According to Le Jeune,

> Flight is to some extent tolerable in Summer, for one can escape to an island or hide in the obscurity of some dense forest; but in Winter, when ice serves as a bridge to enable the enemy to search the Islands, and when the fall of the leaves has laid bare the forest recesses, you do not know where to hide; besides, the tracks on the snow are immediately discovered; and it is, moreover, extremely cold in Winter to sleep long at the sign of the Moon.[39]

The fears rooted in the persistent intimidation by the Iroquois that winter affected all aspects of life within Wendake. Panic took over, and societal customs were put on hold. Indeed, the fact that a Wendat party set to leave for Quebec in the spring of 1636 delayed their plans due to heightened fears of a potential Iroquois assault illustrates the severity of the situation.[40] This annual expedition was essential to Wendat trade by the 1630s, and the Wendat's decision to postpone the trip would not have been an easy one. If the party failed to meet the French that year, trade for the entire season would be undermined.

The Wendat addressed the issue of constant warfare in several ways. One immediate strategy was the bolstering of fortifications of their principal villages. At the village of Ossossane, for instance, the young men began to construct a new palisade.[41] They made the fort square rather than round, and arranged stakes in straight lines in order to create four towers at each corner of the palisade. The four towers had been the suggestion of the Jesuit priests, who had agreed to employ four Frenchmen to keep guard at each tower with a musket.[42] As a result, the war-ridden atmosphere within Wendake led to a working partnership between the French and Wendat, fostering a closer connection than before.

In addition to warfare, the 1630s were simultaneously characterized by devastating epidemics. In the autumn of 1633, smallpox made its first decisive attack on Wendake, reducing its population by approximately 50 percent within six years.[43] The immediate effects of these diseases are made most obvious through firsthand accounts of the situation. The Wendat Confederacy was in a state of desolation. Its people were dying and solutions were limited. Following the introduction of smallpox in 1633, the Wendat experienced their first major epidemic in 1634, this just preceding the initial council meetings organized to discuss the Feast of Souls ceremony for 1636. The epidemic began in the summer and continued to debilitate the population throughout the winter months.[44] The Jesuits observed this epidemic and made notes on the symptoms of the disease. It was described as a "sort of measles and an oppression of the stomach."[45] According to Father Brébeuf, it usually began with a high fever and ended with a bout of diarrhea. This was followed by a rash that looked like "a sort of measles or smallpox, but different from that common in France."[46] Some victims also suffered blindness or blurred vision for several days. The epidemic of 1634 was so severe that communities were unable to harvest food for subsistence during the winter.[47] Although the exact number of people affected by this disease is uncertain, Brébeuf stated that "he personally did not know anyone who had escaped [the epidemic] and that a large number had died."[48]

While the epidemic subsided after the winter and during the early months of 1635, Jesuit records indicate that the death rates within Wendake remained uncharacteristically high in comparison to previous years. This state of remission was only intermediary, however, as another epidemic more devastating than the last attacked Wendat villages in the spring of 1636. It began in May and continued for the next six months.[49] The symptoms of this disease were much more drawn out than those of 1634, as victims were often bedridden for long periods of time before they began to recover or died.[50] The death rates were unprecedented. In the span of eight days, the village of Ossossane lost ten individuals.[51] By the end of the epidemic, this same village lost fifty people in total.[52] Based on the total deaths from Ossossane, Trigger estimates that roughly 500 Wendat died during the 1636 epidemic.[53]

These epidemics, beginning only two years before the initial planning of the Feast of Souls in 1636, instilled a sense of confusion, disillusionment, and ultimately a state of panic within Wendake. Combined, this intense atmosphere, in conjunction with the constant threat of warfare, would have pressed the Wendat to seek out ways to ensure their survival for the future.

The French were the first to approach the Wendat under these circumstances, suggesting a reaffirmation of the loosely defined Wendat-French alliance. Throughout the year preceding the Feast of Souls, the French made two decisive gestures toward the Wendat, signaling a French interest in redefining and confirming an official alliance. The first of these gestures came about in a meeting Samuel de Champlain and Théodore Bochart du Plessis had with several Wendat in 1635. During this meeting, Champlain made explicit inferences concerning the possibility of a French-Wendat alliance. He encouraged the Wendat to adopt the Christian faith, declaring that this was the only means by which a very close alliance with the French could be cemented. Champlain concluded that if this alliance were to be realized, the French "would readily come into [Wendat] Country, marry their daughters, teach them different arts and trades, and assist them against their enemies."[54] The Frenchmen then wrote down the details of the meeting in a letter and requested that the letter be taken to the Jesuits so that it might be presented formally at a general council of the Wendat Confederacy.[55] The opportunity articulated by Champlain was clear: if the Wendat were to convert to Christianity, the French would form an alliance that would foster kinship ties through marriage, cultural exchanges, economic gain, and military strength. The implications of this meeting suggest that the French had a need to create an alliance with the Wendat as well.

The French reiterated similar interest in affirming an alliance with the Wendat later that same year. It was during a large council of the Bear Nation when Father Brébeuf had just made a lengthy speech about the necessity for the Wendat to convert to Christianity. Brébeuf emphasized Champlain's earlier proposal by promising that the Jesuits would help the Wendat in whatever way they could to make this proposal a reality. Brébeuf concluded his speech by presenting the council with a wampum belt of 1,200 porcelain beads.[56] The importance of Brébeuf's gesture lies in an understanding of the use of wampum by the seventeenth-century Wendat. During this period, wampum collars or belts were widely used to confirm agreements or make treaties between Amerindian nations, as well as Amerindian and European nations.[57] Taking this into consideration, Brébeuf's gift of wampum would have been perceived as an attempt by the French to solidify an alliance with the Wendat. In remembering Brébeuf's earlier call for the Wendat to consider Champlain's offer, the general message was that the French desired to contract a solid relationship with the Wendat through a coalition between the two groups.

Overall, there were many reasons for the Wendat to seek an alliance with the French in 1636. The French were present within Wendake, they possessed firearms, and they themselves had made attempts to form an alliance with the Wendat. The inherent effects of disease and warfare only bolstered the necessity for such an alliance. While the Wendat could still depend on their Algonquian allies for support, the intense atmosphere of the 1630s culminated in a Wendat attempt to seek a new alliance through a redefinition of the terms of French-Wendat interaction. Consequently, the Feast of Souls of 1636 served as the means by which the Wendat expressed their urgent desires.

"PRESSING INVITATIONS"

During the early spring of 1635, leaders of the Bear Nation gathered together to discuss the organization of a Feast of Souls. The council of the confederacy had determined that a feast would take place the following spring. Throughout the subsequent year, the French received numerous invitations to take part in the Feast of Souls through various levels of participation. These so-called pressing invitations represented a shift from the more reticent interaction between the Wendat and French from previous years.[58] On the whole, there were several attempts by the Wendat to include the French in their Feast of Souls.

From the initial phase of preparation to the final stages of the ceremony, the French were invited to be active participants. In April 1635, the "Old Men" and headmen of the Bear Nation joined together to plan a Feast of

Souls for the following year. This council, according to Brébeuf, "was one of the most important that the [Wendat] have."[59] He observed that "they have nothing more sacred . . . it was a Council of peace. . . . They call these Councils, *Endionraondaone*, as if one should say, 'A Council even and easy, like the level and reaped fields.'"[60] Significantly, the French missionaries were invited to attend this traditional meeting.[61] During the council, the French were not only encouraged to speak but also allowed to enter fully into discussions on the nature of the ceremonial burial. The Jesuits expressed their wish to have the Bear Nation accept Christianity. They explained that this was so that future generations would not have their souls sent to hell, as was the case with those unconverted souls that were to be buried during the feast. The Wendat men listened respectfully to the Jesuits words and, in the end, appeased the Jesuits by agreeing that, for the most part, they would not wish the experience of hell on any of their friends or family.[62] This invitation to the French to join their discussions on the organization of the Feast of Souls demonstrated a sense of collective desire from the leaders of the Bear Nation to incorporate the French from the very beginning.

French participation in the Feast of Souls also involved a Wendat request to have Frenchmen buried in the ossuary pit. During the winter preceding the feast, a headman approached Brébeuf on behalf of the leaders of the Bear Nation to request the missionary's approval of burying two Frenchmen during the ceremony. The men in question were Guillaume Chaudron and Étienne Brûlé, who had been killed four years earlier and were buried within Wendat territory.[63] The Wendat's invitation for the French to partake in the burial and essentially mix the bones of the Wendat with those of the French was a direct call to unite the French and Wendat in a confirmed alliance. The reburial of Chaudron and Brûlé would have formed the basis of a ritual kinship bond, similar to the enduring link between the Wendat and the Algonquian. By burying the bones side by side, the French would have engaged fully in the ceremony's spiritual, cultural, and diplomatic function.

The invitations extended to the French were by no means light gestures on the part of the Wendat. In fact, Brébeuf stated explicitly that not only had they received "several pressing invitations" from the master of the feast, but also a number of invitations from Anenkhiondic, who was "the chief Captain of the whole Country."[64] Apparently, the Jesuits were given the impression that if they did not attend the feast, the Wendat would have perceived the entire ceremony to be a failure.[65] This makes sense considering that one of the main purposes of the feast for that year was to unify the

French and the Wendat. If the French did not attend, the alliance could not be confirmed, and the feast would have had very little significance in terms of redefining a coalition. This also explains the urgency with which the invitations were sent to the Jesuits. It was crucial that the Jesuits understood the importance of their attendance, as it was equally important for the Wendat to receive confirmation that their attempts to include the French in the feast would be achieved.

The Wendat further demonstrated their desire to create an alliance with the French at the evening council held the night before the official burial ceremony. It was customary for the headmen attending the ceremony to gather together in council the night before the burial. This council included all the leaders of the respective nations involved in the ceremony, whether they were Wendat or from allied tribes. It was at this time that the master of the feast would give presents to his guests, affirming their friendship, kinship, and alliance to each other. It had been assumed, as was the custom of the feast, that the French would join the other visiting nations and the Wendat headmen at the evening council.[66] The French were unaware of this formality and so did not attend.

The extent to which the Wendat desired the French to be involved in the gift-giving council is somewhat ambiguous. Present-day Wendat traditionalists interpret this event as a strategic and purposeful exclusion of the French.[67] It was important for the Wendat to have the visiting nations believe that the French absence from the meeting was merely a miscommunication. This perception would have maintained the notion that the French might still form an official alliance by participating in the feast the next day. In reality, however, the Wendat may have already thought that the French were reticent in attending and participating in aspects of the ceremony and so conveniently misinformed the French of the meeting. This would have alleviated a public refusal by the French in regards to their participation in the council.

Jesuit accounts of the event present a different interpretation. According to Brébeuf, Anenkhiondic confronted the Jesuits the morning after the council. He explained how the participants in the council were disappointed over the abstention of the French the night before and wanted to make amends by giving the French their gift in any case.[68] Anenkhiondic then presented Brébeuf with a new robe of ten beaver skins. He explained that this was a reciprocal exchange in that this gift was in return for the wampum belt given by Brébeuf the year before.[69] Brébeuf's account indicates that there had indeed been a miscommunication and that the Wendat had truly preferred a French presence at the evening council. The inclusion of the French at the night council would have indicated that the Wendat perceived the French to be no different than their Algonquian allies. If the French had participated, they would have not only shared in a highly symbolic component of the feast but also confirmed their commitment to the Wendat Confederacy. Moreover, Anenkiondic's insistence on still presenting the gift to the French the next morning exhibits another attempt by the Wendat to incorporate the French into their system of alliances. Despite the discrepancies between the traditionalist perspective and the written records of Brébeuf, the results remained the same. The French and other nations acknowledged the genuine desire by the Wendat to include the French in the evening council.

In the end, attempts by the Wendat to solidify an alliance with the French were numerous. Through preparations, councils, burials, symbolic material exchanges, and invitations related to the Feast of Souls, the Wendat clearly indicated their intention to create a ritualistic kinship bond with the French that would ultimately lead to a traditional Wendat coalition.

A CUSTOMARY RECIPE

Records indicate that two days past the day of Pentecost, on May 10, 1636, the Wendat held a Feast of Souls at the village of Ossossane.[70] Thousands of people were involved, gifts were exchanged, souls were united, and kinship ties were defined.[71] The extent to which the French were involved in this ceremony, however, was never fully realized in the context of Wendat aspirations. Essentially, "the Kettle" of 1636 had been prepared by the Wendat. It was molded by tradition, heated by desperation, and stirred with persistence. Yet in the end, this work was reduced to a customary recipe, as attempts by the Wendat to integrate the French into their feast came to little avail. Consequently, the traditional ingredients or aspects of the ceremony remained the same as Feasts of Souls performed in the past.

Although the French accepted invitations and attended most of the councils and ceremonies, they outright refused to have Frenchmen reburied in the ossuary pit. Notwithstanding relentless attempts by the Wendat to persuade the missionaries to allow Chaudron and Brûlé to be buried with their dead, Father Brébeuf adamantly rejected the idea. He explained his initial rejection by stating that "that could not be, that it was forbidden to [the French]; that, as they had been baptized and were, as we hoped, in heaven, we respected their bones too much to permit them being mingled with the bones of those who had not been baptized; and, besides, that it was not our custom to raise the bodies."[72]

Brébeuf's understanding of the repercussions of this decision was later portrayed in a reflection on his resolution. The Jesuit demonstrated a good comprehension of the significance of the mingling of the bones and the cultural implications of rejecting such an offer. As a result, he tried to appease the Wendat by suggesting that although he would not allow the French to be buried in the communal pit, he would agree to bury them in a separate grave beside the ossuary pit. He justified his proposal in the following manner: "As it is the greatest pledge of friendship and alliance they have in the Country, we were already granting them on this point what they wished, and were making it appear thereby that we desired to love them as our brothers, and to live and die with them."[73]

Thus it seems that Brébeuf did understand that a refusal to bury the French was the equivalent of refusing an alliance and kinship bond. This said, his later proposal of a separate burial illustrates a lack of full comprehension. Without the actual mixing of the bones within the ossuary pit, the burial of the French would mean very little in terms of the Wendat's concept of alliance formation. Several Wendat men voiced this reality in reaction to Brébeuf's decision. They approached Brébeuf, telling him that they were offended by the actions of the French and were annoyed that they were prevented from "boasting, as they had hoped, to strange Tribes that they were the relations of the French."[74] Furthermore, they were quite certain that other nations "would say that the friendship [between the French and Wendat] was only in appearance, since [the French] had not allowed the bones of [the] Frenchmen to mingle with theirs."[75] Therefore, without the full burial and mixing of bones between the French and the Wendat, the invitation for the French to join the burial resulted in no more than empty gestures of friendship on the part of the French as well as a rejection of a profound kinship bond with the Wendat.

In addition to the ultimate decision by the French to abstain from the burial ceremony, they also refused to accept the beaver robe offered to the missionaries by Anenkhiondic the morning after the evening council. Brébeuf returned the gift immediately. He justified his action in that Anenkhiondic had presented the gift to the French as reciprocation for the wampum belt given to the Wendat the year earlier. Brébeuf explained that the French had only "made [the wampum] present to lead [the Wendat] to embrace [the French] faith."[76] The assertion by Brébeuf that the wampum belt was intended to represent anything but a French desire for religious conversion would have been confusing for the Wendat. The French had used wampum in a nontraditional way, allowing for their motives to be lost in translation as the Wendat still understood the wampum to represent a diplomatic or trade agreement.[77] Moreover, the rejection of the beaver robe by the French would have further marginalized the extent of their participation in the Feast of Souls. Despite significant attempts by the Wendat to incorporate the French into their Feast of Souls and consequently solidify a Wendat-French alliance, the outright rejection by the French in regards to the mixing of French bones in the ossuary pit and the beaver robe incident rendered the invitations inconsequential.

CONCLUSION

The circumstances surrounding the Feast of Souls in 1636 and its aftermath clarify a number of important aspects of Wendat history. First, the feast of 1636 demonstrates that although natives forged alliances in the seventeenth-century eastern woodlands with verbal contracts and the exchange of wampum, burial ceremonies, such as the Feast of Souls, also served as diplomatic vehicles to create military, political, and economic ties. Through this framework, the burial pit was not only a sacred space for spiritual ceremony and a means to display and exchange trade goods but simultaneously served as a metaphorical and physical diplomatic tool used to create alliances.

Wendat attempts to incorporate the French into their Feast of Souls in 1636 also illustrates the intense atmosphere of the 1630s. Engulfed in Iroquois attacks and incessant disease, the timing of the feast remained rooted in a pragmatic effort to stabilize the confederacy. The Wendat became desperate and searched for a solution to their situation; an alliance with the French seemed like a desirable option. Looking beyond this period to the 1640s, one cannot help but consider the repercussions if the French had agreed to actively commit themselves to the cause of the Wendat. The presence of French military and guns would have certainly evened the odds against the Iroquois.[78] In 1703, the Wendat chief Michipichy reflected on these circumstances, blaming the Wendat's loss to the Iroquois in 1649 on the fact that "there were no French among them."[79] If the French had agreed to officially take up arms and join the Wendat, the Iroquois-Wendat conflict might have had a very different outcome.

Although this was the first time that the Wendat had officially invited a European nation to join in the feast (Gabriel Sagard was merely an observer in 1624), their presence did not transgress the tradition of the feast itself.

Rather, invitations to the French stayed consistent with the ceremony's purpose as a mechanism for defining and affirming kinship ties and alliances. The precarious atmosphere of the 1630s forced leaders to pursue creative solutions to address the social and political uncertainty confronting their community. A Wendat attempt to include the French in their feast consequently served as a coping strategy to strengthen the confederacy. Despite these diplomatic efforts, however, the Wendat failed to meet their goal as the French formally rejected any kind of official coalition with them in 1636. In essence, the call by the Wendat to "*faire la chaudière*" became a cultural and temporal indicator of the times as well as a foreboding signal of the overwhelming obstacles to follow.

NOTES

1. The popularized term "Huron" has also been used to describe this same group and "Huronia" as their place of habitation. "Huron" is a European-derived label for this group, and it is for this reason that the term "Wendat" has been selected instead of "Huron." The terms "Wyandot" or "Wyandotte" and "Huron-Wendat" are used to identify Wendat descendants after the seventeenth century.

2. Reuben Gold Thwaites, ed., *The Jesuit Relations and Allied Documents: Travels and Explorations of the Jesuit Missionaries in New France, 1610–1791*, 73 vols. (Cleveland: Burrows Brothers, 1896–1903), 17:209. Until recently, historians seeking to draw from Jesuit sources were relegated to Thwaites's published *Relations* (cited here). Since 1967, however, Jesuit historian Lucien Campeau gained access to the Jesuit archives in Rome and compiled several volumes of unpublished Jesuit documents. These include letters as well as *Relations* in their original languages of French, Latin, and Italian. Campeau's work serves as an additional reference, which I used to verify the translations in Thwaites's editions. See Lucien Campeau, ed., *Monumenta Novae Franciae*, 7 vols. (Quebec: Presses de l'Université Laval, 1967–1987).

3. "Feast of Souls" is used throughout this work in reference to the Wendat's burial ceremony that has more frequently been described in primary and secondary sources as "The Feast of the Dead," or *La fête des morts*. In addition, sources also refer to this ceremony in a metaphorical sense. Primary accounts indicate that when speaking about the Feast of Souls, the Wendat would refer to it as "the Kettle" in English, "*La chaudière*" in French, or "*Yandatsa*" in Wendat. Firsthand accounts of the Feast of Souls indicate that this was indeed

the most important ceremony among the seventeenth-century Wendat. See Samuel de Champlain, *The Works of Samuel de Champlain*, ed. Henry P. Biggar, 6 vols. (Toronto: University of Toronto Press, 1922–1936), 1:161–162; Gabriel Sagard, *The Long Journey to the Country of the Hurons*, ed. George M. Wrong (Toronto: Champlain Society, 1939), 211–214; Thwaites, *Jesuit Relations*, 10:281–305.

4. Francis Parkman, *The Jesuits in North America in the Seventeenth Century* (Toronto: G. N. Morang, 1899), 72.

5. Bruce G. Trigger, *The Children of Aataentsic: A History of the Huron People to 1660* (Montreal and Kingston: McGill-Queen's University Press, 1976), 85.

6. Georges E. Sioui, *Huron-Wendat: The Heritage of the Circle*, trans. Jane Brierley (Vancouver: University of British Columbia Press, 1999), 146.

7. Personal correspondence between the author and Georges Sioui, October 10, 2006.

8. The exception to this rule is Eric Seeman's recent publication, *The Huron-Wendat Feast of the Dead: Indian-European Encounters in Early America* (Baltimore: Johns Hopkins University Press, 2011). For examples of works that touch upon the Feast of Souls, but are not dedicated specifically to this topic, see Allan Greer, ed., *The Jesuit Relations: Natives and Missionaries in Seventeenth-Century North America* (Boston: Bedford/St. Martin's, 2000), 61; Denys Delâge, *Bitter Feast: Amerindians and Europeans in Northeastern North America, 1600–64*, trans. Jane Brierley (Vancouver: University of British Columbia Press, 1993), 73; Sioui, *Huron-Wendat*, 153; Trigger, *Children of Aataentsic*, 88.

9. Jesuit Jean de Brébeuf's observation of a Feast of Souls taking place in 1636 is the most popular source for information on the feast. Most scholars either paraphrase his description or quote his rendition word for word. If there is an analytical component, it usually consists of a few paragraphs. Thwaites, *Jesuit Relations*, 10:281–305.

10. Trigger, *Children of Aataentsic*, 90.

11. Sioui, *Huron-Wendat*, 146.

12. Greer, *Jesuit Relations*, 61.

13. Trigger, *Children of Aataentsic*, 87.

14. In addition to Trigger's, Sioui's, and Greer's assertion that the feast was used to solidify friendly relations within the confederacy and among allied tribes, Seeman's work on the feast and Wendat *deathways* touches briefly on the diplomatic function of the feast of 1636. This said, he focuses more broadly on cultural encounters and the spiritual implications of the feast. See Seeman, *Huron-Wendat Feast of the Dead*, 64.

15. For a broader archaeological analysis of ossuary burial practices of the Wendat and their ancestors, see Ronald F. Williamson and Susan Pfeiffer, eds., *Bones of the Ancestors: The Archeology and Osteobiology of the Moatfield Ossuary* (Gatineau, QC: Canadian Museum of Civilization, 2003).

16. Jean de Brébeuf, *Écrits en Huronie*, ed. Gilles Thérien (Montreal: Bibliothèque nationale du Québec, 1996), 166; Champlain, *Works*, 1:161; Lewis Henry Morgan, *League of the Ho-deno-sau-nee, or Iroquois*, 2 vols. (New York: M. H. Newman, 1851), 1:167.

17. Thwaites, *Jesuit Relations*, 10:279–303.

18. Sagard, *Long Journey*, 211–212; Thwaites, *Jesuit Relations*, 10:279–303.

19. Thwaites, *Jesuit Relations*, 10:293.

20. One beaver robe was made with eight to ten beaver skins. See Sagard, *Long Journey*, 211–212; Thwaites, *Jesuit Relations*, 10:279–303.

21. According to Lewis Henry Morgan, there are two kinds of kinship classes: the descriptive (or natural) and the classificatory (or artificial). The latter has also been described as "fictive kinship," or claimed kinship without evidence of biological descent. This type of relationship is often employed in order to encourage social or political interaction, taking place most commonly among aboriginal societies. In addition, there are special forms of fictitious kinship. In the case of the Wendat Feast of Souls, the use of the ceremony to identify kinship ties between participants defined those relationships as "ritual kinship bonds." This required that a ritual take place in order for the creation of the kinship to be acknowledged as a formal alliance. The confirmation of such associations was regarded as "relations of peace" that required mutual consensus in etiquette and ritual protocol. In other words, through the Feast of Souls, the Wendat defined their alliances among other confederates and allied tribes by creating fictitious kinship bonds through ritual feasting, gift exchange, and the burial of their dead. For more information on the concept of kinship among the Wendat, see Thomas R. Trautmann, "Lewis Henry Morgan and the Invention of Kinship," *Ethnohistory* 36 (Summer 1989): 314; Bruce G. Trigger, *The Huron: Farmers of the North*, 2nd ed. (New York: Holt, Rinehart and Winston, 1990), 54; Beverly Ann Smith, "Systems of Subsistence and Networks of Exchange in the Terminal Woodland and Early Historic Period in the Upper Great Lakes" (Ph.D. diss., Michigan State University, 1996), 281–283. For information concerning the importance of kinship to the Wendat Feast of Souls, see Champlain, *Works*, 1:162.

22. Sagard, *Long Journey*, 211–212; Thwaites, *Jesuit Relations*, 10:279–303.

23. Sagard, *Long Journey*, 213.

24. Champlain, *Works*, 1:190.

25. Pierre-François-Xavier de Charlevoix, *History and General Description of New France*, 6 vols., trans. John Gilmary Shea (Chicago: Loyola University Press, 1962), 1:186.

26. Trigger, *Children of Aataentsic*, 406.

27. Ibid., 597.

28. Ibid.

29. Jean de Brébeuf to Julien Perrault, 3 July 1636, R6275–0-2-F, Jean de Brébeuf Collection, Library and Archives Canada, Ottawa, Ontario[0].

30. Elisabeth Tooker, *An Ethnography of the Huron Indians, 1615–1649* (Syracuse, N.Y.: Syracuse University Press, 1964), 27.

31. Thwaites, *Jesuit Relations*, 24:271–273.

32. Tooker, *Ethnography of the Huron Indians*, 27.

33. Thwaites, *Jesuit Relations*, 10:241.

34. Ibid., 8:61.

35. Ibid., 10:51.

36. Ibid.

37. Trigger, *Children of Aataentsic*, 597.

38. Thwaites, *Jesuit Relations*, 10:51.

39. Ibid.

40. Ibid., 9:245.

41. Ibid., 10:53.

42. Ibid.

43. Conrad E. Heidenreich, *Huronia: A History and Geography of the Huron Indians, 1600–1650* (Toronto: McClelland and Stewart, 1971), 253; Trigger, *Children of Aataentsic*, 499.

44. Trigger, *Children of Aataentsic*, 500.

45. Thwaites, *Jesuit Relations*, 7:221.

46. Ibid., 8:89.

47. Ibid., 8:87–89.

48. Cited in Trigger, *Children of Aataentsic*, 500–501.

49. Jean de Brébeuf to T. R. P. Mutius Vitelleschi, 1636, in *Étude sur les écrits de Saint Jean de Brébeuf*, ed. René Latourelle, 2 vols. (Montreal: Éditions de L'immaculée-Conception, 1952), 2:47–56. This epidemic began at the exact time the Feast of Souls was taking place. The implications of this correlation suggest that Wendake was in a state of insecurity and that the feast was being employed to address such anxieties.

50. Trigger, *Children of Aataentsic*, 527.

51. Thwaites, *Jesuit Relations*, 13:213.

52. Ibid. To put the numerical loss at Ossossane into context, Gary Warrick estimates that between 1634 and 1637, the confederacy as a whole experienced

20 percent depopulation. See Gary Warrick, "A Population History of the Huron-Petun, A.D. 900–1650" (Ph.D. diss., McGill University, 1990), 399.

53. Trigger, *Children of Aataentsic*, 528.

54. Thwaites, *Jesuit Relations*, 10:27.

55. Ibid. The reason behind Champlain's desire to introduce his offer for an alliance at a later council is probably due to the fact that the Wendat at this meeting were not leaders within their communities and had no real authority for making decisions on political diplomacy.

56. Ibid., 10:29.

57. Georges Sioui, *For an Amerindian Autohistory: An Essay on the Foundations of a Social Ethic*, trans. Sheila Fischman (Montreal: McGill-Queen's University Press, 1992), 91. For a more in-depth discussion on wampum, see Jonathan C. Lainey, *La "Monnaie des Sauvages": les colliers de wampum d'hier à aujourd'hui* (Sillery, Q.C.: Éditions du Septentrion, 2004).

58. Thwaites, *Jesuit Relations*, 10:289.

59. Ibid., 10:261.

60. Ibid.

61. Ibid., 10:27.

62. Ibid.

63. Ibid., 10:305.

64. Ibid., 10:289, 301–303.

65. Ibid., 10:289.

66. Ibid., 10:303.

67. According to Sioui, many Wendat today agree upon this interpretation of the evening council. Personal correspondence between the author and Georges Sioui, July 10, 2006.

68. Thwaites, *Jesuit Relations*, 10:303.

69. Ibid.

70. Lucien Campeau, *La mission des Jésuites chez les Hurons, 1634–1650*, ed. Pierrette L. Lagarde (Montreal: Éditions Bellarmin, 1987), 37.

71. Thwaites, *Jesuit Relations*, 10:293–311.

72. Ibid., 10:305.

73. Ibid.

74. Ibid., 10:311.

75. Ibid.

76. Ibid., 10:303.

77. Jonathan C. Lainey, "Les colliers de porcelaine de l'époque coloniale à aujourd'hui," *Recherches amérindiennes au Québec* 35, no. 2 (2005): 62.

78. Although the French had very few soldiers in New France until 1644, they could have supplied guns in the 1630s and later, in 1649, military personnel.

Louise Dechêne, *Le peuple, l'État et la guerre au Canada sous le régime français* (Montreal: Éditions du Boréal, 2008), 94–104; Keith F. Otterbein, "Huron vs. Iroquois: A Case Study in Inter-Tribal Warfare," *Ethnohistory* 26 (Spring 1979): 150.

79. "Conseil tenu par les Hurons, dans lequel se trouvaient les Outaouas, 12 juin 1703," in *Découvertes et établissements des Français dans l'Ouest et dans le Sud de l'Amérique septentrionale*, ed. Pierre Margry, 6 vols. (Paris: D. Jouaust, 1879–1888), 5:292.

Natives, Newcomers, and *Nicotiana*

Tobacco in the History of the Great Lakes Region

CHRISTOPHER M. PARSONS

COMING ASHORE IN A CANOE FROM THE UPPER MISSISSIPPI VALLEY or from the Great Lakes themselves, an exchange of tobacco often mediated the cultural encounters between natives and newcomers in the seventeenth and eighteenth centuries. In the travel accounts of Frenchmen and missionaries, tobacco emerged as a central means by which encounters with the diverse aboriginal cultures of French North America were understood. For French travelers, knowing tobacco meant decoding the performative aspects of its consumption and, increasingly, understanding the symbolism of pipes, dances, and sacrifices. While traders, travelers, and missionaries often came to different conclusions about the significance of tobacco in particular encounters, they nonetheless agreed that the plant acquired meaning only in local use and that it lacked any innate or universal significance. At the same time, tobacco was a sacred plant to the aboriginal cultures of the Great Lakes region; Iroquoian, Algonquian, and Siouan peoples smoked and sacrificed tobacco to try to bring Europeans into relations with other-than-human beings and powers unknown to the newcomers.[1] Knowing tobacco meant understanding the relationships with other-than-human forces that were vital to the survival of indigenous communities. These relationships were reaffirmed each time the sacred and otherworldly plant was consumed, whether it was smoked or sacrificed. Ultimately both natives and newcomers alike used tobacco as a means to make the unfamiliar comprehensible.

Describing an episode in his voyages in the late seventeenth-century Great Lakes, the Baron de Lahontan wrote: "Thus, without stopping at all of the villages, where I would have done nothing but negotiate and waste my time and tobacco, I resolved to go to the principal Village."[2] Lahontan suggests that tobacco had become inseparable from and even synonymous with contact. Yet the precise role of tobacco in the history of the Great Lakes region has remained somewhat elusive. This essay traces the coevolution of understandings of tobacco and conceptions of contact in the seventeenth- and eighteenth-century Great Lakes region. Tying the story of how tobacco was understood and consumed to French and aboriginal experiences of contact, this essay analyzes how natives, newcomers, and species of *Nicotiana* became inseparable in complex encounters that depended upon all but were determined by none.

The work of numerous anthropologists, archaeologists, and historians who have researched the material and ideational facets of early American smoking might appear to make these well-tread subjects. Yet scholars have been unable to agree on how best to study both of these aspects of the plant's North American history. Some, it is clear, assign little merit to the plant itself, and focus instead on the human elements of its history. Studies that have focused on the exchange, burial, and, to some extent, use of pipes, for instance, have emphasized the antiquity of what Alexander von Gernet has named the "Pipe/Tobacco/Smoking complex" and have demonstrated its ubiquity among pre- and early contact populations throughout the Americas.[3] Yet many scholars who have written about the material cultures of smoking seem to go to great lengths to avoid writing about tobacco. In the "Pipe/Tobacco/Smoking complex," tobacco is presented as the simplest and most easily explainable ingredient. Documentary and archaeological records have been used to show the range and distribution of particular pipe styles, but tobacco quickly recedes to the background of narratives that focus instead on the "anthropocentric" dimensions of smoking.[4] Its cultural contribution pales next to the vessels in which it was smoked, and, to generalize grossly, tobacco is presented as little more than a target of symbolic projection. Thus tobacco enters the story only as a holder of the meanings applied to it by humans, and the focus is on those areas where tobacco ceases to become a natural object and enters social worlds. As James Warren Springer has written, the story of smoking is too often told as one of "pipes and their associated materials."[5] In these works, tobacco is almost always a victim of ventriloquism, left to speak for race or class or gender, but with little to add of its own.

Yet in other studies that focus specifically on the history of tobacco in colonial North America, the plant is most often presented as a solid and transcendental biological agent. To know tobacco in this context, scholars such as Joseph Winter and Jordan Goodman turn to Latin species names (most offer *Nicotiana rustica* in the case of aboriginal peoples of northeastern North America), biochemical assays, and physiological descriptions to ground their analyses.[6] In these works that only incidentally discuss the aboriginal and colonial cultures that made the plant their own, tobacco is little more than the sum of its phytochemical parts, a nicotine delivery system. From this perspective, knowing tobacco's history means speaking first of nicotine contents and species range, and then of gods and ritual use. Human histories impinge on the evolutionary history of a deviously addictive and pleasurable plant, and not vice versa.[7] Thus, in an effort to give tobacco a voice, people and cultures are almost inevitably silenced.

Both approaches seem ultimately unsure of how to narrate human/ tobacco encounters. This is not particularly surprising as tobacco has proven itself to be an often reticent subject in the history of the Great Lakes region and of much of North America more generally. If some historians and archaeologists rely on pipes to buttress their arguments, this could be a result of the microscopic nature of tobacco seeds and the difficult methods necessary to prove their presence at archaeological sites.[8] Current research suggests the presence of tobacco in the Illinois region at 20–70 B.C.E. and in the Great Lakes region as early as 500–800 C.E.[9] Yet it is surely telling that, for a plant that produces hundreds of seeds in every pod, the presence of a few single carbonized seeds attests to its presence for much of the geographical region considered in this essay.[10] Even where seeds are found, the nature of archaeological remains makes the differentiation of individual species problematic.[11] Understanding where tobacco grew or was used by aboriginal cultures is undeniably difficult, and understanding the importance of tobacco within aboriginal cultures is more difficult still.

The very nature of the plant seems to resist being pinned down. As Catherine Ferland has recently noted, even one species of tobacco could produce enough chemical and morphological diversity to frustrate colonial growers. In eighteenth-century New France, the variability of tobacco severely limited the market for what administrators had hoped would become a valuable colonial cash crop.[12] For the historian, providing a stable and representative image of tobacco is no easier. This is due, in part, to the fact that tobacco has an enormous natural growing range that has expanded dramatically since the Columbian Exchange. There are seventy-five species of tobacco worldwide with chemical properties that vary according to virtually every ecological condition imaginable. *Nicotiana rustica* has a natural growing range from the Great Lakes to northern Mexico and nicotine contents that range anywhere from 2 to 18 percent.[13] If historians have found coming to terms with tobacco's history difficult, it is a result of the fact that the identity of the plant seems fluid, continually changing what can be said about it and who is capable of speaking for it.[14] Thus it may not be surprising that it has proven a difficult actor to integrate into the history of contact between natives and newcomers. Historical authors, on the other hand, seem to have often been less confused about how to treat the plant.

TOBACCO AND FRANCE'S ENCOUNTER WITH THE INDIGENOUS PEOPLES OF THE GREAT LAKES REGION

Tobacco was already thoroughly integrated in contemporary European cultures by the time the French first arrived in the Great Lakes region. However, it was aboriginal usage of tobacco that first drew the attention of French travelers to the plant. Tobacco does not appear to have been innately important for French authors but rather became relevant because of its perceived prevalence in the aboriginal societies with which they interacted.[15] Jesuit superior at Quebec and missionary to the Innu (Montagnais) Paul Le Jeune, for instance, wrote in 1633, "Oh, how grateful I am to those who sent me some Tobacco last year. The Savages love it to madness."[16] French authors who described cultural encounters with aboriginal cultures in North America valued tobacco because of its importance in indigenous cultures.

This way of viewing tobacco was representative of broader historical trends in early modern Europe, where tobacco accrued economic value as a colonial commodity but gained cultural significance primarily through consumption. While not necessarily verbose, tobacco was nonetheless understood to say a great deal about those who used it and the cultures in which it was situated. Thus in both the Great Lakes region and St. Lawrence valley, understanding cultural encounters increasingly came to mean understanding the significance of the specifics of tobacco usage. At the same time, for French authors in North America, understanding tobacco meant observing aboriginal peoples and the way in which they used it before theorizing the meaning that they gave the plant.

Yet even as French travelers sought to understand tobacco by studying its place in native societies, native societies were seen through the medium of tobacco. The early accounts of Jesuit missionaries in the St. Lawrence valley and eastern Great Lakes region often tied broader critiques of indigenous cultures to tobacco use. In these critiques, smoking became emblematic of more deeply rooted moral failings of aboriginal peoples. Paul Le Jeune's often quoted opinion that one can "say with compassion that they pass their lives in smoke, and at death fall into the fire" is typical and reveals the associations that early missionaries drew between tobacco use and diabolism.[17] Although Le Jeune was writing about the Innu, Jesuit accounts of Wendat tobacco consumption reveal how these types of associations extended to descriptions of the aboriginal peoples of the Great Lakes region as well. For example, after seeing a Wendat man throw tobacco on a fire to ask for success in hunting and for the protection of his cabin, the Jesuit Jean de Brébeuf wrote in 1637 that the missionaries' "hearts ached, that we could not prevent these infamous sacrifices."[18] As the significance of aboriginal smoking changed over time, however, French authors took an increasingly positive view of its role in contact situations. In 1679, a little less than half a century after Brébeuf's account, the Recollect missionary Louis Hennepin interpreted the refusal of the Siouan peoples who had taken him captive to smoke with him as evidence "that their design was to murder us."[19]

These examples resonate with the growing sense in early modern Europe that tobacco was an essentially fluid object that had little innate meaning separate from the contexts of its consumption. That a plant that could be both a killer and savior in the same texts should be loosely defined in the abstract is not surprising. Even its very nature as an accepted panacea meant that it was understood that tobacco could adapt to treat a multitude of different humoral complexions and maladies.[20] In France, stories of reattached severed limbs, cured migraines, and healed wounds accompanied Jean Nicot as he returned with news and seeds of the plant from his post as ambassador to Portugal in 1561. According to first reports, tobacco could do virtually anything, but not to everyone and not everywhere. Accepted within a medical culture that took for granted the mutability and difference of body types, little could be said about any single sickness, let alone remedy, in the absence of a carefully defined context that included patients and what we might now consider their local ecologies.[21] We can read, for instance, that what could be a cure for some was "the same as putting a fire to oil" for others.[22] Tobacco was understood to possess the potential to cure virtually every illness known to early modern Europeans, but it could kill just as easily and was seen as dangerous in the hands of the untrained consumer. Some thought the dangers were not worth the potential costs; the early seventeenth-century author Barthelemy Vincent argued that the plant was nothing less than a new Pandora's box.[23] Thus, as the ontology of tobacco remained essentially uncertain, the texts that described it became resolutely empiricist and carefully noted the circumstances of its consumption. The truth about tobacco was in the details.

While opinion about its medicinal qualities remained mixed, tobacco gradually became a popular form of recreation. Yet as tobacco "leapt the cultural divide" and left its origins in pagan aboriginal cultures behind, certain types of consumption were rendered more or less civilized, and some more or less savage.[24] In the early to mid-seventeenth century, smoking was seen as a particularly dangerous form of consumption. Seventeenth-century French authors such as the Sieur de Prade and Louis Ferrant, for example, told stories of autopsies of shrunken heads and brains blackened with smoke and recounted countless stories of youths killed by a lack of restraint with the dangerous commodity.[25] Smoking was also seen as an aesthetic menace that was both visually and aromatically unpleasant.[26] For those who did smoke, and as a form of consumption of tobacco in both Old France and New, smoking was second only to snuff; it emerged principally as a leisure activity that was constructed in relation with and closely bound to the consumption of alcohol.[27] So certainly it was not that tobacco was devoid of all meaning, but rather that tobacco was consumed and experienced in diverse settings as essentially different things.

Conditioned by aboriginal peoples to locate tobacco at the heart of contact and trained by the French practice to locate the meaning of tobacco in its particular mode of consumption, the French missionaries, merchants, soldiers, and travelers who met aboriginal cultures in the Great Lakes region carefully observed and analyzed the visual dimensions of smoking for clues about the peoples whom they were meeting. It is clear that much of what they could describe had been determined for them by what aboriginal peoples themselves had decided was essential in meeting the newcomers. This included specific spatial arrangements (inclusion/exclusion, processions, etc.), bodily movements (dances, sacrifices, etc.), and the oral elements of the encounter (silence, song, speeches, etc.).[28] Likewise, historians such as Richard White and Robert Morrissey have convincingly argued that these French authors misunderstood much of what they saw and experienced in indigenous cultures even as the French carefully observed and studied the new peoples and cultures that they met.[29] Yet these misunderstandings became the basis of successful diplomatic, economic, and cultural exchanges throughout the Great Lakes region. French observations of indigenous smoking therefore embedded tobacco and its use within French aesthetic, medical, and social discourses even as they used it as the basis for contact with aboriginal cultures.[30] While it may be tempting to see this as a limiting analysis of aboriginal custom, French efforts to abstract smoking from its aboriginal cultural context were in fact generative, forging new associations between European and aboriginal practice and assembling new knowledge about tobacco and the peoples who consumed it.

Localized and individual encounters became the basis for a universalized knowledge of contact. French participants carefully dissected the performance of tobacco consumption, isolating it from other elements of contact and framing it as the key to understanding the significance of larger cultural exchanges. Presented as a coherent assemblage of pipes and behaviors, knowledge about smoking could be stabilized as a sort of dictionary of aboriginal movements and aesthetics centered on the performance of tobacco consumption. When Hennepin became convinced that the failure of the Dakota who had taken him captive in 1680 to smoke signaled their deception, he was abstracting from a field of knowledge that had been built on the careful analysis of aboriginal smoking as it had happened in the countless local encounters of French travelers in the region. Reapplied to his present situation as a set of normative behaviors and visual cues understood to be universal among aboriginal peoples of the Great Lakes, Hennepin was able to use the presence (or in this case absence) of tobacco to claim to understand the significance of the behavior of peoples he had only just met.[31]

Hennepin's account attempted to provide his readers and later travelers with a how-to guide that distilled aboriginal practice and reconstituted it within a French discourse that his readers could comprehend. Echoing many other authors who wrote on this subject, in 1684 Lahontan wrote that "the red calumets are the most in vogue and the most esteemed. The savages use them for negotiations, for their political affairs, and above all in their voyages, being able to travel everywhere in security when they carry this Calumet in their hand."[32] Often these representations had enough in common with aboriginal practices that, from a French point of view, smoking "worked" as a bridge between cultures that could be transported successfully outside of its local cultural contexts and beyond the Great Lakes region. For example, in 1673, when Marquette met indigenous peoples who were likely Chickasaw farther south on the Mississippi River, he claimed that it was the sight of his calumet that "had checked the ardor" of what had initially seemed a hostile reception.[33]

The French looked to their own culture for clues about the significance of aboriginal performances associated with smoking. Smoking together was increasingly understood as a simple means of signaling an accord in both New France and Old, so that the Baron de Lahontan told an Iroquois delegation in 1684, "The intention of this grand monarch [the king of France] is that we smoke, you and I, together in the grand Calumet of peace; as long as you promise me in the name of the *Tsonnontouans, Goyoguans, Onnontagues, Onnoyoutes & Agnies* to give an entire satisfaction and damages to his subjects and to do nothing in the future that could cause an angry rupture."[34] Frequently these authors compared smoking together with aboriginal peoples to drinking a toast. This was particularly true in the case of accounts of the ritual-laden calumet ceremony that became prevalent in the southern Great Lakes and Mississippi regions. The Jesuit Pierre-François-Xavier de Charlevoix made this comparison explicitly when he wrote, "To smoke therefore in the same pipe as a sign of alliance is the same thing as to drink from the same cup, as is commonly practiced in several nations."[35] Jesuit missionary and explorer Claude Allouez similarly wrote of the calumet among the Illinois in 1667, "This ceremony resembles in its significance the French custom of drinking several out of the same glass."[36]

The writings of French travelers show the ruthless dissection of aboriginal cultural practice and a consistent effort to translate experiences of ritual smoking into the terms of a European discourse. Hennepin, for instance, wrote that "when the Nadouessians and the Issati take Tobacco, they look upon the Sun, which they call in their Language *Louis*; and as soon as they have lighted their Pipe, they present it to the Sun with these Words, *Tchendiouba Louis*, that is to say, *Smoke Sun*; which I took for a kind of Adoration."[37] Also describing the use of the calumet, the Jesuit Joseph-François Lafitau wrote: "They walked with solemn steps and lifting their pipes toward the sun, seemed to present these to them to smoke, still without saying a word."[38] We can see a similar attention to the individual postures, behaviors, language, and gestures that formed the basis of knowledge of tobacco in French North America in the writing of Claude-Charles le Roy de Bacqueville de la Potherie, who wrote: "This elder made great exclamations over the iron, who appeared to him a spirit; we lit the Calumet and each smoked. . . . We once again filled the Calumet, those who smoked sent the smoke of the tobacco to the face of the French as the greatest honour that they could render him; whoever saw himself smoked [*se voyait boucaner*] said not a word."[39] Likely this effort to decode aboriginal consumption of tobacco was influenced as well by a more general interest in aboriginal bodies and the conviction that they offered the key to a great deal of knowledge about the moral and natural environments of the New World. If, as Stéphanie Chaffray has shown us, French travelers were far more curious about indigenous bodies than indigenous environments, then what chance did a single plant have?[40]

As the focus of French texts on the act of smoking continued, it was increasingly not what was smoked, but how it was smoked that established claims made about contact between aboriginals and the French in the Great Lakes region. There is a noticeable trajectory here as, over the course of the seventeenth century, tobacco itself received less attention than its consumption in accounts of smoking. This was part of a larger pattern that was also evident in seventeenth- and eighteenth-century Europe, where the dire warnings about smoking were minimized as the plant became an accepted facet of European social life. Tobacco, or even smoking, was increasingly seen less as innately dangerous than as dangerous solely to those who might abuse it. Authors such as the popular scientist Pierre-Joseph Buc'hoz, who wrote in the mid-to-late eighteenth century, continued to draw attention to the risks posed by smoking tobacco and recounted familiar tales of brains blackened by the abuse of tobacco. Yet these accounts were presented as hearsay, and this author suggested that they were less credible than the numerous firsthand observations of tobacco's considerable benefits.[41] Whereas in 1625 Johann Neander told horror stories about people falling victim to tobacco even after light consumption, by the mid-eighteenth century Buc'hoz's cautionary tales featured victims who had regularly consumed as much as three ounces of tobacco a day or who had died after a contest to see who could smoke the most in an afternoon.[42] This should not be surprising as, by the eighteenth century, tobacco use was not only accepted but popular; the plant that had once seemed so foreign was included in botanical texts on plants that were native to Europe.[43]

In the Great Lakes region, tobacco was removed from the act of smoking in accounts that made no reference to the plant itself. It was eventually thought to be enough simply to show a pipe or to choose a particular pipe to smoke with.[44] Tobacco was also separated from smoking in the language used to describe the act. For example, Gabriel Sagard used the verb *"pétuner"* in both his *Histoire du Canada* (1615) and his *Le grand voyage du pays des Hurons situé en l'Amérique* (1632).[45] However, in the late seventeenth century authors almost universally used *"fumer."* The distinction here is a subtle one because the performances they describe seem almost identical. Yet *"pétuner"* did not take a direct object, and *"pétun,"* as tobacco was then known, was implied and inseparable from the action of smoking. Later authors described what it was to *fumer*, and often dropped the explicit mention of tobacco. Smoking, rather than smoking tobacco, had become the essential element. Authors increasingly suggested that it was enough to go through the motions and that the desired effect of peace and commerce could be achieved without smoke, and thus without tobacco.[46] While Sagard and contemporary authors such as Brébeuf wrote about smoking tobacco explicitly, by the late seventeenth century this was implied, and the particular object being consumed added little to the account.

Additionally, tobacco, once and occasionally still seen as an intoxicant, was increasingly rendered inert or even beneficial by authors who described its role in native cultures. Whereas Neander wrote in the 1620s that aboriginal smokers in the New World used religious ceremonies as an excuse to consume tobacco to a point of drunkenness, Charlevoix wrote in the eighteenth century that "the smoke of their tobacco brings down [*abattre*] the vapors of the brain, renders the head free, awakens the mind, and puts us in a state to do business."[47] Lafitau went further still in 1724 when he explicitly wrote against earlier authors who "declaim violently against tobacco and regard it as a pest and poison which came from hell," but who, he believed, "were undoubtedly deceived by the effect which tobacco produces on people who do not know how to smoke and are not accustomed to its odour."[48] If tobacco was smoked properly, it would barely be felt at all, as "it does not cause the same symptoms to those who use it a great deal, like the Americans [aboriginal peoples] who, when they smoke, do not intend to become intoxicated."[49] The assumption that tobacco took on cultural significance only as it was consumed was translated into a consideration of the plant's physiological effects and reiterated its essentially fluid or plastic nature. The result was to further de-emphasize the materiality of the plant, and, indeed, nearly all who wrote about smoking with aboriginal people in the Great Lakes region in the late seventeenth and eighteenth centuries gave the impression that tobacco was the least important part of smoking.

TOBACCO, ABORIGINAL PEOPLES, AND THE RECEPTION OF FRENCH NEWCOMERS IN THE GREAT LAKES REGION

While French accounts of smoking increasingly silenced tobacco, the attention that their accounts gave to the performative aspects of smoking in the Great Lakes region provides ample opportunity to examine diverse aboriginal conceptions of tobacco and to see how these cultures understood the place of the plant in contact situations with the French. Central to this task is to relax our own conceptions of tobacco and to ease out of the constraints imposed by sources that left little room for consideration of the plant itself. Likewise, if we stick to the idea that tobacco was little more than a nicotine delivery vehicle, it soon becomes apparent that aboriginal peoples of the Great Lakes region were getting it all wrong.

A first step in examining aboriginal relationships with tobacco involves reconnecting smoking with what French authors described as the sacrifice of dried tobacco. There are two immediate consequences to this approach. First, it broadens our idea of what it meant to consume tobacco, and, second, it raises questions about who was actually consuming the plant in the ritual uses of tobacco described by French travelers. Most contemporary authors who have focused on smoking and pipes have been quick to mention, and as quick to pass over, the perhaps surprising prevalence of tobacco as either dry or burned offerings to the other-than-human beings that populated aboriginal realities. Yet as von Gernet has recently written, "It was not the pipe but the substances it contained that empowered individuals with a sense of the supernatural and offered a means of communicating with other-than-human potencies."[50]

Historical authors offered accounts of numerous and widespread offerings of tobacco even as they divorced them from their descriptions of smoking in aboriginal cultures. Lafitau, for instance, related that "they throw tobacco and other herbs which they use in place of tobacco into the fire in honour of the Sun; they also throw some into lakes and rivers in honour of the presiding spirits."[51] Describing Wendat customs in 1636, Brébeuf wrote:

> They address themselves to the Earth, to Rivers, to dangerous Rocks, but above all, to the Sky; and believe that all these things are animate, and that some powerful Demon resides there. They are not contented with making simple vows, they often accompany them with a sort of sacrifice. I have remarked two kinds of these. Some are to render them propitious and favourable; others to appease them, when they have received in their opinion some disgrace from them, or believe they incurred their anger or indignation. Here are the ceremonies they employ in these sacrifices. They throw some Tobacco into the fire; and if it is, for example, to the Sky that they address themselves, they say *Aronkiaté onné aonstanias taitenr*, "O Sky, here is what I offer thee in sacrifice, have pity on me, assist me." If it is to implore health *taenguiaens*, "Heal me." They have recourse to the Sky in almost all their necessities and respect the great bodies in it above all creatures, and remark in it in particular something divine.[52]

These sorts of ritual uses of tobacco often seem to have been tied to the sanctity of particular spaces, such as specific rocks or rivers. The Jesuit *Relations*, for instance, describes a certain lake that was thought to be populated by beings who prepared flint for the Haudenosaunee who had need of them and who demanded tobacco in return.[53] Just as often these sorts of offerings were tied to the need to hunt or fish.[54] In all cases they were directed at beings who possessed powers sought after by aboriginal peoples of the Great Lakes region—power named *manidoo* by Algonquian cultures, *orenda* by the Haudenosaunee, and *wašicun* by Siouan cultures. The anthropologist Irving Hallowell wrote that among the Ojibwa whom he had studied, "a natural-supernatural dichotomy has no place."[55] He later added that in a culture in which "natural forces" as such did not exist, these beings were "neither the personification of a natural phenomenon nor an altogether animal-like or human-like being."[56] Rather, these were beings thought able to intervene and influence the human and natural world of the Great Lakes region and who were counted upon to influence the outcome of human interaction with plants, animals, and the physical environment with what Bruce White has referred to as "control power."[57] These beings were fond of or even addicted to tobacco, and, as they sacrificed and smoked the plant, aboriginal peoples sought to engage them in reciprocal relationships.[58]

Thus it is hardly surprising that in 1702 some of the aboriginal converts at the mission of St. François Xavier sprinkled tobacco "all around the church, which is a kind of worship that they pay to their divinities; and, when they go inside, they have not enough of it to satisfy their desire to throw some to the true God, as to the greatest divinity of whom they have ever heard."[59] Accounts in which aboriginal peoples sprinkled tobacco at the feet of French missionaries or explorers suggest that the French themselves were sometimes understood to be other-than-human.[60] Opinions on these sorts of uses of tobacco were not surprisingly mixed. Early seventeenth-century accounts, for instance, saw these sorts of offerings as little more than superstition and excuses for drunkenness and immoral behavior.[61] Those missionaries who held this viewpoint went to pains to attempt to show aboriginal peoples that such offerings, while right in spirit, were misdirected and unnecessary.[62] Others who recognized the intent in such actions, however, saw sacrifices of tobacco to the Christian God as a sign of reverence. The Jesuit Claude Dablon, for example, "could hardly restrain [his] tears of joy at seeing the crucified Jesus Christ worshipped by a Savage," after seeing an unnamed aboriginal man at his mission to the Illinois sprinkle powdered tobacco over his crucifix in 1670.[63]

The centrality of tobacco offerings to aboriginal conceptions of the plant is reinforced if we turn to origin stories and the work of anthropologists who wrote and worked among nineteenth- and twentieth-century Great Lakes aboriginal cultures. In the Oneida creation story, for instance, tobacco is a plant that preexists even the creation of Turtle Island (North America) itself. As Sky Woman fell from Sky World after being pushed through a hole in the sky by the husband who had questioned her fidelity, she grabbed tobacco as she fell and took it, without any specific intent, beyond the reach of the other-than-human beings that continued to populate Sky World. As the desire for tobacco was no less among these other-than-human beings, in the future they were forced into an accommodation with the Iroquoian people who henceforth cultivated it. Thus offering tobacco seems less a sacrifice in the Christian sense of the word than an attempt at maintaining reciprocal relationships with these beings who in turn ensured successful hunts, reliable harvests, and miraculous cures.[64] While this is only one of the eight possible origins of tobacco identified by von Gernet in the oral histories of Iroquoian people, it provides a clear sense of tobacco's other-than-human origins.[65]

Similarly, Paul Radin's retelling of one particular articulation of a Ho-chunk origin story suggests that tobacco was a gift to human beings to facilitate their relationships with beings with powers upon which they depended:

> Earthmaker created the spirits who live above the earth, those who live under the earth, and those that live in the water; all these he created and placed in charge of some powers. Even the minor spirits who move around, Earthmaker caused to have rule over some blessing. In this fashion he created them and only afterwards did he create us. For that reason we were not put in control of any of these blessings. However, Earthmaker did create a weed and put it in our charge, and he told us that none of the spirits he had created would have the power to take this away from us without giving us something in exchange. Thus said Earthmaker. Even he, Earthmaker, would not have the power of taking this from us without giving up something in return. He told us that if we offered him a pipeful of tobacco, if this we poured out for him, he would grant us whatever we asked of him. Now all the spirits came to long for this tobacco as intensely as they longed for anything in creation, and for that reason, they will take pity on us and bestow on us the blessings of which Earthmaker placed them in charge. Indeed so it shall be, for thus Earthmaker created it.[66]

Tobacco is therefore only in a limited sense what might be called a gift of the gods since it was neither created for the Iroquoian or Algonquian peoples in the first place, nor was it intended for their own consumption. The gift was control of the plant and the ability to distribute it. I would therefore suggest that an individuated, pharmacologically defined conception of consumption limits our understanding of tobacco in aboriginal cultures. Indeed, if one looks closely, it is possible to suggest that aboriginal peoples were not the consumers of tobacco but acted as proxies for the other-than-human beings they mobilized when they smoked or sacrificed the plant.

In historical French accounts what emerged is an image of what might therefore be termed an impersonal consumption. While modern authors provide physiological and pharmacological explanations of tobacco's effects on the human body, aboriginal smokers believed that they were simply an intermediary for other-than-human beings who were the real recipients of the plant's power. For instance, Charlevoix commented on how aboriginal people used the calumet, writing that they "have the intention to take the Sun as a witness and in some fashion as a guarantor of their treaties; for they never miss to push the smoke towards this star."[67] This action of pushing the smoke, so meticulously and frequently noted by French observers, suggests that aboriginal peoples, as much as pipes, were vessels for a sacred smoke. According to the research of Jordan Paper, pipe design often reinforced this suggestion, with intended recipients carved into bowls to face the smoker, establishing a bond between the smoking of the one and the consumption of the other.[68]

Aboriginal conceptions of tobacco and contact therefore are made visible when we understand that smoking and sacrifices were inexorably linked in the seventeenth- and eighteenth-century Great Lakes region. Some French-authored accounts that seem to bridge the gap between personal consumption and offering to an other-than-human being demonstrate that French efforts to separate the consumption and sacrifice of tobacco were ultimately mistaken. At Chouskouabika (on the shores of present-day Green Bay), for example, a Potawatomi man "possessed a Stone Idol, which, however, had not the slightest resemblance to the human form. Still, it was his God; he offered it tobacco to smoke, dedicated his feasts in its honor; adorned it with porcelain, and embellished it with paint."[69] An even clearer example comes from Nicolas Perrot, who wrote about the treatment of bears that had been killed by Algonquian hunters. Perrot's account stated that, "as they kill them, they light their pipes and put the pipe in their mouth. They push the smoke out by the nostrils of this animal."[70] Bacqueville de la Potherie added that this was inspired to "weaken their fury and to ask them to have no resentment against them [who killed them] or those who would want to kill others."[71] In spite of the fact that tobacco was clearly offered in these instances, the neat division that French authors tried to construct between sacrifices and smoking no longer seems tenable.

Numerous accounts that suggest that tobacco did not count as a food during fasts further suggest that aboriginal peoples who smoked understood that they were not consuming the plant themselves. At the mission to the Mascouten, for example, Allouez was told by a man "that he had not eaten [any food] for Five days, but had only smoked [a little]."[72] Almost forty years earlier, Brébeuf recounted that a Wendat man, "after having fasted eighteen days without tasting anything, it is said, except tobacco, came to see me; I gave him seven or eight raisins; he thanked me and told me he would eat one every day—that was in order to not break his fast."[73] Joseph Winter has even suggested that cravings that we today associate with addiction may have been seen as the personal embodiment of a need felt by other-than-human beings. By extension, even the pleasure that aboriginal consumers of tobacco felt as they smoked was not necessarily their own and was shared as much as the tobacco itself.[74]

If tobacco was increasingly smoked with rather than offered to French travelers and traders, does this mean an increasing secularization of a sacred crop and, for aboriginal peoples, of contact? Maybe, but likely not. What it might suggest instead is the continued sacred dimension of aboriginal experience in aboriginal-French contact. It might also suggest ongoing attempts to incorporate the French into an aboriginal world populated with a multitude of categories and ontologies alien to French ways of being. In early encounters tobacco was thrown at the feet of French visitors who seemed to possess the powers of other-than-human beings to engage them in the sorts of reciprocal exchanges that such an offering implied. Even as French traders, missionaries, and diplomats were increasingly understood to be thoroughly human, the aboriginal interest in smoking tobacco with them may be seen as an attempt to bond them with the other-than-human beings that peopled the Great Lakes region and who depended on tobacco. Even as Jesuits and other missionaries roamed the Pays d'en Haut working to save pagan souls, aboriginal peoples may have been, if not proselytizing, then at least teaching—teaching the French the proper behavior toward the sacred in encounters that, from the perspective of Great Lakes aboriginal peoples, can no longer be seen as solely involving natives and newcomers.

CONCLUSION

Tracing the ontology of tobacco and its place in aboriginal realities that were far more populous than those of European observers thus reveals that contact was as much both a human and spiritual encounter. Just as the French used tobacco, and increasingly smoking, as a means by which to make aboriginal peoples comprehensible, these same aboriginal peoples of the Great Lakes region used tobacco to make sense of the newcomers to their region and to integrate them into more familiar relations with neighboring nations and other-than-human beings. What is fascinating, then, about what von Gernet has called the "Pipe/Tobacco/Smoking complex" is its ability to support the multiple conceptions of contact developed by French and aboriginal participants simultaneously.[75] The plant, both in and of itself and as it was consumed, allowed for both natives and newcomers to maintain the "creative misunderstandings" on which contact in the Great Lakes region depended,[76] for this was a nearly infinitely malleable toolbox able to simultaneously feed humors and spirits and to make sense of contact for all parties involved. Based on a limited set of shared behaviors toward the plant, tobacco itself could bridge and transcend cultures meeting even for the first time.

The history of tobacco in the Great Lakes region is the history of the encounters between aboriginal peoples and French explorers and missionaries. As a physical mediator of this contact and as an object mobilized by both natives and newcomers to assimilate and make the other knowable, tobacco highlights the ontological dimensions of what are often more narrowly defined as economic or diplomatic exchanges. From what we might today identify as cravings, pleasure, or the smoke produced in its consumption, tobacco provided a host of possible associations, determining none in advance. Ethnobotanist Wade Davis has written that plants should primarily be thought of as providing a base for pharmacological possibility, and that seems very true here.[77] In providing both natives and newcomers with a set of tools with which to make sense of themselves and each other in contact, tobacco had a direct influence on the ways in which knowledge was made and in which contact was experienced. But with what must ultimately be considered a productive force, tobacco must be seen as having opened up rather than simply limited contact, allowing for the encounter of not just natives and newcomers but also their respective realities.

NOTES

1. The anthropologist Irving Hallowell coined the term "other-than-human beings" in his work on twentieth-century Ojibwa communities. Striving to avoid the Western connotations of words such as "supernatural" or "spirits," I use this term to describe those agencies in aboriginal worldviews that were responsible for the character of the natural world and that mediated aboriginal relationships with their immediate physical environments. See A. Irving Hallowell, "Ojibwa Ontology, Behavior, and World View," in *Contributions to Anthropology: Selected Papers of A. Irving Hallowell* (Chicago: University of Chicago Press, 1976), 357–390.

2. Lahontan, *Œuvres complètes*, ed. Réal Ouellet and Alain Beaulieu, 2 vols. (Montreal: Presses de l'Université de Montréal, 1990), 1:407. Unless otherwise noted, all translations have been made by the author.

3. See, for instance, the many essays in Sean Rafferty and Rob Mann, eds., *Smoking and Culture: The Archaeology of Tobacco Pipes in Eastern North America* (Knoxville: University of Tennessee Press, 2004); Alexander von Gernet, "The Transculturation of the Amerindian Pipe/Tobacco/Smoking Complex and Its Impact on the Intellectual Boundaries between 'Savagery' and 'Civilization,' 1535–1935" (Ph.D. diss., McGill University, 1988).

4. For this particular phrasing, see Robert L. Hall, "An Anthropocentric Perspective for Eastern United States Prehistory," *American Antiquity* 42 (1977): 499–518.

5. Springer himself goes beyond this simplification and devotes a significant part of his article to exploring tobacco in and of itself, and yet the phrase that opens his article leaves little question about the relative importance of the ingredients of the "smoking complex." James Warren Springer, "An Ethnohistoric Study of the Smoking Complex in Eastern North America," *Ethnohistory* 28 (1981): 217–218.

6. See the essays in Joseph C. Winter, ed., *Tobacco Use by Native North Americans: Sacred Smoke and Silent Killer* (Norman: University of Oklahoma Press, 2000); and Jordan Goodman, *Tobacco in History: The Cultures of Dependence* (London: Routledge, 1993).

7. Joseph C. Winter, "The Food of the Gods: Biochemistry, Addiction & the Development of Native American Tobacco Use," in *Tobacco Use by Native North Americans: Sacred Smoke and Silent Killer*, ed. Joseph C. Winter (Norman: University of Oklahoma Press, 2000), 325.

8. For a description of the process by which seeds are recovered at archaeological sites, see Thomas W. Haberman, "Evidence for Aboriginal Tobaccos in Eastern North America," *American Antiquity* 49 (1984): 273.

9. Sean Rafferty, "'They Pass Their Lives in Smoke, and at Death Fall into the Fire': Smoking Pipes and Mortuary Ritual during the Early Woodland Period," in Rafferty and Mann, *Smoking and Culture*, 1.

10. Gail E. Wagner, "Tobacco in Prehistoric Eastern North America," in Winter, *Tobacco Use by Native North Americans*, 200.

11. Joseph C. Winter, "Introduction to the North American Tobacco Species," in Winter, *Tobacco Use by Native North Americans*, 8.

12. Catherine Ferland, "Une pratique 'sauvage'? Le tabagisme de l'ancienne à la nouvelle France, XVIIe–XVIIIe siècles," in *abac & fumées: regards multidisciplinaires et indisciplinés sur le tabagisme, XVe–XXe siècles*, ed. Catherine Ferland (Quebec: Presses de l'Université Laval, 2007), 90.

13. Seven of these species seem to have been extant at contact. Winter, "Introduction to the North American Tobacco Species," 4.

14. The theory of fluid objects is discussed in Marianne de Laet and Annemarie Mol, "The Zimbabwe Bush Pump: Mechanics of a Fluid Technology," *Social Studies of Science* 30 (2000): 227.

15. Sylvie Savoie, "La nourriture des Dieux . . . et des humains: le tabac dans les sociétés autochtones du Nord-Est, XVIIᵉ–XVIIIᵉ siècles," in *Les systèmes religieux amérindiens et inuit: perspectives historiques et contemporaines*, ed. Claude Gélinas and Guillaume Teasdale (Quebec and Paris: In Situ and L'Harmattan, 2007), 44.

16. Reuben Gold Thwaites, ed., *The Jesuit Relations and Allied Documents: Travels and Explorations of the Jesuit Missionaries in New France, 1610–1791*, 73 vols. (Cleveland: Burrows Brothers, 1896–1903), 5:109–111.

17. Ibid., 7:133.

18. Ibid., 13:261.

19. Louis Hennepin, *A New Discovery of a Vast Country in America*, ed. Reuben Gold Thwaites (Toronto: Coles Publishing, 1974), 229.

20. von Gernet, "Transculturation of the Amerindian," 60; Goodman, *Tobacco in History*, 54. For the best coverage of the earliest controversies over tobacco, see Sarah Augusta Dickson, *Panacea or Precious Bane: Tobacco in Sixteenth-Century Literature* (New York: New York Public Library, 1954).

21. von Gernet, "Transculturation of the Amerindian," 60. Since the seventeenth century, Nicot's story is recounted by virtually every author interested in tobacco. For a recent recounting, see ibid., 31–40.

22. Jean Ostendorpf, *Traicté de l'usage et abus du tabac* (Bordeaux: A. Castra, 1636), 11.

23. Barthelemy Vincent, "Le traducteur au lecteur," in Johann Neander, *Traicté du tabac, ou nicotiane, panacée, petun: autrement herbe à la reyne, avec sa préparation et son usage*, trans. Barthelemy Vincent (Lyon: B. Vincent, 1625), n.p.

24. Peter C. Mancall, "Tales Tobacco Told in Sixteenth-Century Europe," *Environmental History* 17 (October 2004): 17; Goodman, *Tobacco in History*, 81–84.

25. Jean le Royer, Sieur de Prade, *Discours du tabac: où il est traité particulièrement du tabac en poudre* (Paris: M. le Prest, 1688), 98; Louis Ferrant, *Traité du tabac en sternutatoire* (Bourges: 1655), 10.

26. See, for example, the proscriptions against smoking in civilized company of Antoine de Courtin in his *Nouveau traité de la civilité qui se pratique en France parmi les honnestes gens* (Paris: L. Josse & C. Robustel: 1728), *passim*.

27. Pierre-Joseph Buc'hoz, *Dictionnaire universel des plantes, arbres et arbustes de la France* (Paris: Lacombe, 1770), 356; Ferland, "Une pratique 'sauvage'?," 93;

Goodman, *Tobacco in History*, 66, 81; von Gernet, "Transculturation of the Amerindian," 114.

28. For representative accounts of spatial arrangements see Lahontan, *Œuvres complètes*, 1:406–407; Thwaites, *Jesuit Relations*, 59:113–121, 65:117. For representative accounts of physical performance, see Hennepin, *New Discovery*, 246, 408, 412; Nicolas Perrot, *Mœurs, coutumes et religion des sauvages de l'Amérique septentrionale*, ed. Pierre Berthiaume (Montreal: Presses de l'Université de Montréal, 2004), 195; Thwaites, *Jesuit Relations*, 15:27, 17:93, 51:47. For representative accounts of oral encounters, see François-Xavier de Charlevoix, *Journal d'un voyage fait par ordre du roi dans l'Amérique septentrionale*, ed. Pierre Berthiaume (Montreal: Presses de l'Université de Montréal, 1994), 605; Thwaites, *Jesuit Relations*, 11:209, 12:147, 13:201, 54:231, 59:129–131.

29. White explains, however, that many of these misunderstandings could still lead to productive cultural exchange. These creative misunderstandings became a key facet of what White refers to as "the middle ground." See Richard White, *The Middle Ground: Indians, Empires, and Republics in the Great Lakes Region, 1650–1815* (New York: Cambridge University Press, 1991), 52—53; Robert Morrissey, "Bottomlands, Boderlands: Empires and Identities in the 18th Century Illinois Country" (Ph.D. diss., Yale University, 2006), chapter 3.

30. For a further elaboration of situated sight and embedded objects, see Charles Goodwin and Marjorie Harris Goodwin, "Seeing as a Situated Activity: Formulating Planes," in *Cognition and Communication at Work*, ed. Yrjo Engeström and David Middleton (Cambridge: Cambridge University Press, 1997), 61–95. For a broader consideration of situated knowledges, see Donna Haraway, "Situated Knowledges: The Science Question and the Privilege of Partial Perspective," *Feminist Studies* 14 (Autumn 1988): 575–599.

31. Hennepin, *New Discovery*, 229.

32. Lahontan, *Œuvres complètes*, 1:303.

33. Thwaites, *Jesuit Relations*, 59:149.

34. Lahontan, *Œuvres complètes*, 1:305.

35. Charlevoix, *Journal d'un voyage*, 471.

36. Thwaites, *Jesuit Relations*, 51:47.

37. Hennepin, *New Discovery*, 214.

38. Joseph-François Lafitau, *Customs of the American Indians Compared with the Customs of the First Times*, 2 vols., trans. and ed. William N. Fenton and Elizabeth L. Moore (Toronto: Champlain Society, 1974–1977), 1:176.

39. Claude-Charles le Roy de Bacqueville de la Potherie, *Histoire de l'Amérique septentrionale*, 4 vols. (Paris: J.-L. Nion et F. Didot, 1722), 1:106.

40. Stéphanie Chaffray, "Corps, territoire et paysage à travers les images et les textes viatiques en Nouvelle-France (1701–1756)," *Revue d'histoire de l'Amérique française* 59 (2005): 42, 45.

41. Buc'hoz, *Dictionnaire universel des plantes*, 355–358.

42. Neander, *Traicté du tabac*, 55–56; Buc'hoz, *Dictionnaire universel des plantes*, 355–358.

43. See, for instance, John Pechey, *The Compleat Herbal of Physical Plants, Containing all such English and Foreign Herbs, Shrubs and Trees, as are used in Physick and Surgery . . . the Doses or Quantities of such as are Prescribed by the London-Physicians* (London: H. Bonwicke, 1694).

44. Thwaites, *Jesuit Relations*, 59:149; Hennepin, *New Discovery*, 229.

45. Gabriel Sagard, *Histoire du Canada et voyages que les frères récollets y ont faicts pour la conversion des infidèles depuis l'an 1615* (Paris: Librairie Tross, 1866), 177, 207, 222, 242; Gabriel Sagard, *Le grand voyage du pays des Hurons situé en l'Amérique* (Paris: Chez Denys Moreau, 1632), 106, 122.

46. Thwaites, *Jesuit Relations*, 60:155.

47. Neander, *Traicté du tabac*, 49; Charlevoix, *Journal d'un voyage*, 471.

48. Lafitau, *Customs of the American Indians*, 1:82. A similar quote can be found in Thwaites, *Jesuit Relations*, 44:275.

49. Lafitau, *Customs of the American Indians*, 1:82.

50. Alexander von Gernet, "North American Indigenous *Nicotiana* Use and Tobacco Shamanism: The Early Documentary Record, 1520–1660," in Winter, *Tobacco Use by Native North Americans*, 74.

51. Lafitau, *Customs of the American Indians*, 2:133.

52. Thwaites, *Jesuit Relations*, 10:157–159.

53. Ibid., 10:163, 51:181, 55:191, 67:159.

54. Ibid., 9:211, 67:157–159.

55. Hallowell, "Ojibwa Ontology, Behavior, and World View," 367.

56. Ibid., 367, 369.

57. Bruce M. White, "Encounter with Spirits: Ojibwa and Dakota Theories about the French and Their Merchandise," *Ethnohistory* 41 (Summer 1994): 380–381.

58. Ibid., 377; Alexander von Gernet, "Chapter on Mythology to be included in a book on the Iroquoian tobacco complex," Ms. Coll. 20, Series IV, William N. Fenton Papers, ca. 1933—2000, American Philosophical Society, Philadelphia, 2.

59. Thwaites, *Jesuit Relations*, 67:265.

60. Ibid., 51:43, 54:229–231. Bruce White has argued that this was a common feature of early encounters between aboriginal and French cultures in the Great Lakes region. See White, "Encounter with Spirits."

61. Neander, *Traicté du tabac*, 49.

62. In the "mission to the maskoutech, the Illinois and other tribes," for example, Jesuit missionaries tried "To inspire Them with the respect that they should pay to Churches, and I obtained that no one should smoke, and that they should not converse together in it, at least while I was there." Thwaites, *Jesuit Relations*, 58:23, 55:29.

63. Ibid., 55:219–221.

64. Delmus Elm, Harvey Antone, Floyd Glenn Lounsbury, and Bryan Gick, *The Oneida Creation Story* (Lincoln: University of Nebraska Press, 2000), 28–62; see also von Guernet, "Chapter on Mythology," 4.

65. von Guernet, "Chapter on Mythology," fol. 2–8.

66. Paul Radin, "The Autobiography of a Winnebago Indian," *University of California Publications in American Archaeology and Ethnology* 16 (1920): 450–466, cited in Elisabeth Tooker, ed., *Native North American Spirituality of the Eastern Woodlands: Sacred Myths, Dreams, Visions, Speeches, Healing Formulas, Rituals and Ceremonials* (New York: Paulist Press, 1979), 74–75.

67. Charlevoix, *Journal d'un voyage*, 470.

68. Goodman, *Tobacco in History*, 65.

69. Thwaites, *Jesuit Relations*, 57:275.

70. Perrot, *Mœurs, coutumes et religion des sauvages*, 280.

71. Bacqueville de la Potherie, *Histoire de l'Amérique septentionale*, 2:34–35, cited in Perrot, *Mœurs, coutumes et religion des sauvages*, 281.

72. Thwaites, *Jesuit Relations*, 58:27–29.

73. Ibid., 10:203; see also Perrot, *Mœurs, coutumes et religion des sauvages*, 197.

74. Winter, "Food of the Gods," 308.

75. Tobacco might be profitably thought of as akin to the "boundary objects" discussed in Susan Leigh Starr and James R. Greisemer, "Institutional Ecology, 'Translations' and Boundary Objects: Amateurs and Professionals in Berkeley's Museum of Vertebrate Zoology," *Social Studies of Science* 19 (August 1989): 1907–1939.

76. See note 30 for references to the notion of "creative misunderstandings" and their place in contact between French and aboriginal peoples in the seventeenth- and eighteenth-century Great Lakes region.

77. Wade Davis, *The Clouded Leopard: Travels to Landscapes of Spirit and Desire* (Vancouver: Dougllas & McIntyre, 1998), 2.

The Terms of Encounter

Language and Contested Visions of French Colonization in the Illinois Country, 1673–1702

ROBERT MICHAEL MORRISSEY

DURING THE SPRING AND SUMMER OF 1699, TWO PRIESTS—THE Jesuit Julien Binneteau and Marc Bergier, a priest of the Seminary of Foreign Missions—competed to control a tiny mission at an Indian village on the Mississippi River known as Tamaroa, or Cahokia.[1] Vying for the attentions of local Indians, who must have been perplexed by the feuding priests, Bergier and Binneteau sabotaged each other's religious services. Each priest encouraged Indians not to attend the other's mass. The priests spread rumors about one another to the Indians. And, in a show of surprising aggression, Bergier tried to steal property—in particular an Illinois-language dictionary—from Binneteau.[2]

Over the course of a few months, news of this feud reached Quebec, and the controversy grew. The director of the Jesuits in Quebec sent complaints to his superiors in Europe about the Seminary priests, and high-level Seminary priests in Quebec defended Bergier's actions to their own superiors. François Laval, the eminent former bishop of Quebec, weighed in, defending the jurisdiction of the Seminary priests and attacking the Jesuits. Back in France, the king's confessor, himself a Jesuit, made a direct appeal to Louis XIV on behalf of the Jesuits in the Illinois Country.[3] And so a tiny wilderness mission—the most remote in North America—came to the attention of the highest church and secular authorities in the French empire.

It is fitting that an Illinois-language dictionary was an object of Binneteau and Bergier's struggle, because *language* was a central issue in this mission controversy. Previous historians have treated the 1699 contest for the Tamaroa merely as a petty turf war between jealous priests.[4] But historians have missed the broader context that gave this dispute its significance and made it not just a jurisdictional struggle, but a contest over competing missionary strategies in France's overseas empire. When he founded the Jesuit mission of the Immaculate Conception in the Illinois Country in 1673, the Jesuit Jacques Marquette marked the occasion by delivering a speech to the Illinois in their native language. In so doing, he demonstrated that the priests of this new Illinois mission would continue the well-established Jesuit practice of adapting themselves to local native practice in order to create authentic Christianity in a native context. They viewed the remote Illinois mission as an isolated refuge where they could realize a Jesuit ideal—helping indigenous people to adopt Christianity *on their own terms*, and quite literally *in their own terms*.

But the Jesuits' strategy—in the Illinois Country and elsewhere—was controversial. In the late 1600s, church authorities censured Jesuits for heterodoxy in their missions, especially in China, where the priests were judged too permissive in their adaptations of Christian ritual into the native context.[5] Facing similar suspicions, Jesuits in the Illinois Country soon found themselves defending the Illinois project and its underlying vision of an isolated and idiosyncratic Illinois Christianity from opposing religious and secular authorities who favored missions with the more ambitious goal of radically converting, or *Frenchifying*, Indian peoples and incorporating them into French colonial society, including by teaching them "civilized" lifestyles and the French language. When competing Seminary priests and Recollect priests arrived in the Illinois Country, the resulting struggle was no mere turf war. Rather, it was a fight to determine on what terms, on whose terms, and to what purpose missions should be conducted. Thus the Illinois Country became a front in a worldwide debate about missionary strategy that pitted the Jesuits against imperial authorities and competing missionary officials throughout the Atlantic world and beyond. Fighting over dictionaries and the "terms of encounter," missionaries made the Illinois Country into a battleground to determine the nature of the French-Indian frontier of inclusion.

"FIRST MAKE MEN OF THEM": THE POLITICS OF CONVERSION

When New France became a royal colony in 1663, administrators in Quebec began to look for solutions to the colony's chronic problems of low population and lagging productivity. In 1666, formalizing a policy that came to be known as *francisation*, the minister of finance, Jean-Baptiste Colbert, wrote to New France intendant Jean Talon that the colony should try to assimilate Indians: "To increase the colony . . . the most useful way to achieve it would be to try to civilize the Algonquins, the Hurons, and the other Savages . . . and to persuade them to come to settle in a commune with the French, to live with them, and educate their children in our mores and our customs."[6] The verb used when discussing this process, *franciser*, meant, literally, "to Frenchify," suggesting the goal of complete cultural transformation that French planners envisioned in the seventeenth century.[7]

The government policy of assimilation seemed to go hand-in-hand with the agenda of missionaries laboring in New France to convert Indians to Christianity. As one official wrote in a typical comment on *francisation*, the policy was understood to be good "both for religion and for the service of the King."[8] Indeed, as the people with the closest and most constant contact with Indians, Recollect and Jesuit missionaries were already for much of the first half of the seventeenth century conducting a program of assimilation, and they were enthusiastic advocates. In their early missionary projects, both Recollects and Jesuits deemed it necessary for Indians to assimilate to French lifestyles before they could authentically convert. As the mantra went, "none could ever succeed in converting them, unless they made them men before they made them Christians."[9]

Thus in Sillery, a Jesuit mission founded in 1637 near Quebec, priests taught Indians to farm and abandon their seminomadic lifeways. Attending the academy that Jesuits established in the village of Quebec, Indian children learned to speak Latin and French. Missionaries tried to encourage their neophytes to abandon their "idle and lazy form of life," for farming.[10] Missionaries founded "reserves," or "*réductions*," nearby the French population centers where Indians could live and gradually acquire the habits of the French. One Sulpician priest summed up the logic behind these programs:

> We believe that the Indians profit by living among us, and not in their own land; that they must be taught our language, that their women must wear skirts and their men hats and pants; that they must adopt French housing; learn animal

husbandry; and how to sow wheat and root vegetables; and that they must be able to read [French] and hear mass and be taught the holy rites.[11]

As this quote suggests, administrators and early missionaries deemed the French language an especially important focus of the process of conversion and assimilation.[12] Government officials in New France viewed language instruction as a major part of the program of *francisation*, and particularly encouraged the missionaries to take up this task. "It is necessary to inspire [the Indians] with the desire to learn our language, just as the English teach them theirs," wrote New France governor Louis de Buade de Frontenac in the 1670s.[13]

To the extent that missionaries faithfully pursued these policies, converting Indians not only into Christians but also into civilized and eloquent French people, they were helping pursue the goals of the secular colonial administration. But there was a problem. Jesuits had begun to harbor serious misgivings about *francisation* by the time Colbert encouraged it as an official policy. Around 1634, as Jesuit activity in New France increased, the Jesuits began to doubt that Indians needed to adopt French ways of living as a precursor to religious faith. As Colbert wrote, this was not mere laziness by the Jesuits, but rather a conscious strategic decision. They actually *preferred* not to assimilate the Indians, "because they [the Jesuits] thought they might better preserve the tenets and holiness of our Religion by keeping the converted Indians' ordinary lifestyle than by bringing them among the French."[14] The 1630s and 1640s marked the beginning of the classic era of the Jesuits' peripatetic Huron missions, where heroic men like Paul Le Jeune, Jean de Brébeuf, and Jérôme Lalemant followed Indians into the wilderness, lived in native villages, and spoke native tongues as they pursued conversions far from the security of the French population.[15]

A concise and classic summary of the new Jesuit approach came from Jérôme Lalemant's 1642 *Relation*. Rather than assimilating the Indians to French culture, he wrote, the Jesuit himself should "penetrate" the culture of the Indians, adapt himself to their customs, and thus win over the natives:

> To make a Christian out of a Barbarian is not the work of a day. The seed that is sown one year in the earth does not bear fruit so soon. A great step is gained when one has learned to know those with whom he has to deal; has penetrated their thoughts; has adapted himself to their language, their customs, and their manner of living; and, when necessary, has been a Barbarian with them, in order to win them over to Jesus Christ.[16]

In the 1660s, after an interim caused by Iroquois attacks in the Pays d'en Haut, the Jesuits increased their efforts to meet the Indians on their own native ground, to adapt themselves to the Indians' ways. And they made more and more missions in the distant country, *away* from French settlements and in places where Colbert's vision of assimilation was a near impossibility. In so doing, they aligned their New France missions with other Jesuit projects in India, China, and Paraguay, all of which famously functioned according to a "Jesuit Way of Proceeding," which was articulated by Ignatius Loyola himself in his *Constitutions* and other writings. As Loyola wrote, in every mission, the important thing was to teach and live "in a way that is accommodated to those people, [and their] understanding."[17]

But while Jesuits pursued this new strategy throughout the mid-seventeenth century, proponents of *francisation* within the colonial government looked on these Jesuit missions with indifference, if not suspicion. In 1672, the new governor Frontenac complained openly that the "distant missions" did nothing but contribute to the colony's problem with illegal traders, or *coureurs de bois*. And the mission Indians themselves? They were hardly Christians, let alone assimilated subjects of the French king. "The majority of their missions are pure mockeries," wrote Frontenac, "and I don't think that [the Jesuits] should be permitted to extend them any further than they already have until we see in one of these places a church of Indians better formed."[18] Frontenac's views were shared within the administration. Colbert wrote to condemn the Jesuits' method of "keeping the converted Indians' ordinary lifestyle [rather than] bringing them among the French."[19] To this end, the intendant Talon in 1667 made a "civil reproach" toward the Jesuits for their failure to affect changes in the "customs" and "manners" of the "savages" in their faraway missions. Talon made the Jesuits promise to change their ways: "They have promised me that they will work to change these Barbarians in all their missions, beginning with their language."[20] Six years later, the Jesuits had apparently not changed their policy, and the king wrote with his own opinion on the matter:

> Regarding the request that the Jesuits have made to continue their missions in the distant country, His Majesty esteems that it would be much more advantageous for the good of the Religion and for that of His Service to apply themselves to that which is close, and at the same time that they convert the Savages, to attract them into a civil society and to quit their form of living, with which they will never be able to become good Christians.[21]

In spite of these arguments, many Jesuits continued to idealize the potential of a wilderness church, and Jesuit writings glorified the "innocence" and authenticity of primitive religious practice in the distant missions. Rejecting the administration's arguments in favor of *francisation*, the Jesuits countered that such methods only served to alienate Indians from both Christianity *and* French alliance in general. The Jesuit historian of New France, Pierre-François Charlevoix, wrote in 1741 how the Jesuits' convictions against *francisation* only became *more* steadfast over time: "Experience has taught us that the worst system of governing these people and maintaining them in our interest, is to bring them in contact with the French, whom they would have esteemed more, had they seen them less closely." So long as *francisation* was the government policy, the Jesuits could not be on board: "The best mode of Christianizing them was to avoid Frenchifying them."[22]

The Jesuits' priorities were clearly out of step with those of the government in the 1660s and 1670s. Rather than changing their strategy to conform to the wishes of the government, the Jesuits did something quite the opposite. In 1672, just as Governor Frontenac was criticizing the Jesuit missions in the backcountry as "pure mockeries," the future leader of the Jesuit order in Canada, Claude Dablon, announced the Jesuits' next great project. They would establish a mission among a previously isolated group of Indians who had recently visited the mission at St. Esprit on Lake Superior. These Indians lived beyond the Mississippi valley watershed, farther in the upper country than any Jesuits had thus far served, many weeks' journey from Montreal. Rejecting the government's call to pursue only nearby missions, the Jesuits launched this new mission project to this far distant country, the country of the Illinois. And while the government wanted Jesuits to try to make Indians adopt French customs, Jesuit missionary Jacques Marquette, setting out for the Illinois in the 1670s, predicted that he would soon be living on *their* terms:

> After the fashion of the Savages, [we go] in order that we may share their miseries with them, and suffer every imaginable hardship of barbarism. They are lost sheep, that must be sought for among the thickets and woods, since for the most part they cry so loudly that one hastens to rescue them from the jaws of the Wolf.[23]

And so, ignoring the administration's campaign for *francisation*, the Jesuits founded their Illinois mission as a place where they could create a new, isolated Christian community apart from corrupting French influence and built in the terms of the Indians themselves. Pursuing this alternative vision, Marquette and fellow Jesuit missionary Claude Allouez began in the 1670s to learn the Illinois language and to follow the Illinois lifestyle.[24] All of this was directed not at imperial goals of consolidation and strengthening the empire, but rather at the quite different goal of creating an idiosyncratic local Christianity *on the Illinois' own terms.*

IN THEIR OWN WAY

The early history of the Jesuits' mission in the Illinois Country has been often told as a heroic wilderness trial, and it was that. The first two priests, Jacques Marquette and Claude Allouez, suffered enormous hardships in establishing the outpost, and Marquette died in Michigan while returning to Michilimackinac after his first strenuous Illinois Country winter. Yet these two priests—along with their successors Jacques Gravier, Gabriel Marest, and Pierre-François Pinet—persisted, and by 1690 had established the mission on such solid footing that they celebrated the Immaculate Conception as a jewel in the Jesuit system. But while the early years of the Illinois Country have been often told as a story of self-denying priests imposing Christianity in the wilderness, the more significant story of these early years is how the priests embraced and idealized the Illinois's own contributions to the creation of an idiosyncratic mission Christianity.[25] By translating and transposing Christian ideas into Illinois language and worldviews, the Jesuits embraced the Illinois as active partners in the creation of mission Christianity in their own fashion.

During the age of exploration and conquest, Europeans symbolically took possession of the New World in elaborate ceremonies layered with many codes and traditions.[26] After performing such ceremonies, they then wrote narratives to discursively represent their domination over native peoples.[27] For historians inclined to such readings of the first moments of contact and conquest, the early French explorations of the Mississippi valley, together with the accounts that explorers and missionaries wrote to describe it, are a fertile ground for examination. Simon François Daumont de St. Lusson's dramatic ceremony of possession at Sault Ste. Marie in 1671, for example, was a rich display full of legal protocol and ritual, visual symbols, verbal cues, songs, crosses, and theatrical gestures, all of which combined to communicate the possession of this new landscape in distinctive French terms.[28]

But if such ceremonies and narratives by Europeans argued for the European possession of the landscape, it is significant that when Marquette arrived in the Illinois Country, he spent the majority of his narrative describing not how he took possession of the Illinois, but rather how the Illinois ceremoniously took possession *of him.* The longest passage in Marquette's account from his exploration of the Illinois Country is a description of the calumet ceremony, and it provides a dramatic first example of his strategy of accommodation to native life in the Illinois Country. Describing the ceremony, Marquette flattered himself that the calumet was a special "compliment" intended "to do us Honor," and accompanied by "kind Attentions." In parts of his description, he wrote as if to imply that the Indians, in *honoring* him, were assuming a submissive posture toward him and the French authority that they thought he represented. But Marquette's participation in the ceremony, he understood, simultaneously implied the opposite—his willingness to accommodate to an Illinois worldview and Illinois authority.[29]

Marquette could tell that the ceremony was intended to advance an idea of Illinois supremacy and power; it was a demonstration of the Indians' control over their environment. One of the dances featured a "lofty discourse, delivered by him who holds the Calumet," concerning "the victories that he has won, the names of the Nations, the places, and the Captives whom he has made."[30] Performing an elaborate dance featuring a great deal of war imagery, the warrior signaled the extension of the tribe's power over both the land and the people in it. In some versions of the ceremony described in later accounts, the Illinois planted a post in the ground, "where those who wish to make known their great deeds in war, striking the post, declaim on the deeds they have done."[31]

If participating in the ceremony implied the Jesuits' submission to the military power of the village, their tolerance of the obvious religious significance of the calumet also demonstrated the Jesuits' willingness to accommodate themselves to Indian worldviews. Religious imagery ran throughout the ceremony, as Marquette and other Jesuits noted. Allouez commented that the ceremony was meant as a sacrifice to the spirits worshipped by the Illinois.[32] Throughout the ritual, chiefs gestured with the pipe toward the sun, signaling their consideration of the sun as deity. In other ways, the calumet clearly was used to honor the manitous of animals and other spirits. In some versions of the ceremony, a chief could offer smoke to six directions—east, west, north, south, sky, and earth—and to manitou statues representing spirits in the local geography.[33] Participating in this ceremony conveyed the Jesuits' initial willingness to accommodate themselves not only to local patterns but even to what they might have considered idolatrous religious worldviews.

Like Jesuits in China who dressed themselves in Confucian scholarly robes in order to accommodate to indigenous expectations, the Jesuits accommodated to local patterns in the Illinois Country through participation in the calumet ceremony.[34] They understood this accommodation to be an active strategy for the creation of community in the Illinois Country. Of course the Jesuits' ultimate aim was to *change* and even *destroy* idolatrous local customs reflected in the calumet ceremony, as much of their writings made clear. But their intention was to do this *from within*. It is significant that both Marquette and Allouez, the first Jesuits in the Illinois Country, emphasized the role of the pipe ceremony in establishing community. The ceremony created a common ground, a "sacred trust," and a "sure pledge of peace," according to Allouez.[35] To Marquette, the significance was similar: "They use it to strengthen their alliances . . . and to speak to Strangers."[36] The creation of community was the necessary first condition for conversion, and the Jesuits gave their first lessons and catechisms within the context of this Indian religious ceremony, on Indian ground. This stands in sharp contrast to the ceremonies of possession conducted by St. Lusson and others, in which Indians were a passive audience expected to watch the French-controlled pageantry and accept the supremacy of the French empire. The Jesuits' partaking in the calumet ceremony reflected their understanding that the Illinois would be active participants in, not passive recipients of, colonial Christianity. Indeed, while Allouez raised a cross to signal the possession of this landscape within the kingdom of God, he also noted with satisfaction the Indians' own agency in the initial steps of religious conversion. Baptizing an Illinois man at his deathbed, Allouez noted significantly that the convert went "to go take possession of paradise in the name of the whole nation."[37] The Jesuits thus assigned an active role to the Indians in the creation of their own Christianity.

As noted above, part of the function of the calumet ceremony for the Illinois was that it made it possible to *speak to strangers*. Thus Marquette made the ceremony the occasion for his first important speech, in which he gave his initial ten lessons about the Catholic faith. Again conforming to their customs, Marquette preceded each individual lesson with a gift. But if this accommodation lubricated the wheels of intercultural communication, Marquette's ability to *speak to strangers* across the frontier was probably owing to the more important fact that he spoke their language. Indeed, Marquette had begun to learn the Illinois language from a slave in 1670 while he lived at St. Esprit. Though he probably did not speak fluently, he almost certainly carried a prayer book containing transcripts of several prayers translated into the Illinois language that he or Allouez made with the help of their first translators. With this book, Marquette would have been able to read several translations to the audience such as the Paternoster, a short catechism, and others.[38]

Thus Marquette put his lessons *on Indian ground* and *in Indian terms* at the first ceremony of the calumet. But for both Marquette and Allouez, these initial steps were part of a broader strategy that would continue to characterize their Illinois mission well beyond its initial founding. After opening the mission, Allouez began to encourage Indians to use their own traditional ceremonies in their approach to the new Catholicism that he taught. Allouez observed how many useful parallels existed between Illinois spirituality and Catholicism. He noted, for example, that the Illinois recognized one spirit above all others, a concept he could exploit in his explanation of the one Catholic God. He noted the importance of dreams in the Illinois worldview, and he did not object when some Illinois neophytes spoke of their hopes of seeing the Christian God in their sleep.[39] Allouez was pleased when the Illinois used traditional customs of fasting and feasting in their veneration of the Christian God. And he seemed thrilled when the Illinois placed an image of Christ at the center of one of their great feast celebrations, offering food to the icon as a sacrifice. Even if these ceremonies clearly bore the marks of traditional Illinois customs, Allouez considered them a basis for Christian practice. In response, Allouez announced proudly, "They honor our Lord among themselves in their own way."[40]

Allowing the Illinois to "honor our Lord among themselves in their own way" was right at the center of the Jesuits' strategy for creating an Illinois mission. Allouez noted how some Illinois threw tobacco around the base of the church when they visited the mission at St. François Xavier (Green Bay) in 1670. "When they pass by here they throw tobacco all around the church, which is a kind of devotion to their divinity," he wrote.[41] Even though this risked a confusion and possibly unorthodox translation of the Catholic ritual, and even pushed against the boundary of idolatry, Allouez considered it a good foundation for the establishment of Catholicism. It reflected the Indians' obvious enthusiasm for Christianity and the fact that "they at least esteem Prayer," even though they only knew how to worship "in their own way."[42]

On another occasion, Illinois neophytes addressed some speeches to the church, as if the building itself were an "animate being." Allouez considered this a hopeful sign as well, even if it was far from orthodox.[43] The Illinois' attempts to win favors from God by offering presents at the altar also represented a holdover from traditional Indian practices, but Allouez was thrilled to report "the honors they pay to our Holy Church, after their fashion."[44] Claude Dablon, observing a group of Illinois who visited St. Esprit, reported that they were about to construct their own church, using Indian materials. Though we can only imagine it, the image of such a structure, which likely would have taken the form of a long wood hut, covered with *apacois*—the reedy mats that were the main component of the distinctive architectural style of the Illinois—would have made a good symbol for the kind of church that the first Jesuits created in the Illinois Country. Christian ritual was housed within a decidedly indigenous structure of which the Illinois themselves were the creators.[45]

While all of this reflected Jesuit efforts to create Christianity *on their terms*, perhaps the key element of the strategy was translation and the creation of an Illinois spiritual vocabulary. Very significantly, Jesuits sought words in the Illinois language through which they could express the new meanings of Catholicism. The best example here is manitou, the concept that Marquette and Allouez both used in order to communicate notions of the Christian God. Although not unprecedented, it was an important decision to use this word, and one that reflected the priests' confidence that they could render Christianity within familiar Illinois terms without imposing whole new conceptual schemes.[46] It appears that the two priests viewed this concept of manitou as useful in translating the idea of a single, Christian God. Marquette wrote in one of his accounts that the "great *Manitou . . .* is the name which they give to God."[47] Tellingly, Marquette here reveals that he let the Indians themselves provide the word for God, rather than supplying it himself. This was the name "*which they gave.*" For both Marquette and Allouez, manitou was, if not an exact equivalent, then at least a workable translation for the concept of a single creator.[48]

Thus Marquette's prayer book, which was apparently used by both Allouez and Marquette during the early mission years, employs the concept of manitou—the specific translation was *Kichemanit8a*—to convey the idea of God in various prayer translations. Notably, the early Jesuits in the Illinois Country did not use the French word *Dieu* to communicate the notion of God, as some missionaries in other regions did.[49] This reflects their willingness, again, to place Catholicism within the terms of the Illinois themselves, and their confidence that such transpositions accurately reflected the meanings they strove for.

Thanks to compatibilities they found in language and spiritual practices, Allouez was enthusiastic about the Illinois mission. "The greatest field of the gospel appears to be [there]," he wrote.[50] Conversion in Illinois required no radical *francisation*, but simply minor adjustments. Specifically, Allouez wrote, the Illinois initially worshipped *the sun*. But "when they are instructed in the truths of our Religion, they will speedily change this worship and render it to the *Creator of the Sun*, as some have already begun to do."[51] This optimism—that Indians would *speedily* change their beliefs—was based on Allouez's conviction that the beliefs were already pretty close to the mark. This is what Marquette meant when he wrote of his early mission that "we keep a little of their usage, and take from it all that is bad."[52]

This understanding of the success and purity of the mission helps to explain the Jesuits' preference for an isolated and distant mission *on the Indians' terms*. However, in 1680 another group of missionaries arrived who were more skeptical about the strength of this strategy for creating Christianity in Illinois. In particular, these Recollect priests, who included the famous explorer Father Louis Hennepin, were skeptical about the efficacy of the Jesuits' translations. Harboring much different plans for the *terms of encounter*, the Recollects clashed from the start with the Jesuits over strategy.

"SO BRUTAL AND NARROW A MIND"

The Jesuits' idyllic mission did not remain isolated for long. As explorers and officials began to see the prospects for colonization beyond the Great Lakes and into the Mississippi valley, the Illinois River became the thoroughfare between New France and the nascent Louisiana colony. Indeed, René-Robert Cavelier de La Salle's party arrived in 1680 to establish Fort Crèvecoeur only a short distance from the main village of the Illinois where the Jesuits centered their mission. La Salle brought with his party three Recollect priests: Louis Hennepin, Zenobe Membre, and Jacques Gabriel. And they in turn brought a completely different concept of colonial missions to the Illinois Country. Soon they were heaping criticism on the Jesuits, revealing a deep disagreement over missionary strategy and the missionaries' purpose in Illinois.

Hennepin arrived in Illinois in 1680 and wrote about his first impression of the local Indians in the Kaskaskia village, one of the main villages of the Illinois where the Jesuits had been working. Where Allouez, Marquette and Dablon had found many virtues in the Illinois' traditions that made the priests confident about the conversion of these people, Hennepin disagreed:

> The Illinois, as most of the savages of America, being brutish, wild and stupid, and their Manners being so opposite to the Morals of the Gospel, their Conversion is to be despaired of, till Time and Commerce with the Europeans, has removed their natural Fierceness and Ignorance, and thereby made them more apt to be sensible of the Charms of Christianity.[53]

Hennepin's discussions of the Illinois seemed almost the opposite of the Jesuits' enthusiastic descriptions. To Hennepin, the Illinois were "Lazy, Vagabonds, Timorous, Pettish, Thieves, and so fond of their Liberty, that they have no great Respect for their Chiefs."[54] Hennepin denied that the Indians had any religion whatsoever, apart from simple-minded superstitions: "As to their Religion I observed that they are very superstitious; but I could never discover that they had any Worship, nor any Reason for their Superstition."[55] Reading Hennepin side by side with early Jesuit accounts of the Illinois, therefore, the contrast is overwhelming. The Jesuits saw a set of preexisting cultural practices and virtues that would prove a useful basis for a Christian mission; Hennepin rejected the very idea of accommodation. To him, indigenous practices could never provide a foundation for Catholicism: "They are naturally very vicious, and addicted to some Superstitions that signify nothing; their Customs are savage, brutal, and barbarous."[56]

Because of his initial prejudices, Hennepin and his partners developed a strategy for converting the Indians that also contrasted sharply with the Jesuits' strategy. As they saw it, converting the Illinois would require missionaries to impose an entirely new set of practices, keeping nothing of traditional Illinois customs. Father Membre wrote, "With regard to conversions, I cannot rely on any. . . . There is in these savages such an alienation from the faith, so brutal and narrow a mind, such corrupt and un-Christian morals, that great time would be needed to hope for any fruit."[57] The Recollects concluded that the concepts of Christianity simply had no close equivalents in Indian spirituality, which made the simplest translation impossible. As Hennepin wrote, "The Truths of Christianity are so sublime, that I fear, neither my words nor Signs and Actions have been able to give them an Idea of what I preach'd unto them."[58] Hennepin himself finally gave up trying to translate Christian concepts, expressing the common understanding that conceptual gaps in the Indian language made the expression of Christianity futile:

> I don't know whether their Predecessors had any Knowledge of a God; but 'tis certain their Language, which is very natural and expressive in everything else, is so barren on this subject, that we can't find any expression in it to signify the Deity, or any one of our Mysteries, not even the most common: this gives us great perplexity when we would convert them.[59]

Since Hennepin concluded that translation was impossible, his only option was to start from scratch and rely on rote instruction. He taught Indians to perform rituals, and tried to conduct elaborate and impressive ceremonies to engage the Indians where verbal communication failed. In some cases he tried to teach the Indians to recite prayers in French, a strategy that was difficult not just because the Indians could not understand the language, but because the Illinois were not accustomed to certain sounds necessary for French pronunciation. Nevertheless, Hennepin charged on with a disciplined, stern approach: "We forc'd their children to pronounce as we did, by inculcating to them the Labial Letters, and obliging them to frequent[ly] converse with the Children of the Europeans that inhabited the Fort."[60] But he was pessimistic about the value of the resulting religious practice. He noted that the Indians used Catholic ritual purely for entertainment and diversion, and rarely, if ever, *understood* what their words and rituals actually meant. When they came to talk, Indians did not give much effort toward understanding what the priests were saying: "They come to us, and attend to what we say, purely out of Idleness, and natural Curiosity to converse with us, as we with them; or rather they are tempted to follow us, by the Kindness and Flatteries we express toward them."[61]

Concluding that the Illinois were basically a lost cause, Hennepin gave his assessment of the Jesuits' optimistic reports of conversions among the Illinois. These conversions were worthless, he wrote, as the Illinois hardly adopted Christianity at all: "[Had I followed] the Example of those other Missionaries, I could have boasted of many Conversions; for I might have easily baptized all those Nations, and then say, as, I am afraid [the Jesuits] do without any ground, that I had converted them."[62] All of this was a critique not just of the Illinois, but moreover of the Jesuits' strategy. Jesuits worked to find ways to transpose Christianity within the local lifeways of the Illinois. The Recollects found very little of value in the Illinois customs, concluding that the only way to convert these people was through a total elimination of Indian traditions and their replacement with French lifeways, language, and beliefs. As his initial assessment suggests, Hennepin believed that the best way to convert the Indians was to promote their interaction with the French people. Conversion to Christianity would require "time and commerce with the Europeans" in order to make the Illinois "sensible to the Charms of Christ."[63]

> Our ancient Missionary Recollects of Canada, and those that succeeded them in that work, have always given it for their opinion, as I now own 'tis mine, that the way to succeed in converting the Barbarians, is to endeavor to make them men before we go about to make them Christians. Now in order to civilize them, 'tis necessary that the Europeans should mix with them, and that they should dwell together, which can never be done for certain till the Colonies are augmented.[64]

And so the disagreement came down to this—two very different assessments of the capacity of Native Americans for religious conversion. The Recollects, as Baron de Lahontan wrote in the late 1600s, considered the unassimilated Indians "stupid, gross, and rustick Persons, incapable of Thought or Reflection."[65] For the Jesuits, the Indians rather were characterized by "good Sense, a tenacious Memory, and a quick Apprehension season'd with a solid Judgment."[66] These differences in the perceptions of Indians underlay two very different strategies in the Illinois Country.

Hennepin's mission in Illinois never took off, and he left the Illinois Country after only a short stay. But his reports prompted Frontenac and his allies in New France to oppose the Jesuits in remote missions like Illinois. Founding the new colony of Detroit at the end of the seventeenth century, for example, members of Frontenac's faction looked to reduce Jesuit power by opening up the surrounding region to competing missionaries and different methods.[67] Like Hennepin, the founders of Detroit, especially Antoine Laumet dit de Lamothe, Sieur de Cadillac, wanted to use the French language and assimilation to bring the Illinois *within* a single, unified imperial community. Cadillac explicitly complained about the Jesuits' refusal to teach Indians to speak French and to adopt the *francisation* policy. As he saw it, the Jesuits' use of Illinois language in the mission reflected their own political ambitions to remain outside of the larger imperial program.[68] Agreeing with this critique, Frontenac in 1698 expelled Jesuit Father Pierre-François Pinet from the mission at Chicagou, a recent Jesuit establishment just two days' journey from Marquette's original Immaculate Conception mission. In a letter that year to François de Laval, Gravier appealed to the former bishop of Quebec for help in the conflict with Frontenac, complaining that the governor was trying to "drive us from our Missions, as he has already done from that of l'Ange gardien of the Miamis."[69] But the real danger to the Illinois mission came when a group of three Seminary priests arrived in Illinois in May 1698 carrying orders this time from the bishop of Quebec, Jean-Baptiste de la Croix de Chevrières de Saint-Vallier. The orders gave the Seminary priests permission to establish a new mission among the Tamaroa, a branch of the Illinois. For the Jesuits, this was a major threat.

DEBATING THE TERMS OF ENCOUNTER

Through the 1690s, the Jesuits had held their own in the Illinois Country. The Jesuits could stand up to La Salle and Frontenac, since the priests were technically not under secular authority anyway. The difference in 1698 was that the bishop of Quebec himself had issued these orders to the Seminary priests. And the bishop was someone the Jesuits could not ignore. As it happened, Saint-Vallier had become quite suspicious of the Jesuit way of proceeding. While in France in 1697, he observed from up close the controversy over the Chinese Rites and, like many in the Seminary of the Foreign Missions, consequently turned heavily against the Jesuit order. Like many others, Saint-Vallier was convinced that the Jesuit way of proceeding was too permissive, and resulted in unorthodox and even idolatrous practices when indigenous neophytes were allowed to preserve much of their culture intact. Returning to New France the next year, he turned the Illinois Country into a front in the battle against Jesuit unorthodoxies.[70]

Beginning in 1698, Saint-Vallier immediately began to harass Jesuits wherever he could. He shut down their grammar school and passed it to the Seminary priests. He forced curricular changes at their college at Quebec. He seized the Jesuit property at the Huron mission of Old Lorette and handed it over to the Seminary of the Foreign Missions. But if these were all attempts to register his displeasure with the Jesuits over the recent controversies in China, none of these actions seemed pertinent to the actual Chinese Rites dispute. Now, as reports from Hennepin and others detailed the behavior of the Jesuits in the Illinois Country, Saint-Vallier could easily see the reflection of China in the unorthodox religious practices the Jesuits allowed among the Illinois "Christians." Here were Christians who spoke no French, worshipped a manitou, and lived like savages. As in China, where Jesuits dressed as Confucian monks and Indians worshipped ancestors in holy temples, the Christianity in the Illinois mission was highly questionable. Saint-Vallier thus called upon the Seminary priests to begin a new competing mission, knowing that they would sponsor a totally different missionary strategy in the Illinois Country.

Saint-Vallier sent four priests—François de Montigny, Jean-François Buisson de Saint-Cosme, Antoine Davion, and Thaumur de la Source—to the Illinois Country in May 1698. Since the Seminary priests initially promised not to encroach on any specific mission field that the Jesuits had already worked, the two orders got along well, and the Jesuits even helped the Seminary priests as they passed through the village of Kaskaskia.[71] But even in their cooperation the Jesuits and Seminary priests demonstrated their underlying differences. For example, while praising the Jesuits' efforts, the Seminary priest Montigny disapprovingly commented on the rough conditions in the Jesuit missions and the way in which Jesuits seemed to be living rather too close to savagery. "I declare to you that I have been highly edified by their zeal," he wrote back to Quebec, "though of a surety I do not believe that they can bear up much longer under the severe hardships which they endure. I believe that you ought to tell them not to take so much upon themselves."[72] This ostensible praise was also an implicit critique of rudeness of the lifestyle the Jesuits embraced. For their part, the Jesuits reported back to their superiors how friendly the Seminary priests were, but also were sure to note how incompetent the interlopers would have been without the assistance of the generous and expert Jesuit hosts. In addition to composing short speeches in Illinois as introductions for the Seminary priests, the Jesuits demonstrated their generosity by giving them comfortable accommodations, even as the Jesuits themselves lived in the "scarcity of the Indians."

> We received them as well as we were able, lodging them in our own house, and sharing with them what we could possess amid a scarcity as great as that which prevailed in the village, throughout the year. On leaving, we also induced them to take seven sacks of corn that we had left, concealing our poverty from them.[73]

In short, while relations were civil between the two orders, the Jesuits and the Seminary priests regarded one another coolly, each thinly concealing their contempt for the strategies of the other.

Relations worsened when the Seminary priests established their mission at the Tamaroa village. Although they initially promised not to settle in this place, the Seminary priests soon decided that it was a necessary key to more distant tribes in the Mississippi valley, such as the Arkansas. As the Jesuits saw it, the creation of this Cahokia mission was a dangerous encroachment on their territory. Following on Frontenac's recent expulsion of Pinet from Chicagou, this suggested to Gravier a conspiracy to exclude the Jesuits altogether from the Illinois Country. Thus the Jesuits prepared to fight back. As soon as St. Cosme planted a cross to open the mission at the Tamaroa village, Jesuits arrived to contend the establishment. As St. Cosme remembered it, "We . . . planted there a beautiful cross, but I was surprised to see Father Binneteau arrive, who had left Pimiteoui [Peoria], in order to come and establish himself in this mission."[74]

At this point the conflict was open, and Jesuits began treating the Seminary men with "haughtiness." St. Cosme, the Seminary priest, wrote to complain that Jesuits Binneteau and Marest, positioned across the river from the Seminary priests' church, tried to interfere with the new missionaries' operations. "[Binneteau] had wished to prevent [Bergier] from saying his prayers in his chapel and from helping the Christians," St. Cosme wrote.[75]

Montigny complained of the "scandals spread abroad against him by the Jesuits" in the Illinois Country.[76] For their part, the Seminary priests, better funded, offered gifts to Indians to entice them to stay on their side. When 1,000 Kaskaskia arrived in the region in 1700 after having abandoned Peoria, the Jesuits gained a huge advantage, because the Kaskaskia, loyal to the Jesuits, influenced many Cahokia and Tamaroa to join the Jesuit mission. The Jesuits thus had approximately 2,000 neophytes and the Seminary significantly fewer.

As they clashed, the two orders of priests revealed their fundamentally different strategies and purposes in their respective missions. The priests of the Seminary asserted their claim in the Tamaroa on the grounds of their impressive installation. After only a brief time in the mission, St. Cosme wrote about how they had made thirty baptisms, built a chapel, erected a bell, and planted a cross "with the greatest ceremony." Dismissing the Jesuits' claim to this territory, the Seminary priests noted that the Jesuits had no permanent building in the Cahokia village, and therefore no legitimate claim to a mission there: "It is incomprehensible that [the Jesuits] should describe [this] as a mission cultivated for ten years," when "[they have] set up neither house, chapel, nor cross."[77] Indeed, writing to superiors back in Quebec, Montigny suggested that the Jesuits' mission had made no impact on the Illinois before the arrival of the Seminary men, because they had failed to settle the Indians in one place. As Montigny wrote to his superior, "It is necessary that we seek every sort of means to fix our Indians in place because without this there is nothing or very little we can do for the religion of the savages."[78] The implication here was that the Jesuits had no claim on the Illinois mission, and that the priests had achieved nothing in their many years here.

Meanwhile, the Jesuits asserted their claim in different terms altogether. While admitting that they had not officially installed a chapel in Tamaroa prior to the Seminary priests' arrival, the Jesuits declared their authority by virtue, significantly, of language. The Jesuits should control the Tamaroa mission, Gravier maintained, because the Tamaroa spoke Illinois. As the Jesuits argued, and as the Seminary priests would learn, the Tamaroa were a "wandering nation," like the rest of the Illinois.[79] What mattered more than permanent mission buildings was the Jesuits' twenty years' experience of traveling with the Illinois "to their towns, to their hunting grounds, to their fishing spots."[80] It was by living on Indian ground, in Indian terms, that the Jesuits had established their claim. While the Seminary priests expressed that they were "astonished to see the Jesuits complaining of a mission situated 90 leagues from their nearest establishment," Jesuits nevertheless considered the Tamaroa part of their territory.[81]

And so their conflict revealed the fundamental disagreement over strategy. The Seminary priests, like other non-Jesuit missionaries, brought with them certain expectations about the proper *terms* on which missionary activity should proceed, which meant settlements, farming, and *francisation.*[82] But as the Jesuits argued, the Seminary priests would not be effective missionaries, since they were not prepared to live *on the terms* of the Illinois. "The gentlemen of the seminary, who work less than we do, will continually receive both grants and pensions for living in missions where they do nothing, and which they abandon at once," complained Marest. Positioning the Jesuits against the Seminary priests in terms of strategy, Marest added, "All those gentlemen do not even take the trouble to learn the Savage Tongues."[83] Notwithstanding the prayer book that the Jesuits reportedly gave the Seminary priests, the latter apparently were largely unsuccessful— and even unwilling—in their efforts to learn the language. Nor were they willing to adapt themselves to Indian practices when it came to lifestyle. The Seminary priests themselves wrote of their necessity, even in the wilds of the Illinois Country, to "live in the European manner, because one tires easily of the Savage provisions." As one Seminary priest wrote, "very few men can accustom themselves or rather withstand" the "Savage" lifestyle.[84]

To the Jesuits, all of this suggested the wrong priorities, not to mention a basic futility in the design of the Seminary mission. The Seminary priests, wrote Marest, would fail: "I am convinced that these missions will receive rude shocks. They were beginning to be on a good footing. This caused Jealousy in the minds of the gentlemen of the foreign missions, who have come to take them from us."[85] Significantly, the Jesuits attributed the Seminary priests' hardships to their language problems, problems that the Jesuits themselves did not share. Writing of the difficulties that the Seminary priest Bergier faced in Tamaroa, Marest noted that "he had to bear rude attacks from the Charlatans [non-Christian Indians], who, availing themselves of his slight knowledge of the Savage language, everyday took away from him some Christians."[86] During his travels down the Mississippi River in the early 1700s, Gravier contrasted mission work done by Seminary priests and Jesuits throughout this new Louisiana jurisdiction. All the Jesuits, he observed, were excellent and diligent at learning languages.[87] Seminary priests, he wrote, were not diligent, and most lacked language skills. The Seminary priest Alexandre Huvé, for example, worked in a Natchez mission, though he "knows not a word of their language."[88] Gravier continued, "He hears confessions, baptizes, marries, and administers Communion and extreme unction, without understanding the savages. What would be said if a Jesuit were to do as much?"[89]

And so the Jesuits' strategy of linguistic accommodation gave them an obvious advantage, which they defended from the interlopers. Bergier himself recognized his disadvantage. After he gained control of the Cahokia mission, he reflected on his inadequacy: "Not knowing the language except very poorly, it is not possible for me to maintain the mission on the footing on which the [Jesuit] Father [Pinet] would have placed it, as he speaks the language perfectly and better than the Indians themselves."[90] Jealous and frustrated, it was at this point that Bergier allegedly tried to take the Jesuits' advantage away from them by *stealing* one of their dictionaries.[91] The Seminary priests complained, "What could one think moreover of the conduct of the Jesuit fathers both at Chicago and at the Tamaroa where they would not share with Mr. Bergier their dictionaries and other writings in order to give him a means of learning the language?"[92]

For their part, the Jesuits did view their strategy as under siege, and they understood their situation as part of a larger political contest beyond the bounds of the Illinois Country itself. The issue in the Illinois Country was not simple jealousy between missionaries. As in China, the Seminarians attacked the Jesuits' strategy. "After having chased [the Jesuits] from China," wrote a Jesuit in Canada, "[the Seminary priests] also want to make them abandon Louisiana."[93] Back in France, the Jesuit François de la Chaise, the king's confessor, echoed his understanding that the Illinois Country was a front in a larger battle: "All I know Sir, is that we have been pursued everywhere by these Gentlemen [of the foreign missions]. They have chased us from Cochin China and from Tonkin, they wish to again chase us from Canada."[94] On the ground in the Kaskaskia mission, Gravier worried about how "to maintain ourselves in this new colony—where we shall be no less persecuted than in China and elsewhere."[95] If the Jesuits' crime in China had been to tolerate too much of the natives' own practices, to put Christianity on native terms, it was easy to see how their Illinois mission was attacked on the same grounds.

RESOLUTION

Regarding the mission of the Tamaroa, a final decision was made in 1702 by a committee of church and secular authorities led by the archbishop of Auch, one of the highest church authorities in France. The committee's decision was interesting, and significant. Steering a middle course through the controversy, the resolution was a compromise that effectively recognized *both* Jesuit and Seminary missionaries. Unlike in China, neither order would be forced to shut down or discontinue its mission practices. Significantly, too, the resolution recognized that both missionary groups should continue to pursue their respective missions according to their characteristic strategies. The Seminary priests would be allowed to preserve their mission in Tamaroa and Cahokia, proceeding on the principle that it was necessary "to gather our savages in one place" and *Frenchify* them.[96] Meanwhile the Jesuits would retain the right to pass through the Tamaroa village as they followed the Indians on their "wanderings":

> The Gentlemen of the Foreign Missions will stay alone [separate], established in the place named Tamarois [Cahokia] and they will receive in a brotherly way the Jesuit fathers when they pass there to go assist the Illinois and Tamarois in the places of their hunting and their fishing, which places of hunting and fishing the Jesuit fathers can establish if they judge it appropriate, as long as it is pleasing to the king and under the consent of the bishop of Quebec.[97]

Thus the compromise of 1702 recognized and accepted both strategies and enshrined a permanent competition in the Illinois Country over the *terms of encounter*. But this compromise really did cut against the Jesuits' way of proceeding. Marquette had founded the Immaculate Conception as an isolated and remote mission where Indians would not be polluted by French ways. While the 1702 ruling made it possible for the Jesuits to continue to try to live *on the Indians' own terms*, the presence of these new interlopers, their establishment at Tamaroa, and the presence of ever greater numbers of traders and colonists at outposts like Kaskaskia meant that the dream of isolation was really at an end. Charlevoix had noted that the best way of creating an Indian Catholic community "was to avoid Frenchifying them." But the Jesuits could not preserve the "innocent" and "primitive" Christianity that they idealized now that the Illinois Country was no longer the remote outpost that it had been in the 1670s. Furthermore, by the early 1700s the Jesuits began to change their own minds about missionary strategy, for reasons I discuss elsewhere.[98]

As this essay has demonstrated, the conflict in the Illinois Country in 1699 was no mere turf war among jealous missionaries. Instead, it was the culmination of a three-decades-long debate within the French Atlantic about how missionaries should operate, and to what purpose. In the 1670s, the Jesuits had a particular vision, one based on a premise that Indians could be good Christians and good allies without being assimilated to French "civilization." Instead, they thought, the Indians could remain essentially as they were—semisedentary, outwardly "savage," fascinated by dreams and calumets. Indeed, the Jesuits believed, Indians in their native state could achieve a kind of ideal primitive Christianity. But of course the Jesuits' plan put them at odds with colonial authorities and other missionaries, and this essay has shown how the Illinois Country was invaded by people with competing agendas in the 1690s. Motivated by dreams of a Colbertian program of *francisation*, competitors such as Hennepin and the Seminary priests tried to create colonial missions on much different terms at the end of the seventeenth century.

Focusing on the issue of language—the *terms of encounter*—helps to illuminate these competing visions for a frontier of inclusion. Colonial planners recognized the importance of language in shaping an imperial community. Early imperialists fantasized about a future day when all the various nations of Indian people would be assimilated into one uniform linguistic and cultural community under the control of the colonial authority.[99] Many missionaries, for their part, agreed with this project, since they regarded Indian languages as incapable either of expressing the sophisticated ideas of Christianity or of fostering logical thought and civilized values.[100] For all of these people, the linguistic diversity of America seemed an obstacle in the way of empire. The solution was to eliminate local, idiosyncratic languages in favor of uniformity.

But Jesuits disagreed, consciously pursuing a missionary strategy based on the Indians' own terms, and literally *in their own terms*. Historians have long commented on the exceptional linguistic sophistication of the priests in seventeenth-century Illinois, at least two of whom might have been among the most talented Jesuit linguists in New France.[101] When viewed in light of the important debates about missionary strategy, the linguistic strivings and successes of the Illinois missionaries take on a political significance. The Illinois missionaries used indigenous language to create an authentic Christianity in native terms at the precise moment that this strategy was coming under fire. They then used their mastery of that language as a tool to control and protect their wilderness church from competing agendas.[102]

The task of creating a shared language is fundamental to human interaction and community. But local languages and idiosyncratic cultures can be the bane of empire. When Jesuits and Seminary priests fought over the dictionaries that the Jesuits had made for communicating a syncretic Christianity to the Illinois, this was for the Jesuits a fight to preserve a missionary strategy from the influence of outsiders and from the unwelcome priorities of an emerging empire in the Mississippi valley. At the start, Jesuits reveled in their exclusive access to their local Christian community in the Illinois

Country, and they fought to maintain it. Unable to impose a uniform vision from France, religious officials in 1702 resolved that frontier missionaries and colonists themselves should decide the *terms of encounter*.

NOTES

1. Located across the river from modern St. Louis, Missouri.
2. The events of 1699 were recounted in voluminous correspondence, much of which survived in archives of Jesuits and the Seminary of Foreign Missions. See especially manuscripts from the Archives du Séminaire de Québec (hereafter cited as ASQ), Colonies, SME 12.1, including 009/024, 009/025, 009/080, 009/026, 009/055, 009/056. See also the report made in 1849 on the affair by E. A. Taschereau, "Mission du Séminaire de Québec chez les Tamarois," ASQ Transcripts, Illinois Historical Survey.
3. For these letters, and many others, see ASQ, Colonies, SME 12.1; Taschereau, "Mission du Séminaire de Québec." See also Gilbert J. Garraghan, S.J., "New Light on Old Cahokia," *Illinois Catholic Historical Review* 11 (October 1928): 99–147.
4. The major treatment of this event in historical scholarship is Garraghan, "New Light on Old Cahokia." Other historians barely mention its importance, and the best recent work on Illinois missions concentrates on other themes. See Tracy Leavelle, "Religion, Encounter, and Community in French and Indian North America" (Ph.D. diss., Arizona State University, 2001).
5. The literature on the so-called Chinese Rites controversy is expansive. For the key turning points and arguments in this most important early modern dispute over theology and cross-cultural relations, see George Minamiki, *The Chinese Rites Controversy: From Its Beginning to Modern Times* (Chicago: Loyola University Press, 1985), especially chapter 3, "The Age of Controversy." For more on Jesuit missions in China, and the Jesuit strategy that became so controversial, see also Liam Matthew Brockey, *Journey to the East: The Jesuit Mission to China, 1579–1724* (Cambridge, Mass.: Belknap Press of Harvard University Press, 2007).
6. Colbert to Jean Talon, January 5, 1666, quoted in Saliha Belmessous, "Assimilation and Racialism in Seventeenth- and Eighteenth-Century French Colonial Policy," *American Historical Review* 110 (April 2005): 322–350.
7. While discussion of this policy increased in the 1660s under the new administrations of Talon and Colbert, *Frenchification* was not at all a new notion in the history of New France. Various previous colonial officials had believed

in the potential to grow the population through assimilation. Champlain famously looked forward to an assimilationist policy at the very beginning of New France when he promised the Ottawa and Huron that "our young men will marry your daughters, and we shall be one people." Reuben Gold Thwaites, ed., *The Jesuit Relations and Allied Documents: Travels and Explorations of the Jesuit Missionaries in New France, 1610–1791*, 73 vols. (Cleveland: Burrows Brothers, 1896–1903), 5:211. The 1630 charter of the Company of New France looked forward to incorporating Indians into the population and stipulated that the Indians were automatically to become French subjects, with all the rights that attended to this status. Inheriting this old dream and echoing Champlain, Colbert himself wrote that "in the course of time, having but one law and one master, [Indians and the French] may likewise constitute one people and one race." Quoted in William J. Eccles, *France in America* (East Lansing: Michigan State University Press, 1990), 41.

8. Minister to Denonville, 1686, in Theodore C. Pease and Raymond C. Verner, "French Foundations, 1680–1693," in *Collections of the Illinois State Historical Library*, ed. Illinois State Historical Library, 38 vols. (Springfield: Illinois State Historical Library, 1934), 23:115.

9. Recollect, 1616, quoted in James Axtell, *The Invasion Within: The Contest of Cultures in Colonial North America* (New York: Oxford University Press, 1985), 53. This notion was ever-present in the writings of mostly non-Jesuit missionaries throughout the seventeenth century. It became a mainstay of government policy at the beginning of the era of *Frenchification*. As New France governor Louis de Buade de Frontenac wrote to Minister of Finance Jean-Baptiste Colbert in 1672, "[The missionaries] should try to make them more sedentary, and to make them quit a [nomadic] life so opposed to the spirit of Christianity, since the real method of making them into Christians is to make them into men." Frontenac to Colbert, November 2, 1672, in *Découvertes et établissements des Français dans l'Ouest et dans le Sud de l'Amérique septentrionale*, ed. Pierre Margry, 6 vols. (Paris: D. Jouaust, 1879–1888), 1:247. All quotes from Margry translated by the author.

10. Axtell, *Invasion Within*, 60–64.

11. A Sulpician quoted in Louise Dechêne, *Habitants and Merchants in Seventeenth-Century Montreal*, trans. Liana Vardi (Montreal: McGill-Queen's University Press, 1992), 9.

12. As scholars have noted, for many of the European colonial powers, one of the most important early dreams for cultural conversion in the New World involved teaching Indians to use "civilized" languages. This project, which Stephen Greenblatt has termed "linguistic colonialism," was based on the assumption that language fundamentally enabled civilized living and thought.

Uniform language also enabled more efficient governance over a subject population. At the same time as they were initially colonizing America, European states were engaged in a project to standardize the vernaculars within European kingdoms in order to create the foundation for emerging national communities. Linguistic conformity instilled loyalty and regularity, at the same time that it reduced local and provincial autonomy. This strategy of statecraft translated easily to dreams about the New World, where European powers imagined the proliferation of uniform European language among native populations as a precursor to incorporating them as loyal subjects. While the diversity of languages and dialects in the New World made this difficult, many considered it essential. Administrators in New Spain in the sixteenth century actually took measures to *restrict* priests from conducting missions in indigenous languages, considering the native tongues to be an ineffective, if not dangerous, basis for the creation of colonial communities. Stephen Greenblatt, "Learning to Curse: Aspects of Linguistic Colonialism in the Sixteenth Century," in *First Images of America*, ed. Fredi Chiapelli (Berkeley: University of California Press, 1976), 16–32; Tzvetan Todorov, *The Conquest of America: The Question of the Other* (New York: Harper & Row, 1984).

13. Frontenac, 1672, in Margry, *Découvertes et établissements*, 1:247–251.

14. Colbert to Talon, April 5, 1666, Archives nationales de France, Colonies (hereafter cited as AN, Col.), C^{11A}, vol. 2, fol. 205, quoted in Dechêne, *Habitants and Merchants*, 9.

15. In the 1630s, Jesuits began to write their famous *Relations*, in which they detailed these arduous journeys through the wilderness in pursuit of souls. A hagiographic engraving created in Paris to honor the memory of Jean de Brébeuf reflected the most important elements of this new strategy, recalling the heroic priest's achievements in "following them into the deep forest," and "reducing the principles of their own language." Brébeuf engraving, in Carole Blackburn, *Harvest of Souls: The Jesuit Missions and Colonialism in North America, 1632–1650* (Montreal: McGill-Queen's University Press, 2000), frontispiece.

16. Thwaites, *Jesuit Relations*, 23:207.

17. Ignatius Loyola's credo explicitly endorsed the idea that priests meet the indigenous people on their own terms. Rather than making them live as Europeans, Loyola urged Jesuits to sponsor Christianity even as they themselves lived in indigenous ways. As he quoted from St. Paul, "Be all things to all men in order to win all to Jesus Christ." Quoted in Peter A. Dorsey, "Going to School with the Savages: Authorship and Authority among the Jesuits of New France," *William and Mary Quarterly*, 3rd series, 55 (July 1998): 399. See Loyola's letter to Joao Nunes Barreto, in *Jesuit Writings of the Early*

Modern Period, 1540–1640, ed. John Patrick Donnelly (Indianapolis: Hackett, 2006), 25. See also Axtell, *Invasion Within*, chapter 5, "When in Rome."

18. Frontenac to Colbert, 1672, in Margry, *Découvertes et établissements*, 1:248–250.

19. Colbert to Talon, April 5, 1666, AN, Col., C[11A], vol. 2, fol. 205. All quotes from AN translated by the author.

20. Talon to Colbert, October 10, 1667, AN, Col., C[11A], vol. 2, fol. 306–320v.

21. King's decree paraphrased by Frontenac, in Margry, *Découvertes et établissements*, 1:249.

22. Charlevoix, 1741, quoted in Axtell, *Invasion Within*, 69.

23. Thwaites, *Jesuit Relations*, 54:185.

24. Axtell, *Invasion Within*, chapter 5.

25. For a still-useful example of the traditional approach, see Mary P. Palm, "The Jesuit Missions of the Illinois Country, 1673–1763" (Ph.D. diss., St. Louis University, 1931).

26. See Patricia Seed, *Ceremonies of Possession in Europe's Conquest of the New World, 1492–1640* (Cambridge: Cambridge University Press, 1995).

27. Stephen Greenblatt, *Marvelous Possessions: The Wonder of the New World* (Chicago: University of Chicago Press, 1991); Todorov, *Conquest of America*.

28. Lusson's ceremony is described in many places, including Talon to Colbert, November 2, 1671, AN, Col., C[11A], vol. 3, fol. 159–171; Margry, *Découvertes et établissements*, 1:96–99. Later explorers and missionaries performed similarly self-conscious actions to symbolize their possession of parts of the Mississippi valley, including by raising crosses, carving in trees, singing songs, performing dances, burying plaques, and shouting into the woods. Narratives written and published later by explorers such as Hennepin, Lahontan, Perrot, La Salle, and others discursively advanced the project of colonial domination by providing simplistic, sometimes even fictional, images of Indian savages, which served to justify dispossession and conquest. See Tracy Neal Leavelle, "Geographies of Encounter: Religion and Contested Spaces in Colonial North America," *American Quarterly* 56 (December 2004): 913–943; Richard White, "Discovering Nature in North America," *Journal of American History* 79 (December 1992): 874–891; Gordon M. Sayre, *Les Sauvages Américains: Representations of Native Americans in French and English Colonial Literature* (Chapel Hill: University of North Carolina Press, 1997). Fundamentally, these writings tried to put a strange landscape into familiar, European terms. See Mary Louise Pratt, *Imperial Eyes: Travel Writing and Transculturation* (London: Routledge, 1992).

29. Thwaites, *Jesuit Relations*, 59:119. While the calumet was clearly a show of welcome to the "strangers," Marquette understood that he was nevertheless

expected to participate in specific, inflexible ways. "[The calumet] must not be refused, unless one wishes to be considered an Enemy," wrote Marquette. He had to puff the disagreeable smoke. And he also had to eat the distasteful food offered during the ceremony. While the music was pleasant, sung "in perfect harmony" (Marquette was in fact so pleased by it that he took down the melody and lyrics in his notes), there were some aspects of the ceremony that were repulsive. But as Marquette recognized, he would have to adapt himself to this ceremony in order to achieve his goals. And as his interpretation of the ceremony makes clear, this required him to accept Indian meanings as much as they accepted his. The following description is based on the first part of Marquette's journal in ibid.

30. Ibid., 59:137.

31. Tonty's 1698 Memoir on La Salle's Discoveries, in *Early Narratives of the Northwest, 1634–1699,* ed. Louise Phelps Kellogg (New York: C. Scribner's Sons, 1917), 288. Two years after Marquette's initial arrival in the Illinois Country, Claude Allouez would also remark on the war imagery of the calumet dance, understanding it to be a demonstration of Indian power to which the priests had to subject themselves: "The performer makes war in rhythmic time, preparing his arms, attiring himself, running, discovering the foe, raising the cry, slaying the enemy, removing his scalp, and returning home with a song of victory—and all with an astonishing exactness, promptitude and agility." Thwaites, *Jesuit Relations,* 51:49.

32. Ibid.

33. Robert L. Hall, *An Archaeology of the Soul: North American Indian Belief and Ritual* (Urbana: University of Illinois Press, 1997), 1–9.

34. See Minamiki, *Chinese Rites Controversy,* 16.

35. As Allouez wrote, "This ceremony resembles in its significance the French custom of drinking, several out of the same glass." Thwaites, *Jesuit Relations,* 51:49.

36. Ibid., 59:129.

37. Ibid., 60:163.

38. The prayer book survives and has been published. Claude Jean Allouez, J. L. Hubert Neilson, and Literary and Historical Society of Quebec, *Facsimile of Père Marquette's Illinois Prayer Book* (Quebec City: Quebec Literary and Historical Society, 1908).

39. Thwaites, *Jesuit Relations,* 51:51.

40. Ibid.

41. Ibid., 58:265.

42. Ibid. These aspects of the Jesuit mission in Illinois have been noted before, but here I stress the ways in which they reflected a conscious strategy by the

Jesuits to create a locally appropriate Catholicism. See Christopher Bilodeau, " 'They Honor Our Lord among Themselves in Their Own Way': Colonial Christianity and the Illinois Indians," *American Indian Quarterly* 25 (Summer 2001): 352–377.

43. Thwaites, *Jesuit Relations*, 58:265.

44. Allouez narrative quoted in Dablon's Relation of 1674, in ibid., 58:265–267.

45. Ibid., 55:217. As Allouez wrote, "Upon our return thither, we hope to find a Chapel, which they are preparing to build themselves, in order to begin there in good earnest the functions of Christianity." Marquette and Allouez found many parallels that they could exploit in their initial attempts to create a local Christianity, *after their fashion*. Marquette thrilled when he saw some Kickapoo performing sacrifices to what looked like a cross erected in the middle of a village. Even though this cross was full of non-Christian imagery, "adorned with many white skins, red Belts, and bows and arrows, which these good people had offered to the great *Manitou*," Marquette looked on it as a hopeful foundation for Catholicism, or perhaps even evidence that they had already learned a bit of the faith from some other source. Marquette's first mass at the newly dedicated mission took place in an open field that was also the setting for the "great Council" where the Illinois sometimes worshipped manitous. This place was likely the same one where the calumet and local *midewinwin* dance were regularly performed in the summer months, as Marquette had only recently observed. In any event, it is significant that for mass Marquette used *this* place, already invested with spiritual meaning for the Indians, rather than moving to a new setting that was free of these traditional associations. The fact that he did so reflects his willingness to graft Christianity onto preexisting spiritual landscapes.

46. On this point, see Edward G. Gray and Norman Fiering, eds., *The Language Encounter in the Americas, 1492–1800: A Collection of Essays* (New York: Berghahn Books, 2000), introduction.

47. Thwaites, *Jesuit Relations*, 59:103.

48. Marquette did recognize some slippages here, to be sure. For example, he knew that the status of manitou could sometimes inhere in a person who was thought to possess exceptional powers. Ibid., 59:127. For an excellent discussion of "manitou" and translation in Illinois missions, see Tracy Neal Leavelle, " 'Bad Things' and 'Good Hearts': Mediation, Meaning, and the Language of Illinois Christianity," *Church History* 76 (June 2007): 363–394.

49. Such decisions were an attempt to gain better control over the meaning that was conveyed in translation of Christian concepts. Critics of the Jesuits noted the multiplicity of meanings that could result when the priests used indigenous terms and phrases as a basis for communicating Christianity. See Blackburn, *Harvest of Souls*, 7, 136.

50. Thwaites, *Jesuit Relations*, 51:51.

51. Ibid., 55:184.

52. Ibid., 54:181.

53. Compare this with Dablon's initial assessment: "His [the chief of the Illinois] countenance, moreover, is as gentle and winning as it is possible to see; and, although he is regarded as a great warrior, he has a mildness of expression that delights all beholders. The inner nature does not belie the external appearance, for he is of a tender and affectionate disposition. And what we say of the chief may be said of all the rest of this nation, in whom we have noted the same disposition, together with a docility which has no savor of the barbarians." For both quotations, see George R. Healy, "The French Jesuits and the Idea of the Noble Savage," *William and Mary Quarterly*, 3rd series, 15 (April 1958): 146.

54. Louis Hennepin, *A New Discovery of a Vast Country in America*, ed. Reuben Gold Thwaites, 2 vols. (Chicago: A. C. McClurg, 1903), 1:167. The Jesuit Dablon, by contrast, had singled the Illinois out for having a well-defined manner of government, which, while not equivalent to the European style, gave the Illinois a decidedly ordered way of life. Thwaites, *Jesuit Relations*, 55:207–215.

55. Hennepin, *New Discovery*, 1:168.

56. Ibid., 2:460.

57. Quoted in Palm, "Jesuit Missions," 22.

58. Hennepin, *New Discovery*, 1:217.

59. Ibid., 2:467–468.

60. This quote actually describes Hennepin's missionizing at Fort Frontenac, where he labored before arriving in the Illinois Country in the 1680s. It is likely that he would have employed the same strategy when he arrived in Illinois. Ibid., 2:20.

61. As for the memorized prayers, Hennepin wrote that they were meaningless. "These miserable dark Creatures listen to all we say concerning our Mysteries," he wrote, "just as if 'twere a Song." Ibid., 2:460. Another quote to the same effect: "We Teach them Prayers; but they repeat them like Songs, without any distinction by Faith. Those we have catechized a long time, are very wavering, except some few: They renounce all, return into their Woods, and take up their old Superstitions upon the least Crotchet that comes into their Heads." Ibid., 2:467–468.

62. Ibid., 2:168. Hennepin believed that the willingness by the Jesuits to baptize Indians was foolish, because the Indians had ulterior motives for embracing the faith: "They will suffer themselves to be baptized ten times a Day for a Glass of Brandy, or a Pipe of Tobacco, and offer their Children to be baptized but all without any Religious Motive." Ibid., 2:460.

63. Ibid., 2:168.
64. Ibid., 2:457. If this was the Recollect inclination, it is also significant that Hennepin was aligned with a whole colonial project that aimed to make a colonial community along this basic outline. As leader of the project of which the Recollects were a part, La Salle hoped to increase the French population in Illinois as quickly as possible after 1680, and to encourage the mixing of French and Indians in the colonial mission. La Salle's prior experience led him to favor *Frenchification* as the proper *terms* of colonialism in Illinois. In particular, his experience in founding Fort Frontenac on Lake Ontario in the 1670s gave him confidence that the best means of creating a colonial community was gradually to help Indians adopt the customs of the French. At Fort Frontenac, La Salle wrote, "[the Indians] consented willingly that the two [Recollect] Priests, who have built a house and a church, should raise their children in the French manner." As a result, La Salle reported, "there is room to hope that very soon these two different villages should compose one township of good Christians and Frenchmen." Upon arriving in Illinois, La Salle wrote excitedly that he had already begun to teach the French language, and even Latin, to the Illinois. La Salle's faith in *Frenchification* is also demonstrated in the narrative of his early settlement in Illinois. Commenting on the Miami, who were polygamists, the narrator of this account relates La Salle's own belief that "they can hardly be induced to give up this evil custom, nor that of repudiating the wife at the first whim, until there shall have been established among them colonies of Frenchmen who, by their example, fortified by the exhortations of Churchmen and by the authority of the laws and of governors, shall lead them to an exact observance of the chief rules of Christianity." Also importantly, La Salle's main sponsor was Governor Frontenac, himself a strong proponent of *Frenchification* and openly critical of the Jesuits' isolated, distant missions. As Frontenac wrote, "I have given [the Jesuits] an example and made them see that when they want to make useful the credit and the power they have with the savages, they will make them sociable, and [raise] their children in the way that I have." Father Hennepin's plan was consistent with this. He would teach the French language to Indian children. He would inculcate French lifestyles, aiming first and foremost to "persuade the Barbarians to dwell Constantly in one place." He would try to teach Indians to farm using iron tools, a practice that they abandoned to his dismay. But above all, Hennepin would look toward "commerce with the French" as a means to civilizing the natives. See Robert Cavelier de La Salle, *Relation of the Discoveries and Voyages of Cavelier de La Salle from 1679 to 1681; the Official Narrative*, trans. Melville Best Anderson (Chicago: Caxton Club,

1901), 295; Frontenac to Colbert, November 14, 1674, in Margry, *Découvertes et établissements*, 1:230; Hennepin, *New Discovery*, 2:457.

65. Louis Armand de Lom d'Arce de Lahontan, *New Voyages to North America*, ed. Rueben Gold Thwaites (Chicago: McClurg, 1905), 2:413.

66. Quoted in Axtell, *Invasion Within*, 77.

67. LaSalle's lieutenant Henri de Tonty had long tried to get the Illinois transferred officially to a Recollect jurisdiction and to replace the Jesuits at Illinois; this effort had been frustrated: "M. de Tonty having been unable to obtain from my Lord the Bishop a Recollect Father, told me on arriving here, that he was going once more to Quebec to get one." Gravier to Villermont, March 17, 1694, "De la mission de l'Immaculée Conception de N. D. au fort St. Louis des Ilinois," Bibliothèque nationale de France, MSS Français, 22804, 59–60v, Manuscripts in Illinois Historical Survey.

68. Cadillac envisioned an explicit *Frenchification* program for his missionaries, including bringing Recollect missionaries to Detroit "with particular orders to teach the little Indians the French language, this being the only method to civilize them, humanize them, and plant inside their heart the spirit of law and religion and of Monarchy." As he argued, "Parroqueets and magpies speek [French] well; why should reasonable creatures find it difficult?" He knew that the Jesuits believed that "*fréquentation*" between the French and the Indians "is dangerous and corrupts their customs . . . and there is nothing but the distancing of the French habitations from the Indians that will preserve and guarantee [the latter] from this corruption." Cadillac totally disagreed. He looked forward to a time when Indians and French people intermarried, and their offspring "would not speak anything *but* French." These *Frenchified* Indians would become "the strongest pillar of the Colony." Cadillac's Memoir on Detroit, in Margry, *Découvertes et établissements*, 5:146.

69. Thwaites, *Jesuit Relations*, 65:53.

70. See Alfred Rambaud, "Jean-Baptiste de la Croix de Chevrières de Saint-Vallier," in *Dictionary of Canadian Biography Online*, http://www.biographi.ca.

71. The story of the Seminary-Jesuit dispute in Illinois is recounted in Garraghan, "New Light on Old Cahokia," and also in several detailed contemporary accounts. See also "Mémoire de l'abbé Joseph de la Colombière sur l'établissement des Tamarois," ca. 1700, ASQ, SME, 12.1/ 009/017.

72. Quoted in Garraghan, "New Light on Old Cahokia," 105.

73. An Illinois Jesuit, quoted in ibid., 106.

74. Letter of St. Cosme to Laval, From the Tamarois, March 1700, ASQ Extracts, Manuscripts in Illinois Historical Survey.

75. Taschereau, "Mission du Séminaire de Québec chez les Tamarois," 12.

76. Ibid., 14.
77. Quoted in Garraghan, "New Light on Old Cahokia," 111.
78. ASQ, Missions SME, 12.1. 009/024.
79. Taschereau, "Mission du Séminaire de Québec chez les Tamarois," 19.
80. ASQ Missions, SME, 12.1/009/025, "Exposé des Jésuites du Canada sur leur différend avec Mgr de Laval et son Séminaire au sujet de la mission des Tamarois."
81. Taschereau, "Mission du Séminaire de Québec chez les Tamarois," 6.
82. ASQ, SME 12–1, 009/056, 1699. Saint-Vallier critiqued how the Jesuits wandered, "leav[ing] one place in order to go to another." As he saw it, there was a clear preference for "a settled priest," as the Seminary priests intended to become, over "a passing mission," like the ones the Jesuits maintained. This was a disagreement over strategy, and Saint-Vallier knew it was crucial to pick the correct one. "The most essential thing of all," he wrote to Gravier, "is that the Bishops charged with the conduct and with the conversion of souls of their dioceses should take the measures most likely to succeed." As he saw it, the Jesuits were not likely to succeed since "[the Jesuit missions] are not even bound to establishments but to individuals or to communities."
83. Thwaites, *Jesuit Relations*, 66:39.
84. Montigny himself wanted to find a way to get European food into the Illinois Country. Laval Manuscripts, "Mémoire touchant la mission des Tamarois, la nécessité de son union au Séminaire de Québec," July 17, 1700, ASQ Transcripts, Manuscripts in Illinois Historical Survey.
85. Thwaites, *Jesuit Relations*, 66:35.
86. Ibid., 66:263.
87. Ibid., 65:151, 167.
88. Ibid., 66:129.
89. Ibid.
90. Bergier, 1702, quoted in Palm, "Jesuit Missions," 39.
91. Taschereau, "Mission du Séminaire de Québec chez les Tamarois," 9.
92. ASQ SME, 12.1, 009/024.
93. Ibid., 4.
94. Ibid., 5.
95. Thwaites, *Jesuit Relations*, 66:35.
96. Laval Manuscripts, "Mémoire touchant la mission des Tamarois."
97. Ruling on the dispute between Jesuits and Seminary priests in Illinois, Laval Manuscripts, 1701, ASQ Transcripts.
98. See Robert Michael Morrissey, "I Speak It Well: Language, Communication, and the End of a Missionary Middle Ground in Illinois, 1673–1712," *Early American Studies* 9, no. 3 (September 2011): 617–648.

99. On "linguistic colonialism," see Greenblatt, "Learning to Curse."

100. Edward G. Gray provides an interesting discussion of colonists' understandings of native languages and the question of whether they could contain Christian meanings in *New World Babel: Languages and Nations in Early America* (Princeton, N.J.: Princeton University Press, 1999), chapters 1–3.

101. Victor Egon Hanzeli, *Missionary Linguistics in New France: A Study of Seventeenth- and Eighteenth-Century Descriptions of American Indian Languages* (The Hague: Mouton, 1969), chapter 1.

102. Far from assimilating the Illinois into a larger, uniform empire, Jesuits used their own language skills to achieve what might be considered a contrary agenda to Greenblatt's linguistic imperialism, that is, *linguistic localism.* Exploiting their language abilities to preserve their mission community opaque to outside influence, Jesuits created a version of Christianity and a community that was intelligible only to insiders, and focused on the local world of the mission. Once this mission was established, Jesuits resisted efforts by other missionaries and Illinois *commandants* to infiltrate their territory and align it to different imperial agendas. Significantly, as language was the foundation and symbol of the Jesuits' strategy, language quickly became the focus of these controversies, too.

"Gascon Exaggerations"

The Rise of Antoine Laumet dit de Lamothe, Sieur de Cadillac, the Foundation of Colonial Detroit, and the Origins of the Fox Wars

RICHARD WEYHING

IN 1701, FRENCH COLONIAL AUTHORITIES EMBARKED UPON AN AMBItious, though ill-fated, quest to create a center of empire deep in the Great Lakes region, or the Pays d'en Haut, along the waterways joining Lakes Erie and Huron—a vital crossroads of the early American West known simply as "the straits," or *le détroit*. As envisioned by its founder, Antoine Laumet dit de Lamothe, Sieur de Cadillac, and endorsed at Versailles by Louis XIV and the Minister of the Marine, the Comte de Pontchartrain, Detroit was intended to serve as a linchpin of French dominance in North America, where an array of native groups from the surrounding regions—often referred to collectively by colonial officials as the *nations des lacs*—could be gathered to assist in the Crown's impending imperial wars against England.[1]

Though Cadillac succeeded in convincing the minister that Detroit would "cause the certain ruin of the English colonies," he was a seemingly unlikely figure to lead such an important enterprise. He had arrived in the colonies less than two decades earlier as a mysterious immigrant from rural Gascony and spent five years roaming the eastern seaboard as a vagabond smuggler before assuming a false noble title and entering the service of the state during the Nine Years' War (1688–1697). Citing this shadowy past, Cadillac's many detractors warned Versailles of his ulterior designs to master the contraband fur trade in the Great Lakes region, and insisted that the Indian alliances that he proposed to consolidate at Detroit were far too fragile to be relied upon for such grand imperial plans. In previous decades, colonial governors had only been able to enlist broad support among the diverse, and historically antagonistic, *nations des lacs* due to the existence of a common, though recently subdued, enemy: the Five Nations of the Iroquois who, after gaining access to muskets, powder, and shot from Dutch, and later English, trading operations in the Hudson River valley in the 1640s, emerged as the single greatest fighting force in North America. Simultaneously reeling from epidemics that accompanied these European traders into the interior, the Iroquois launched concerted attacks upon New France and the villages of the *nations des lacs* throughout the second half of the seventeenth century, attempting to replenish their populations with scores of captive slaves and dominate the fur-trading routes of the continental interior that could ensure their continued access to European arms. While the Iroquois specter loomed over the Great Lakes region, French colonial governors had been able to sustain the illusion that they could act as proper Indian "fathers" to their diverse "children" in the region, championing Indian diplomatic rituals to preserve peace between them, providing them with arms through their own networks of trade in the Pays d'en Haut, and then leading combined war parties against the Five Nations. Such rhetoric of fictive kinship, however, had always masked what was a highly contingent set of relationships between traditional rivals—hardly the ready instrument of state power that officials at Versailles might have imagined.[2]

When Cadillac arrived at court in the winter of 1698 promising to mobilize thousands of Indian warriors at Detroit, the circumstances that had once allowed the alliance to survive in previous years had largely ceased to prevail. Following years of combined French and Indian assaults, Iroquois power had finally been broken, and their chiefs began arriving in Montreal suing for much-needed peace. Moreover, saturated French markets for North American furs had recently prompted the minister to order the closure of the western trading posts where, for decades, French officials had struggled to maintain the loose allegiance of the *nations des lacs*. Already, the old alliance was disintegrating into cycles of violence between its erstwhile members, who were no longer bound together by a shared Iroquois threat and the continual mediation of French agents in their midst. Gathering the diverse peoples of the Pays d'en Haut at Detroit under these conditions, Cadillac's critics asserted, would likely lead to conflict. Because deadly European diseases continued to travel along the waterways of the Great Lakes sustaining the demand for captive slaves to replace the dead within Indian communities, competition among those who resettled at Detroit over access to French arms that could empower their villages in this precarious environment would produce a general war—one that the colonial state would find difficult to ignore if it wanted to preserve its influence among the region's most powerful peoples.

Although Cadillac and his political allies were well aware of these dangers, they were ultimately willing to risk everything for an opportunity to batten off the region's ongoing contraband trade, and to eventually monopolize the commerce of the interior once French markets for Great Lakes pelts had recovered. As widely predicted, however, their gamble eventuated in catastrophe. Following the foundation of Detroit, violence broke out almost immediately between the villages of the Odawa, Miami, Wyandot, and others whom Cadillac managed to attract there, and by 1710 the straits had become a war zone in which, as one Potawatomi chief declared to Governor Philippe de Rigaud de Vaudreuil in Montreal, "everyone wished to be master."[3] Despite strenuous efforts to remain in power, Cadillac was eventually relieved of command at Detroit, but over the ensuing months Jacques-Charles Renaud Dubuisson, the post's interim commander, failed to halt escalating intervillage disputes. In June 1712, they culminated in the slaughter of nearly 1,000 men, women, and children from the Meskwaki (or Fox), Mascoutin, and Kickapoo peoples outside Detroit—groups whom Cadillac had recklessly encouraged to migrate from Wisconsin just months before his removal. The massacre at Detroit was one of the most horrific episodes in the history of early America, and it ignited three decades of conflicts—often glossed by historians as "the Fox Wars"—that pitted the colonial state and its most important Indian allies against the victims of these atrocities throughout the Great Lakes and Mississippi River valley.

Recent ethnohistorians have largely echoed the language of Cadillac's seventeenth-century critics, and presented the tragic events outside Detroit as an inevitable development: the logical consequence of a "naive" colonial policy that created an "intertribal powder keg" doomed to explode.[4] According to these scholars, the intervillage violence that erupted along the straits was the result of Indian peoples redetermining the parameters of the alliance themselves, drawing colonial forces into long-standing feuds to eliminate their rivals from sources of trade and diplomacy. While agreeing with much of the substance of these claims, this essay argues that the origins of the Fox Wars are best understood with greater attention to historical developments on both sides of the Atlantic.[5] The conflicts that began outside of Detroit were as much the product of Cadillac's high political machinations to reconfigure the French colonial presence in the Great Lakes region as they were the preexisting animosities between the region's native peoples that were subsequently exacerbated. It was the often chaotic entanglement of these two complex systems—the patron-client networks of the French state into which Cadillac rapidly integrated himself, and the fluctuating village politics of the *nations des lacs*—that made the Pays d'en Haut a place of such uncertainty, and eventual violence, at the onset of the eighteenth century. Albeit separated by thousands of miles and layers of cultural misunderstanding, the Indian villages of Detroit and the interior of Versailles were joined in fate, and interconnected by the words and actions of men such as Cadillac who moved back and forth between these two important nodes of the Atlantic world.

THE EMERGENCE OF AN "EXPERT": FROM ANONYMITY TO AUTHORITY IN THE FRENCH ATLANTIC

From the very beginning the basic ingredients that would produce the horrors of the massacre outside Detroit were evident, but Cadillac ardently refused to acknowledge the gathering unrest. In September 1708, for instance, he dispatched one of many appeals to the Minister of the Marine defending his embattled brainchild. Brandishing the same rhetorical flourish he had once used to persuade Versailles of Detroit's promise back in 1698, he now lashed out at his detractors in the colonies, claiming they could offer nothing but "abomination, blasphemy . . . and incompetent quarrels" regarding conditions at Detroit.[6] After nearly seven years of troubling uncertainty, however, Pontchartrain's confidence in Cadillac had been greatly shaken, and the minister's marginalia revealed a patron-client relationship in deepening crisis. Evoking a stereotype for the hotheaded characters of Cadillac's natal region, the minister responded with a simple, yet barbed, quip: "*exagérations gasconnes.*"[7]

The nineteenth-century French romantic novelist Alexandre Dumas later memorialized this typecast with his own fictional son of Gascony, the impetuous musketeer D'Artagnan. Although Cadillac's service to the Crown would ultimately prove less magnanimous than the exploits of Dumas's hero, his career was arguably no less storied. By 1708, his characteristic *gasconades* had finally begun to tire his readers at Versailles, but such bravado would not result in an end to his colonial career, or even his removal from ministerial protection. Relieved of command at Detroit, Cadillac was swiftly appointed to the governorship of Louisiana. And despite an encore of controversy and dismissal at this colonial post (as well as four and a half months of imprisonment in the Bastille on related charges of treason), he ended his life governing the town of Castelsarrasin near his birthplace in the metropole itself. Following Louis XIV's death, he continued to submit *mémoires* suggesting colonial policy to the regency government, and in recognition of his toils in the Americas the Crown eventually anointed him a knight in the *Ordre royal et militaire de Saint-Louis*, a highly coveted honor introduced by the "Sun King" in 1693 to decorate some of his most prized military officers.[8] For several decades Cadillac was regarded as a useful, if often controversial, expert in colonial affairs, adept at building, and rebuilding, his own political capital. During the tenures of four successive colonial ministers from the Marquis de Seignelay to the powerful Phélypeaux family—represented by Louis, Comte de Pontchartrain; then his son and successor, Jérôme (who assumed the title of Pontchartrain in late 1699); and finally his grandson, Jean Frédéric, Comte de Maurepas—Cadillac remained an influential voice in the French Atlantic, and an agent of the most militarily powerful and opulent court in all of Europe.

Despite his persistent involvement in the events of the French empire, however, Cadillac's career has surprisingly attracted little scholarly attention.[9] Less intrigued by his resilience as an imperial agent, professional historians have only offered brief discussions of his role in the French Atlantic. Citing, among other abuses of power, his constant pursuit of contraband trade and frequent deception of metropolitan officials, these works have reduced his career to a lurching, and frequently preposterous, quest for personal profit, one worthy of only a few lines in the *longue durée* of French North America.[10] In highlighting how colonial projects—despite the language of idealism in which they are often cloaked—have historically attracted such disingenuous profiteers, these portrayals of Cadillac as the "worst scoundrel ever to set foot in New France" have thankfully replaced an earlier hagiographic tradition that hailed him as a "knight errant of the wilderness."[11] But such indictments of Cadillac's character have left larger, and I would argue more important, questions unanswered. How was he, among myriad other ambitious adventurers seeking self-aggrandizement in the Americas, able to gain enough stature at Versailles to propose such a risky project as Detroit in the first place? And more important, how can an examination of his fateful rise to power advance our understanding of the violent instability that punctuated, if not truly characterized, French and Indian interaction in the Pays d'en Haut?

Providing answers to these questions first requires situating Cadillac in the proper category. Perhaps in the most general sense, he represents an archetype of European expansion into the Americas: a "military entrepreneur," in the words of historical sociologist Thomas Gallant, who pledged to lead auxiliary forces in the colonies (namely foreign mercenaries, privateers, and allied Indian groups) in return for lands, titles, trading prerogatives, or other spoils of war more difficult to attain in the "Old World." Often faced with insufficient resources to project formal state power across the ocean, European monarchs frequently struck deals with figures such as Cadillac, who initially stood outside existing political institutions but emerged opportunistically from the colonial hinterland, offering creative solutions to the strategic dilemmas of the Crown. Though subsequently appointed to great positions of authority in the colonies, these men had entered European courts, so to speak, through the back door.[12]

To be sure, throughout his long reign Louis XIV's preoccupation with dynastic warfare in Europe fostered an increased reliance upon such men in the state's neglected colonies. But Cadillac's ability to gain, and regain, royal support as a military entrepreneur comes into even sharper focus when emphasizing a premise long understood by historians, but only recently addressed by Kenneth Banks's study of the French Atlantic. "The state," he writes, "could only be as strong as its most recent dispatches."[13] Banks reminds us that logistical constraints upon travel (and hence communication) in the early modern period always impeded Versailles's efforts to solidify its hold upon the Americas. Because the king, the Minister of the Marine, and the clerks (*commis*) of the Bureau du Ponant (later renamed the Bureau des Colonies) never crossed the Atlantic themselves, they depended not only upon effective military leaders but also on testimony from appointed colonial officials to devise policy and organize the allocation of resources.[14] As Banks explains, the process of colonial governance often resembled an "exchange—information for promotions and honors—[that] formed the primary basis upon which the Marine managed all of France's overseas possessions."[15] For Banks, oceanic France was a "reporting hierarchy" composed of an "information elite" whose ranks Cadillac also entered: an eclectic array of administrators, explorers, geographers, hydrographers, lawyers, diplomats, and spies employed to provide the state with intelligence.[16]

Charged with administering distant colonial possessions, officials at Versailles certainly wanted details, a commodity the profuse Cadillac excelled at providing as he aggressively integrated himself into the reciprocal patron-client networks of the Marine.[17] Though he often emphasized his soldierly competence by styling himself as a "*guerrier*" equal to the great colonial military leaders of his day (namely the Sieur d'Iberville and l'Amiral Jean-Baptiste du Casse, whose feats during the Nine Years' War became the stuff of legend), Cadillac's career was ultimately preserved by the pen rather than the sword.[18] Continuously plying the Marine with timely expertise, he claimed to lend vicarious vision to Versailles through a range of *mémoires*, dispatches, cartographic and hydrographic charts, as well as periodic audiences with figures in France. It was with savvy aim, for instance, that he once wrote the Sieur de Lagny, a key official at Versailles, that his reports of the English colonies would be so clear that "henceforth you will speak shrewdly of them as if you had been to these places yourself."[19] For three decades he thrived as a political chameleon in this manner, overcoming great setbacks to his career by expediently shifting his ambitions when outlooks in the ministry changed. As he cynically assured his patrons in the naval ministry in 1696, he was a *"créature la plus attachée"* to the designs of his patrons, even as they fluctuated over time.[20]

The results of his efforts would have a profound effect upon the development of French North America. While Cadillac was never a fixture at court, or in the king's councils determining the highest affairs of state, he did gain a considerable amount of influence within the personnel of the Marine. And as his stature rose within this organ of government, he became increasingly tempted to gamble with what power he wielded, hoping to effect major changes in colonial policy that might further his interests. As we shall see, his proposal for Detroit was a masterpiece of high political manipulation, in which he persuaded the Marine to support a new colonial project that might accord him unprecedented riches, but whose plans he secretly knew harbored inordinate risks to the security of New France.

Born in 1658 as Antoine Laumet, the son of a minor official in the village of Saint-Nicolas-de-la-Grave, Cadillac's early life is largely undocumented. Although he would later claim to have served in two infantry regiments as a young man, his contradictory statements on the matter raise considerable doubt. His elegant prose, often adorned with biblical allusion and Latin aphorisms, suggests instead that he received a formal education, likely in law at the nearby Recollect or Jesuit colleges in Moissac, Montauban, or perhaps the regional metropolis of Toulouse.[21] By his mid-twenties, however, unknown events compelled him to flee France. He arrived in the Americas around 1683 and began a scandalous career in the contraband fur trade as a *coureur de bois* along the North Atlantic coast before marrying into the prominent Guyon family of merchants and privateers in 1687, and acquiring a *seigneurie* from the governor of New France, the Marquis de Denonville, in Port Royal, Acadia (present-day Nova Scotia).[22] His marriage contract, in fact, is the earliest surviving record of his presence in North America, which he used to register a nom de guerre he had presumably been operating under since his arrival in the colonies: Antoine Laumet, de Lamothe, Sieur de Cadillac.[23]

As Antoine Laumet emerged as the Sieur de Cadillac, the Atlantic world itself was on the verge of dramatic changes that would create a prime venue for such determined colonial parvenus. In 1688, dynastic conflicts in Europe led to the outbreak of the Nine Years' War, initiating a new era of North American history in which colonial settlements and Indian communities became increasingly implicated in imperial struggles between the monarchies of France and England that were waged from the edges of the Great Lakes to the Indian Ocean. Cadillac's ostensible expertise along the nautical frontiers of French Acadia and New England—gained during his days of itinerant smuggling—soon brought him to the attention of the royal government, and in the early months of the war Governor Denonville recommended him as a pilot for ongoing naval operations in the North Atlantic.

In October 1689, Cadillac departed aboard the frigate *Embuscade* with a handful of other "*spécialistes*" to perform a reconnaissance mission off the New England coastline.[24] This voyage—to be the first of many in his swiftly developing career—would transform the history of North America by inadvertently ushering him into the chambers of Versailles itself. Once at sea, severe autumn storms prevented the *Embuscade* from returning to Acadia and forced the ship's captain to sail for France itself, where he landed in the naval ministry's principal administrative center of Rochefort. Once again in France, Cadillac wasted little time in directly appealing to the minister of the Marine, the Marquis de Seignelay, and penned in very careful handwriting a two-page letter advertising his qualifications. As his initial entry into the realm of high politics, it merits substantial quotation:

Monseigneur,

If I may be bold enough to take the liberty of presenting my most humble respects, I feel obliged to inform you of my recent voyage . . . aboard the *Embuscade* of M. de la Caffinière to perform a campaign of one month. The natural inclination I have always had for serving the King, and indeed the desire to win the honor of your own protection, I accepted [Caffinière's] proposition without hesitation. [But] after sailing for some time to the west, the winds became so contrary and so violent, that it was impossible to put ashore, and we were forced to seek a port in Europe. . . . My Lord, Your Greatness does not yet dispose of the majority of Acadia, but if you would allow me to inform you of my conduct there, and if you find it worthy of continuance, or have some other use for my employment, I could, and would, redouble my efforts to contribute to your prosperity and success. . . . I could inform you of all matters that concern this vast country from Acadia, New England, New Netherlands (English New York), all the way to Carolina. I know better than anyone, having made numerous voyages by both land and sea, and even traveled two hundred and fifty leagues into the depths of these lands. I have seen the most significant places [of the enemy], examined their forts, their cannon, and I know approximately the number of their inhabitants, and the diversity of their religion. And beyond this, My Lord, I speak English, Spanish and Indian. I beg you to consider that I am the first gentleman established in this place [Acadia] where I have made great expense for its safety. I proposed to Mr. de la Caffinière means by which Your Greatness could sustain a strong Garrison at Port Royal without costing His Majesty a *sol*. I do not doubt at all that they have spoken to you of this. . . . I beseech your protection, My Lord, and assure Your Greatness that I am with very profound respect your humble and very obedient servant,

De Lamothe Cadillac.[25]

Though likely read with a measure of skepticism, these boasts of wartime expertise eventually won Cadillac an invitation to Paris, where he met with the *commis des bureaux de la Marine*, Joseph de la Touche, as well as the *Intendant du commerce au département de la Marine*, the Sieur de Lagny. Both men listened to his plans for striking New England and New York, and arranged an audience with the minister, who was similarly impressed by his seemingly exhaustive familiarity with the region.

Based upon these successful interviews, Cadillac remained in France for the duration of the year, living off a gratification of the Marine amid Parisian and Versaillaise society, serving as Seignelay's spokesperson, or "*porte-parole*"—a direct source of information to garner support for the Marine's colonial policies before members of the king's government who were unconvinced of New France's strategic importance.[26] Following Seignelay's death in November 1690, Cadillac continued this role under the new minister, Louis Phélypeaux, Comte de Pontchartrain, and in the spring of 1691 was dispatched to Quebec with orders for the new governor, Louis de Buade, Comte de Frontenac, to appoint him an officer in the colonial Troupes de la Marine. Without his fortuitous voyage to Rochefort, it is difficult to imagine Cadillac's colonial career taking off so rapidly, but after a year at the center of political authority, he returned to the colonies a favorite of two successive naval ministers with close connections to their administrative personnel, and assumed the rank of lieutenant, eager to fulfill his mandate as a hand-picked, if accidentally delivered, agent of the state.[27]

But in recrossing the Atlantic Cadillac exchanged the splendor of Versailles for a ruinous theater of colonial warfare. While he was away in the metropole, the English had planned their own offensive from Boston, and launched a fleet under Sir William Phips that destroyed the French settlements of Acadia (including Cadillac's own *seigneurie*) before entering the Gulf of St. Lawrence and nearly seizing Quebec in October 1690. Cadillac now took up residence in the colonial capital, where he, along with other key military leaders surrounding the governor, began devising strategies to retaliate against English bases of power. In Frontenac—aptly described by the historian William J. Eccles as the "courtier governor"—Cadillac found a natural ally. Both men harbored great political and economic ambitions in the colonies and knew how to finesse metropolitan authorities to profit from the business of empire.

With Frontenac's support, Cadillac occupied an increasingly influential position as one of the state's chosen experts on the issue of invading the northern English colonies.[28] During this time, he was in seemingly perpetual motion, collaborating with officials in New France, performing naval reconnaissance off the Atlantic Coast, drafting lengthy reports, and verifying charts.[29] His efforts were closely followed by figures in the metropole, and in the spring of 1692 Pontchartrain summoned a collection of military experts from New France to "study the matter in greater detail" and finalize plans for the capture of New England and New York. Personally requested by the king, Cadillac figured prominently among them when he boarded the *Poli* for Rochefort. [30]

That winter in Versailles, he presented the fruits of labors. His *mémoires* minutely re-created the geography of the North Atlantic coastline and sketched the various communities French forces would have to contend with—villages of Anabaptists, "*protestants français*," Dutch traders, and New England fishermen, whom he presciently described as "republicans in their souls, enemies of government and domination."[31] For the cities of Boston and New York themselves, he described the surrounding topography; the extent of their fortifications; amounts of ordnance, small arms, and munitions; and the likely size of their garrisons and militias in the event of an attack. Accompanying these reports were the charts of the royal hydrographer, Jean-Baptiste-Louis Franquelin, "*autorisé par La Motte* [Cadillac]," providing detailed street maps that indicated the homes of English colonial elites, among them William Phips of Boston, whose fleet had pillaged Cadillac's estate just three years earlier.[32]

Though likely embellished for effect, we know that his *mémoires* contained enough viable detail to captivate his patrons at Versailles. In the end, his latest trip to the metropole cemented his status as a "*homme de confiance*," and when he arrived back in Quebec he once again carried letters for the governor that confirmed his importance to the Marine.[33] Between his accidental landing in Rochefort in 1689 and his departure from Versailles in 1693, Cadillac had crossed the Atlantic four times to consult with the minister and his advisers, and on the basis of these strenuous efforts had risen from veritable anonymity to budding authority.

"*LES FATIGUES EXTRAORDINAIRES*": COMMANDING IN THE PAYS D'EN HAUT

Returning to New France, however, Cadillac's career would take another dramatic turn. While he was absent at Versailles, the Crown's military fortunes in Europe had declined precipitously following the twin naval disasters of La Hogue and Barfleur in the English Channel. With little hope of additional military support arriving from the metropole, Frontenac now shifted the colony's wartime objectives away from major offensive campaigns against the principal English ports, to what he called "*la petite guerre*," or the use of smaller raiding parties of allied Indians, militia, and colonial Troupes de la Marine to harass the frontiers.[34]

Now that the colony's war effort increasingly relied upon the cooperation of its Indian allies, Cadillac's eye was drawn west, to the distant Great Lakes, where considerable profits were to be made participating in the fur trade while mobilizing support among the *nations des lacs*. Rather than employing his talents in an amphibious assault upon Manhattan, then, Frontenac promoted Cadillac to *capitaine en pied* and offered him the command of Fort de Buade de Michilimackinac, the principal French post in the Pays d'en Haut.

Aside from his relatively brief experience negotiating with Indian delegations at Montreal prior to departing for Fort de Buade, however, little qualified Cadillac to manage the complex relations of these nations. Frontenac probably appointed him under an agreement to share in his eventual profits from the fur trade, contraband or otherwise. But whatever underlying motives contributed to his appointment, Cadillac's shift from amphibious military planner to western Indian negotiator suggests the fluidity with which "expertise" was regarded in the French Atlantic. If men possessed the right connections and had demonstrated a capacity to withstand the volatile conditions of the Atlantic world, they could be shuffled around the state's colonial possessions and entrusted with a variety of responsibilities. In the

French colonial system "expertise" could denote an ambitious versatility (or "*zèle pour le service du roi*" as it was euphemistically phrased in the administrative correspondence) rather than specialization.[35] As Frontenac reported to the Marine, Cadillac was distinguished by this very type of adaptability: "the Sieur de la Mothe-Cadillac," he assured the minister, "is a man of distinction, full of abilities and expertise (*valeur*)."[36]

His appointment to this post would become a fateful exchange of personnel. Cadillac was sent west to replace Louis de la Porte de Louvigny, who had requested to return to France to attend to family matters. Like Cadillac, Louvigny had arrived in the colonies in the early 1680s and first entered the service of the state under Governor Denonville. But he had spent his entire career in the far western country and was renowned for his influence among the *nations des lacs*. Cadillac's tenure at Michilimackinac would eventually qualify him in the eyes of the metropole to present his plans for Detroit, and following the turmoil he helped create at this new post, Louvigny was ultimately charged with restoring stability to the region and mobilizing an Indian coalition to march against the Meskwaki in Wisconsin with whom he brokered a short-lived armistice in 1716.[37]

Perched along the straits of Lakes Huron and Michigan, nearly 1,000 miles from Montreal, Michilimackinac had been both a crossroads and gathering place for the region's diverse Indian groups for hundreds of years before the arrival of Europeans in the Pays d'en Haut. When the French established a military presence on the site in 1683, however, the straits subsequently became the primary rendezvous point for allied coalitions descending upon the powerful Iroquois nations of New York, whose warriors had been ravaging the Pays d'en Haut and threatening the security of New France for nearly half a century.[38] As conflict with these groups and their English trading partners escalated after 1689, imperial survival in North America hinged upon the competency of commanders stationed there as they labored to build the "*pax gallica*" of Indian groups that could sustain New France against its numerically superior rivals.[39]

Undaunted, Cadillac arrived at Michilimackinac prepared to continue his career as a liaison with Versailles, promising to "clarify and dispel the obscurities that great distances often engender." "Just like the charts of the coasts from Acadia to Virginia . . . that I had the honor of presenting to you, and which are now in your office," he wrote to the minister in 1694 or 1695, "I am currently occupied here in drafting a similar report for this country, of its lakes and rivers, and making observations that I measure none have encountered up to the present."[40] His duties, however, would soon prove more demanding than that.

Unlike the maritime enclaves of Acadia and Quebec, where he had initially forged his career, the Pays d'en Haut was a world far from the reaches of metropolitan military power, where a semblance of French sovereignty was barely maintained by a sparse collection of lightly garrisoned trading posts. At Fort de Buade Cadillac was now situated at the center of a heterogeneous and shifting world of Indian villages—communities of Wyandot, Odawa, visiting Potawatomi, Ojibwa, Sioux, Meskwaki, and others—whose seminomadic lifestyle and noncoercive notions of political authority (in which chiefs built consensus in councils rather than issued orders) rendered them difficult to direct in the fashion of a European commandant. Imagining the patriarchal order of France, Louis XIV may have styled himself as a "father" to these Indian "children." But such terms were only embraced by the peoples of the Pays d'en Haut because in their own cultures, a father's social role prescribed the bestowal of gifts and promises of protection rather than demands for subordination to his will. Among the *nations des lacs*, Cadillac held little political authority in the Western sense of the term, and under these conditions Indian warfare was not easily orchestrated according to the logics of European empires.[41]

Beyond these basic cultural differences, several realities of the region's geopolitics also worked against Cadillac's efforts. Although many of the groups surrounding Michilimackinac shared a common hatred of the Iroquois, the groups French officials often glossed as the *nations des lacs* were, in fact, an uneasy assemblage of historic rivals, and friction between them continually frustrated Cadillac's ability to build a united front against the king's enemies. "I am here in the midst of thirty or thirty-three nations who are uncivilized and ungoverned," he wrote to the minister, "who are all enemies of each other and have always had war together. Just in passing one observes that the Wyandots make war upon the Sioux, the Sioux upon the Miamis, Mascoutins, and Mesquakies. These people make war upon Sauteurs, and the Iroquois, make war upon everyone." Referring back to the "*désordres*" of religious and feudal violence that had ravaged France before Louis XIV's reign, Cadillac offered an accessible analogy: "France itself was once like this," he opined, "when war was fought province against province, city against city, and parish against parish."[42]

In addition to these internal fissures, the "*pax gallica*" was also prey to foreign threats. Throughout Cadillac's command at Michilimackinac, rival English officials in New York—who were armed with cheaper and more abundant trade goods at Albany—dispatched Iroquois emissaries into the Pays d'en Haut to negotiate the defection of the *nations des lacs* to their own orbits of trade and diplomacy. Just months after arriving at his post,

Cadillac discovered that a prominent Wyandot band had received Iroquois *colliers*, or wampum belts, inviting the villages near Michilimackinac to fashion a vast coalition against the French presence.[43] At Fort de Buade, Cadillac constantly feared that the alliance was on the verge of collapsing from both internal divisions and external pressures: "I do not have moments of rest here," he wrote to the minister, "since the commandant of this post must always have his eyes a quarter open to remedy everything."[44] After two years of commanding in the Pays d'en Haut, the once tireless *homme de confiance* found himself complaining of the "*fatigues extraordinaires*" of representing the Crown in these contested regions, and openly criticizing officials "at court" who imagined French sovereignty in the Great Lakes as a fait accompli.

Given the Crown's persistent difficulties in subjecting the peoples of the Pays d'en Haut to royal authority, Cadillac suggested, relying upon the *nations des lacs* to sustain French empire in North America was a doomed strategy. "He [the '*sauvage*'] is born here and he wants to die here," Cadillac wrote to the minister. "It is a life to which he has been accustomed since Adam. Do we wish for him to build palaces and for him to adorn them with beautiful furniture? He, who will never exchange his wigwam [*cabine*] and the mat upon which he sits like an ape for the Louvre? That would be working for the impossible."[45] Instead of endeavoring to transform these "*sauvages*" into subjects, he argued, the Marine should reconsider an invasion of the northern English colonies whose existence polarized European power in North America and allowed the *nations des lacs* to occupy a strategic middle ground where defection to Albany was a constant, and compelling, threat. "I will never dissuade myself of the necessity of taking Manhattan," he insisted, "since if this place remains, we will never be masters of these nations and it will still provide them with occasions . . . to make incredible offenses against us."[46]

Despite the immense profits he was making in the fur trade, in fact, Cadillac submitted several requests for a promotion to the rank of *lieutenant de vaisseau* while at Fort de Buade (a highly prestigious naval rank one step below that of *capitaine de vaisseau*), hoping to resume work upon these plans aboard the king's ships linking Versailles with the colonies.[47] Ironically, just months before staking his career upon an auspicious proposal for a new settlement in the Great Lakes region, Cadillac had come to regard his service there as a disagreeable, if remunerative, interruption of these earlier ambitions. Given the state's current position, he concluded, the Pays d'en Haut was an unsuitable space for empire. An unusual crisis, however, would soon prompt him to refocus his ambitions upon the Great Lakes, and perform a striking about-face.

"*UNE IDÉE INSOUTENABLE*": THE SUSPENSION OF THE FUR TRADE, CRISIS IN THE PAYS D'EN HAUT, AND THE GENESIS OF DETROIT

During his struggles to unify the Indians of Michilimackinac in war against the English and Iroquois, Cadillac had enjoyed no tools of coercion and precious little leverage. What influence he continued to exert depended heavily upon his ability to provide the *nations des lacs* with the trade goods (namely firearms, ammunition, and brandy) that they desired. As evidence of the French "father's" goodwill toward his figurative "children," such exchanges had always been fundamental to the maintenance of the alliance.[48] Although Cadillac had requested the command at Michilimackinac to personally profit from this arrangement (and regularly abused his powers in these pursuits by promoting contraband trade), he always understood its greater importance, and during his years at Michilimackinac desperately advocated an expansion of the trade in order to fulfill Indians' needs, or *besoins*.[49]

But Cadillac's frequent endorsements of the fur trade's diplomatic functions never registered with his patrons in Versailles, and when the European market for North American pelts reached saturation, Pontchartrain officially suspended the twenty-five *congés*, or permits, that had constituted the western trade, and ordered the evacuation of all posts in the Pays d'en Haut in 1696. The *nations des lacs* were now expected to make the long journey to Montreal themselves in order to exchange their furs for goods and thereby renew their diplomatic ties with the Crown. By shifting the locus of western Indian relations from the villages of the Great Lakes region to the St. Lawrence valley, Pontchartrain hoped to alleviate the glut of furs in French storehouses that had sent prices plummeting on the European market. Although the fur trade was the primary industry of New France (and certainly enriched well-connected individuals in the colonies such as Cadillac), its overall returns had never been enough to offset the royal expenses for supporting the colony. What little profit that was made needed to be guarded jealously, lest New France become too great a financial burden to the Crown.[50]

Short-term mercantilist considerations alone had not guided the minister's decision, however. For decades metropolitan administrators had more generally bemoaned the fur trade's tendency to threaten the idealized social order of the colony: a cohesive "New France" carved out of the wilderness. If the lure of profit in the West induced enough *habitants* to abandon the colony's principal settlements, administrators feared that fields outside Quebec and Montreal would turn fallow, church pews would become empty, militia ranks would be depleted, and colonial loyalties to the Crown would fray. Although the majority of New France's population never ventured into the Pays d'en Haut, significant numbers of young men—many of them formerly licensed traders, or voyageurs, and soldiers who deserted their posts in the Great Lakes region—chose to become *coureur de bois* in the western country. These men, administrators claimed, were in open revolt against the state, and rumors of their activities continually reminded Versailles how the fur trade fostered undeniably centripetal forces when the collective governing ethos of metropolitan France was one of centralization and royal control. Until the fall of New France in 1763, Versailles viewed the fur trade with ambivalence and periodic hostility, and fought a continuous battle to control its excesses, both real and perceived.[51]

Within this longer history, however, the 1696 edict was arguably the most disastrous restriction Versailles ever imposed upon the western country, since in Indian eyes French withdrawal represented a harsh repudiation of their long partnership. Although peace with England was being negotiated in Europe, the Crown's struggle against the Iroquois continued, and Quebec still relied upon the assistance of the *nations des lacs*. In the ensuing months a wide spectrum of colonial officials and merchants drafted dispatches protesting the minister's decision, and after arriving in Quebec from Fort de Buade, Cadillac became prominent among them. The 1696 edict, he informed Pontchartrain, was simply "*une idée insoutenable*" that would transform Indian allies into enemies and cause the downfall of the colony.[52] His admonishments were seconded by Governor Frontenac, who claimed that Cadillac was the "best suited" to advise the court in the "minds of the savages."[53] In view of their complaints, Pontchartrain subsequently allowed the retention of two garrisoned posts (Michilimackinac and St. Joseph, near the southeast shore of Lake Michigan), but without sanctioning trade at these sites, such measures would have little effect.

Despite their own economic interest in reinstating the trade, both Frontenac and Cadillac were raising valid points that historians now generally confirm. As Catherine Desbarats has written, for example, "Canada could not dictate the terms of its Indian relations. Ties had to be continually renegotiated in face-to-face encounters and continually embodied in material offerings."[54] James Pritchard has been even more direct. "More than an air of unreality surrounded his [Pontchartrain's] orders," he has written. "They reflected a complete lack of knowledge of France's position in North America" and quickly jeopardized the colony's safety.[55] As everyone in New France understood, the minister's new western policy all but invited the powerful *nations des lacs* to find common cause with the English and Iroquois, who for years had eagerly sought to dismantle the Crown's relations with these powerful western groups.

It is in this specific context that Cadillac's fateful proposal for Detroit—the most famous of his "Gascon exaggerations"—should be understood. It was a desperate crossroads in his career: not only had Pontchartrain rebuffed Cadillac's entreaties to restore trading rights in the Pays d'en Haut, he was also facing charges in Quebec for abuses against voyageurs during his tenure at Michilimackinac.[56] Although Frontenac vigorously defended his client, there was a sense that Cadillac's political stature in both the metropole and the colony was crumbling. Only his presence at Versailles, it seemed, could rescue the situation.

In Quebec, Cadillac was aware that many of the Crown's key allies among the *nations des lacs* had begun to push back the Iroquois tide and settle far to the southeast of Michilimackinac along the straits joining Lakes Erie and Huron guarding the entrance to the upper Great Lakes—an area endowed with fertile soil, abundant game, and rich fishing grounds referred to by the Odawa as Bkejwanong.[57] Cadillac also knew that changes were imminent in the political landscape of Versailles as well, since Jérôme Phélypeaux, Comte de Maurepas, was preparing to assume his father's noble title and role as Minister of the Marine. Perhaps the new Comte de Pontchartrain would be more receptive to proposals for an outpost along this critical junction of the Pays d'en Haut, known to colonial officials as *le détroit*, where diplomatic and trade relations with all of the *nations des lacs* could be resumed under conditions more tolerable to the Crown.

Given his frustrations with the rigors of command at Michilimackinac, Cadillac may have seemed an unlikely candidate to personally champion another project in the Great Lakes region. But he knew that with the western country in disarray, the entire colonial system might falter, and with it his career as an expert in North American affairs. Above all, Cadillac was a hardened political survivor. He could not consign himself to such an outcome, and in the gathering crisis the ever-resourceful Gascon glimpsed an opportunity to return to the Great Lakes under far more favorable conditions than he had previously enjoyed. If he succeeded in convincing the minister to grant him sole authority over the western country at *le détroit*, he would eventually be able to monopolize the entire fur trade of the Pays d'en Haut once the market recovered. Cadillac was fully aware, of course, that the difficulties of suppressing intervillage violence among the *nations des lacs* that he had experienced at Fort de Buade would be magnified at Detroit. But the potential rewards had suddenly become much higher.

As he boarded the last ship for France, then, he held carefully crafted plans for the construction of a revolutionary new settlement in the Great Lakes region that pledged to accomplish everything that the minister desired: a veritable "Paris" in the Pays d'en Haut that could solidify the colony's hold over the Great Lakes without promoting the economic, social, and political "*désordres*" that had historically accompanied western expansion. Designed to sell at Versailles, Cadillac's plan promised more than he knew he could accomplish. But if his ruse succeeded he would at least have a chance to salvage the colony's faltering hinterland, and in time he might become the most powerful and wealthy representative of a European state in the heart of North America.

CADILLAC'S HOUR: SELLING DETROIT AT VERSAILLES

Meanwhile, overarching shifts in the geopolitics of empire would also come to Cadillac's aid. Though the Nine Years' War had recently been concluded by the Treaty of Ryswick, a resumption of even greater transatlantic hostilities over the succession to the Spanish throne and its sprawling "New World" empire (to which Louis XIV now laid claim) was greatly anticipated. Under these heightened tensions, Jérôme Maurepas, who was indeed assuming formal oversight of the Marine, came under great pressure from leading figures in the government to surrender his father's reticence over colonial expansion.[58] Under this new administration, the narrow mercantile considerations that just months earlier had motivated Pontchartrain senior's evacuation of the Pays d'en Haut were now replaced by a colonial policy designed to establish proper military footing in the North American interior before the outbreak of a major transatlantic conflict that, as the famed Marquis de Vauban impressed upon the young minister, could very well decide the "monarch of the world."[59]

Through his connections in France, Cadillac was soon enough apprised of the situation. As he arrived in the metropole, his colleague and rival, Pierre Le Moyne, le Sieur D'Iberville, had secured ministerial support for his own ambitious project: the foundation of a new colony, Louisiana, along the Gulf Coast. Cadillac was determined to follow suit in taking advantage of the Marine's new imperialist outlook, but he would not place his trust in such larger political developments alone. As the 1696 edict had illustrated, Versailles continued to view New France as a place whose economic profitability, strategic importance, and loyalty to the Crown were in serious doubt. While his plans perfectly echoed the visions for French global mastery advanced by the likes of Vauban, then, they also abounded in finer points that left little doubt of Detroit's potential to finally remake the Pays d'en Haut according to metropolitan ideals.

There were two basic components of his project as presented in France beginning that winter. The first copiously allayed traditional metropolitan anxieties over the westward expansion of New France by proposing to concentrate all activity within the Pays d'en Haut in a more central and compact colony at Detroit. To this end, Cadillac proposed a strong seat of government (and would eventually request his own governorship of a separate colony centered at the straits), an increased royal garrison, a collection of religious orders, and an influx of settlers to create a militarily powerful and economically self-sufficient community rather than a far-flung trading post inhabited by rebellious *coureurs de bois*. Whatever traffic in pelts continued, he promised, would be closely regulated to avoid the marketplace disasters of the preceding years and stripped of its attenuating effects upon royal authority.[60]

The second, and by far most ambitious, aspect of his proposal, however, outlined a new strategy of resettling (*ramassant*) all of the Indians of the Pays d'en Haut at Detroit. The *nations des lacs* had been so difficult to manage in the past, he now argued, because they were dispersed throughout the region. At Detroit, he could gather them together around a single fulcrum of trade, diplomacy, and religious life that would allow the processes of alliance to finally flourish. If all went according to plan, Cadillac claimed he could amass vast leagues of Indian warriors, perhaps as many as 5,000—an incredible figure given that many administrators at Versailles knew that previous war parties drawn from the region by colonial officials had numbered in the mere hundreds and had demonstrated little obedience to their French "commanders" in the field.[61] When launched in concert with efforts from Montreal, Cadillac nonetheless promised, these French and Indian armies could encircle the English and their Iroquois allies, trapping them, as he wrote to the minister, "between two fires."[62]

After nearly a decade of service to the Crown, Cadillac's stature within the Marine lent his promises an air of credibility. After all, from the very outset he had forged his career with such bold strategies for military success in the Americas, beginning with his detailed plans for the conquest of New England and New York in the early 1690s. Moreover, Pontchartrain could see that *le détroit* was of obvious strategic significance in the event of future conflict with the English and Iroquois, and with Iberville's colony of Louisiana now securing the mouth of the Mississippi, Cadillac's new settlement could solidify French control over the main arteries of the continent. Intrigued by his assurances, and under great pressure to sponsor new sites of French influence in North America before the outbreak of war, the minister dispatched Cadillac back to Quebec in the spring of 1699, bearing orders for the colonial administration to see the project through if they deemed it "*bon et praticable.*"[63]

This partial victory, however, presented Cadillac with a new challenge. Antagonism toward his plans to seize control of the western country would no doubt be significant in the colony. He likely anticipated the greatest resistance to be furnished by certain members of the Montreal merchant community and their political backers (whose traditional market for western furs he sought to appropriate at Detroit) as well as the Jesuits (whose proselytizing efforts in the Pays d'en Haut he had always disrupted with the illegal brandy trade). But opposition to his plan would be more formidable than that. While away in France, his chief supporter, Frontenac, had died, and the new administration, composed of Governor Louis-Hector Callière and Intendant Jean-Bochart de Champigny, was less supportive of his extravagant schemes.

While both men urged a reoccupation of the western country, they knew that Cadillac's proposal deliberately distorted any official's ability to easily dictate the Indian affairs of the Pays d'en Haut, and they raised a number of serious concerns. Champigny in particular worried that any seizure of *le détroit* would disrupt delicate peace negotiations under way with the Iroquois, since these peoples still claimed the regions surrounding the straits as their hunting grounds. Additionally, he feared, refocusing French enterprise in the Great Lakes region so far to the south of Michilimackinac would wrench the alliance off its historic axis, and facilitate further attempts by the English to lure the *nations des lacs* to their own trade networks in New York that extended to Detroit's eastern doorstep. Most important, however, the intendant predicted what Cadillac himself must have privately feared: catastrophic levels of violence within the ranks of the alliance should too many rival Indian villages resettle in the vicinity of Detroit. Instead, he and Callière suggested reestablishing a network of posts throughout the Pays d'en Haut, furnished with sufficient *congés*, to reconnect with the Crown's disaffected allies in trade while avoiding the dangers of a compact Indian policy at Detroit. Like Cadillac, they guaranteed that this renewed traffic in pelts would be closely watched to avoid a recurrence of the 1696 crisis.[64]

Such proposals, of course, were anathema to Cadillac's visions of increased authority in the western country. Unwilling to share power with other commandants in the Pays d'en Haut as he had done at Fort de Buade, he departed again for France in the autumn of 1699 to redouble his efforts and counter the colonial government's opposition. At Versailles, however, he first had to contend with the minister's wrath. As Cadillac later confessed, Champigny's critiques had been so trenchant that Pontchartrain threatened to send him to the Bastille for misleading the Marine.[65] Had the minister done so, much trouble might have been avoided. But once Cadillac had managed to assuage his fears, European diplomatic confrontations over the Spanish succession intensified, forcing Pontchartrain's hand in Detroit's favor. On November 1, 1700, Carlos II of Spain died, and on November 24 Louis XIV proclaimed his grandson, the Duc d'Anjou, the inheritor of the Spanish throne. The resumption of imperial warfare in the Americas was now expected daily.[66]

Left with little time to equivocate, the minister allowed the urgency of the situation to drown out cautionary voices from the colonies. Conferring once again with the king, Pontchartrain sent Cadillac back to Quebec armed with a *mémoire du roi* ordering the foundation of Detroit.[67] Though the new post was to remain under the close administrative watch of Quebec, and the limited fur trade allowed there would be controlled by a new commercial outfit of Montreal merchants known as *la Compagnie de la Colonie*, Cadillac was now free to reenter the lakes as the most powerful representative of the king, and would have ample resources to eventually ensure his own profits.

But in 1700 as he sailed back to New France, Cadillac had only completed the first step of his plan. The hard work of forging a new settlement deep in the Pays d'en Haut remained before him, and in the end, his risky wager at Versailles would emerge as something of an original sin. Tethered to his initial promises, and, in turn, manipulated by powerful Indian leaders who converged upon Detroit with their own interests, Cadillac was soon surrounded by a dangerous diversity of groups and unable to halt the rising violence between them. Though he would continue to maneuver his way through the officialdom of the Marine following his removal from Detroit, decades after his departure the ghost of his "Gascon exaggerations" would still haunt the landscapes of the Pays d'en Haut with their violent repercussions.

POSSESSING "SPEECH LIKE HONEY": POWER AND PERSUASION IN THE FRENCH ATLANTIC

Despite its importance to the history of French and Indian interaction in North America, Cadillac's manipulation of figures at Versailles has in some ways contributed to his status as a historiographic outlier. In view of his proclivity for political intrigue, modern historians seeking to describe the realities of life in the French colonies have often found only limited use for his archival legacy, rightly deemed to be poisoned by disingenuous political posturing. Given his prominent role as a liaison between the high politics of Versailles and the Indian village politics of the Pays d'en Haut, however, Cadillac's machinations deserve closer scrutiny as an important feature of the system.

In this sense we might add another chapter to Kenneth Banks's work on the French Atlantic that helped frame this essay's analysis of Cadillac's career. There was indeed a "hierarchy of reporting" shaping colonial governance, but the hierarchy did not always fulfill its own mandate to excavate and reward the truth of colonial affairs. In order to rise in the ranks, Banks's "information elites" could deliberately act as "*mis*information elites." As Cadillac demonstrated, honesty was not always the most efficient instrument for extracting power from Versailles.

His duplicity, in fact, can be readily explained with reference to a host of scholarly works on the political culture of early modern Europe, first inspired by Norbert Elias's groundbreaking 1939 study of the emergence of "civilized" discourse and manners in European court society. Historians of ancien régime France in Elias's wake (for example, proponents of the so-called linguistic turn such as Roger Chartier) have since explored in great detail the "instrumentalization of language" within the courts of the Bourbon monarchs.[68] Providing an academic vocabulary for the aged truism that politicians are prone to lie, they have deeply contextualized "language games" and "linguistic performances" in which the modalities of political discourse—far from reflections of historical reality or even personal conviction—are best viewed as a series of expedient "representations" of identity, employed by clients to integrate themselves into Versailles's networks of patronage.[69]

Cadillac, of course, fits easily into this interpretive mold. As even his most devoted biographer, Jean Boutennet, once wrote, perhaps his greatest strength lay as a *beau parleur* who excelled at cloaking his many self-interested ambitions in the idiom of royal service and the monarchy's international prestige, or *gloire*. More cynically, Dale Miquelon has evoked the "theatre" of political life at Versailles to envision him as the contemporary court playwright Molière's Scapin, "casting spells" upon the officials of the Marine with his silver-tongued schemes, or *fourberies*.[70] Cadillac himself, in fact, offered such a self-interpretation: when caught up in his own rhetorical successes, he could not resist claiming that he possessed, among other charms, "speech like honey."[71]

While such "language games" were an important element of politics at Versailles, historians such as Anthony Pagden have noted that their role was perhaps more crucial in the case of colonial governance.[72] Far from the periphery of empire, administrators in France were especially susceptible to determined officials such as Cadillac, whose "linguistic performances" were more easily passed off as authentic "*connaissances*" of colonial conditions. Although historians can only speculate upon Cadillac's doubtlessly theatrical presentations during ministerial audiences, his skill at the "language games" of the ancien régime are still visible as a set of *epistolary performances* within the many folios of his written correspondence with the Marine. Despite frequent professions that his primary "*métier*" was that of a "*guerrier*," rather than a self-promoting "*écrivain*," Cadillac possessed an unusual aptitude for both endorsing and exonerating himself with the pen.[73]

Cadillac's ability to write his way into positions of power, of course, was evident early on. As we have seen, just months after the outbreak of the Nine Years' War his intelligence reports of the North Atlantic coast succeeded in transforming him from a scurrilous *coureur de bois* to a respected military attaché at Versailles. It was during the bitter controversies that ensued following Detroit's establishment, however, that his skills at epistolary self-promotion revealed their full extent. Throughout Detroit's tumultuous early years, Cadillac survived by crafting the image of a loyal, though unjustly disparaged, servant of the Crown—a persona he sustained rhetorically by drafting many of his dispatches in the third person. "Lamothe," he always claimed, was as a voice of objective imperial reason in a colony paralyzed by "intrigue and cabal." In asserting such sanctity before the Marine, he was not afraid to deploy profound religious allegory. Styling himself as a New World "Moses" protecting the interests of the king, he once labeled his enemies "pharaohs" and accused them of attempting to "sign the crucifixion" of Detroit in order to establish their own tyranny in the western country.[74] In another instance, Cadillac presented himself as a reincarnation of "St. John of the Golden Mouth," a fourth-century church father canonized for his eloquent oratory and passionate denunciation of abuses of authority.[75] "I have no other patron than the truth itself," he once insisted, before adding, "so great is my confidence in it that I believe I shall be invincible so long as I fight under its standard."[76] Despite the combined opposition of the Jesuits, the Montreal merchant community, and the colonial government at Quebec (led by Governor Philippe de Rigaud de Vaudreuil following Callière's death in 1703), Cadillac was able to maintain the conceit for nearly a decade that he was "as innocent as the angels are of sin."[77]

This required, of course, anything but angelic behavior. Hoping to buy more time, he recklessly supplied the minister with an array of half-truths, wild exaggerations, and, as we have seen, outright denials of the very real dangers he witnessed mounting at Detroit. Although officials at Versailles were not entirely trusting of his behavior, detecting such fraud was no simple task. Just receiving word from the Pays d'en Haut with which to modify policy was a monumental labor, and those controlling the output of "information" had all the power to bend it.[78] It was only in 1708, when negative reports from Detroit began to outweigh even the most forceful of Cadillac's "Gascon exaggerations," that Pontchartrain finally dispatched an allegedly impartial official, François Clairambault d'Aigremont, to venture into the western country and settle the matter. His eventual account toppled Cadillac's rhetorical house of cards and revealed in scathing detail his protracted deceit. Far from a "Paris" in the Pays d'en Haut, d'Aigremont confirmed, Cadillac's settlement—which amounted to a rotting palisade and little more than sixty impoverished settlers and soldiers—was surrounded by a patchwork of fortified Indian villages, locked in violent competition that threatened to plunge the entire Pays d'en Haut into warfare. Fraudulence, d'Aigremont alleged, was the very "principle" upon which Cadillac had operated from the beginning, since "he knew, as we all did, that this post is very detrimental to the colony of Canada."[79]

Despite the extent of the fiasco, however, Pontchartrain could not publicly admit the folly of his long association with Cadillac, and the scheming Gascon (who continued to defend himself effusively) was sent to govern Louisiana while officials in New France struggled to repair the damage he had done in the Pays d'en Haut. The minister's expedient displacement of his client to nominally higher stations was perhaps predictable, but Pontchartrain's next move was more shocking. Like Detroit, Louisiana had been established amid much idealistic fervor and was now failing to meet expectations. By 1710, the colony was on the verge of financial collapse, and much maligned within political circles in France.[80] Such flagging outposts needed skilled apologists—indeed, *beau parleurs*—to facilitate continued investment. Regardless of the troubles he had created in the Great Lakes region, Cadillac was still someone who knew how to arouse great speculation, and set events in motion. Having learned firsthand the power of his "Gascon exaggerations," the minister now turned them to his own use. Hoping that Cadillac's difficulties in the Pays d'en Haut would inspire more prudence in this next endeavor, Pontchartrain now charged him with convincing the king's financial secretary, Antoine Crozat, to assume fiscal responsibility for the colony under a new joint stock company.

But Cadillac's ambition could not be restrained—he was once again intoxicated by the prospects of wealth and power in the colonies. Although he had never set foot in Louisiana, he drafted a *mémoire* that painted, in the words of the historian Marcel Giraud, such a "seductive picture" of the colony's economic future that Crozat eventually complied.[81] His glowing reports of great mineral deposits in the lower Mississippi valley, however, never produced returns, and after several years of failed prospecting Crozat scornfully withdrew his support from the colony. This latest debacle triggered a bitter legal feud that eventuated in Cadillac's imprisonment in the Bastille and, at last, a slow decline to his once meteoric career.[82]

Wherever Cadillac went, it seems, trouble and controversy were not far behind, but his activities as an agent of the state always reinforced how Versailles and its colonial possessions were closely linked. By virtue of a centralized absolutist state, the Marine's patron-client networks formed a chain of command that reached deep into the North American interior and could greatly impact events on the ground, even if the results were at diametric odds with the initial intent of the king's ministers. As an important figure within this transatlantic view of the empire, Cadillac biography should not be overlooked. Without his exploitation of troubled colonial communication, savvy patron-client networking, disingenuous schemes for colonial success, and increasingly reckless drive for power, it is difficult to envision the tragic events of early Detroit, and by extension French empire in the Pays d'en Haut, transpiring as they did.

In all its sordid detail, then, his tenure as a colonial officer highlights an important paradox of power in the French Atlantic. Such "military entrepreneurs" and "information elites" were a self-selecting group of unusually intrepid individuals upon whose services the Marine relied. But at the same time, the very traits that endowed them with the dexterity to act as Versailles's vanguard in the colonies—above all, an intense and often unprincipled desire for personal aggrandizement under the auspices of the state—also drove them to take extraordinary risks with what power they came to wield. Managing this paradox was a difficult task for distant metropolitan administrators, and, as Pontchartrain learned all too late, could result in grave colonial crises if such men were granted too much latitude. It was in just such a system, one marked by its slippages of knowledge and power, that restive colonial adventurers such as Cadillac could carve out a lucrative career on the very edges of the empire, even if their own flickering successes seemed to continually court that very empire's demise.

NOTES

1. Officials in New France used the term *Pays d'en Haut* to distinguish the Great Lakes from the principal sites of settlement to the southeast in the St. Lawrence River valley (namely Montreal, Trois-Rivières, and Quebec), which they called *le Pays d'en Bas*, or "the lower country." All French-to-English translations are the author's.

2. The best analysis of the fragility of these alliances remains Gilles Havard, *Empire et métissages: Indiens et Français dans le Pays d'en Haut, 1660–1715* (Sillery, Q.C., and Paris: Éditions du Septentrion and Presses de l'Université de Paris-Sorbonne, 2003), 439–490.

3. "Paroles de Makisabe, chef potéouatomi," August 17, 1712, Archives nationales de France, Colonies (hereafter cited as AN, Col.), C^{11A}, vol. 33, fol. 85.

4. See Richard White, *The Middle Ground: Indians, Empires, and Republics in the Great Lakes Region, 1650–1815* (Cambridge: Cambridge University Press, 1991), 82–90, 149–159; Brett Rushforth, "Slavery, the Fox Wars, and the Limits of Alliance," *William and Mary Quarterly*, 3rd series, 63, no. 1 (2006): 53–80; Brett Rushforth, "Savage Bonds: Indian Slavery and Alliance in New France" (Ph.D. diss., University of California, Davis, 2003); David Edmunds and Joseph L. Peyser, *The Fox Wars: The Mesquakie Challenge to New France* (Norman: University of Oklahoma Press, 1993), 55–86.

5. In this I follow Gilles Havard's more transatlantic view of the French presence in the Great Lakes region. For these administrative links between the Great Lakes and Versailles, see Havard, *Empire et métissages*, 267–282. For an earlier iteration of this perspective view, see J. M. S. Careless, "Frontierism, Metropolitanism and Canadian History," *Canadian Historical Review* 35 (1954): 1–21.

6. Cadillac to Pontchartrain, September 15, 1708, AN, Col., C^{11E}, (Transcripts) vol. 15, p. 39.

7. Ibid.

8. For the Order of Saint-Louis, see Albert Babeau, *La vie militaire sous l'Ancien Régime*, 2 vols. (Paris: Librairie de Firmin-Didot et Cie., 1889–1890), 2:113.

9. The most useful works for empirically tracing Cadillac's career are authored by local historians in France. Though somewhat laudatory, and in scant circulation in the United States and Canada, they offer the most thorough narratives of Cadillac's life and are essential to any biographical assessment. See Jean Boutonnet (late president of the *Société archéologique et historique du Tarn et Garonne*), *Lamothe-Cadillac, le gascon qui fonda Détroit (1658–1730)* (Paris: Guénégaud, 2001); René Toujas, (late archivist of Montauban and Toulouse), *Le destin extraordinaire du Gascon Lamothe Cadillac de Saint-Nicolas*

de-la-Grave, fondateur de Détroit (Montauban: Atliers du Moustier, 2000); Édouard Forestié, *Lamothe-Cadillac: Fondateur de la ville de Détroit (Michigan), Gouverneur de la Louisiane, et de Castelsarrasin* (Montauban: Forestié Père et Fils, 1907); H. A. Verneau (l'abbé), *Quelques notes sur Antoine de Lamothe de Cadillac offerte à Margry* (Montauban: Publisher, 1904).

10. These critical interpretations grew out of a new postwar historiography championed by William J. Eccles, whose groundbreaking and iconoclastic study of Cadillac's supporter, Governor Frontenac, exposed rampant corruption within the government of New France. See William J. Eccles, *Frontenac: The Courtier Governor* (Toronto: McClelland & Stewart, 1959). For matching characterizations of Cadillac, see Yves Zoltvany, "Antoine Laumet, dit de Lamothe Cadillac," in *Dictionary of Canadian Biography Online*, http://www.biographi.ca; Dale Miquelon, *New France, 1701–1744: A Supplement to Europe* (Toronto: McClelland & Stewart, 1987), 33–36; Jean Delanglez, "The Genesis and Building of Detroit," *Mid America* 30 (1948): 75–104; Jean Delanglez, "Cadillac at Detroit," *Mid America* 30 (1948): 233–256; Jean Delanglez, "Cadillac: The Proprietor of Detroit," *Mid America* 32 (1950): 155–188, 226–258. Gilles Havard has recently elaborated from these works to describe the widespread practices of illegal trade by officers in the *Pays d'en Haut* as "*le syndrome Cadillac.*" See Harvard, *Empire et métissages*, 344.

11. These hagiographic works initially grew out of the efforts of civic-minded Detroiters such as Clarence M. Burton, whose local histories valorized the city's founder and eventually found resonance in more widely circulated popular history. See, for example, Clarence M. Burton, *"Cadillac's village," or "Detroit under Cadillac"* (Detroit: 1896); Agnes Laut, *Cadillac: Knight Errant of the Wilderness, Founder of Detroit, Governor of Louisiana from the Great Lakes to the Gulf* (Indianapolis: Bobbs-Merrill, 1931).

12. For an overview of this dynamic, see Janice Thompson, *Pirates, Mercenaries, and Sovereigns: State-Building and Extraterritorial Violence in Early Modern Europe* (Princeton, N.J.: Princeton University Press, 1994). For the concept of "military entrepreneur," see Thomas Gallant, "Brigandage, Piracy, Capitalism and State Formation: Transnational Crime from a World Historical Perspective," in *States and Illegal Practices*, ed. Josiah McConnell Heyman (Oxford: Berg, 1999), 40; Charles Tilly, "War Making and State Making as Organized Crime," in *Bringing the State Back In*, ed. Peter B. Evans, Dietrich Rueschemeyer, and Theda Skocpol (Cambridge: Cambridge University Press, 1985), 169–191.

13. Kenneth Banks, *Chasing Empire across the Sea: Communications and the State in the French Atlantic, 1713–1763* (Montreal and Kingston: McGill-Queen's University Press, 2003), 64.

14. In France itself, the state had already constructed sophisticated systems of intelligence gathering to direct the king's governing bureaus, which informed the Marine's subsequent efforts. See Jacob Soll, *The Information Master: Jean-Baptiste Colbert's Secret State Intelligence System* (Ann Arbor: University of Michigan Press, 2009).

15. Banks, *Chasing Empire across the Sea*, 188.

16. For the role of cartography in these intelligence networks, see Dale Miquelon, "Les Pontchartrain se penchent sur leurs cartes de l'Amérique: les cartes de l'impérialisme," *Revue d'histoire de l'Amérique française* 59 (Summer/Autumn 2005): 53–72.

17. Cadillac may have only glimpsed the lavish aristocratic court life of Versailles since I have found no evidence that he ever enjoyed a personal audience with the king—something he would not have been afraid to advertise. But at times he became a veritable fixture at the true sources of power, in the adjoining bureaus of the king's ministers where policy was forged. For the increasing transfer of political power from the court to the personal networks of the king's ministries during the reigns of Louis XIV and Louis XV, see Michel Antoine, *Le Conseil du Roi sous le règne de Louis XV* (Paris: Librairie Droz, 1970). Under Louis XV, the ministries of Louis XIV were replaced by councils (*conseils*), but the exercise of power remained largely removed from the court and placed under the jurisdiction of senior officials. Antoine has termed this transformation an "administrative revolution." For patronage networks within the Ministry of the Marine during Cadillac's career, see Sara Chapman, *Private Ambition and Political Alliances: The Phélypeaux de Pontchartrain Family and Louis XIV's Government, 1650–1715* (Rochester, N.Y.: University of Rochester Press, 2004); Charles Frostin, *Les Pontchartrain, Ministres de Louis XIV: Alliances et réseau d'influence sous l'Ancien Régime* (Rennes: Presses universitaires de Rennes, 2006).

18. For Cadillac's self-presentation as a "warrior," see Cadillac to Pontchartrain, August 6, 1701, AN, Marine, C[7] (Personal Dossiers), carton 163, document 4, p. 1. For d'Iberville and Du Casse, see Nellie Crouse, *Lemoyne d'Iberville: Soldier of New France* (Ithaca, N.Y.: Cornell University Press, 1954); Phillipe Hrodej, *L'Amiral du Casse: l'élévation d'un gascon sous Louis XIV* (Paris: Librairie de l'Inde, 1999).

19. Quoted in Boutonnet, *Lamothe-Cadillac*, 327. For similar statements, see Cadillac to Pontchartrain (likely written while commanding at Michilimackinac in 1694 or 1695), Bibliothèque nationale de France (hereafter cited as BnF), Collection Clairambault, vol. 882, fol. 145r-147; Cadillac to Seignelay, December 29, 1689, BnF, Collection Clairambault, vol. 882, fol. 143–144.

20. Quoted in Toujas, *Le destin extraordinaire du Gascon Lamothe Cadillac*, 26.

21. For Cadillac's youth in France, see Boutonnet, *Lamothe-Cadillac*, 17–23; Toujas, *Le destin extraordinaire du Gascon Lamothe Cadillac*, 9–14.

22. For complaints of Cadillac's early activities in Acadia, see Governor Meneval to Seignelay, September 7, 1689, AN, Col., C11D 2 Do you mean C^{11D}, vol. 2, fol. 121v; Meneval to Seignelay, 1690, AN, Col., C11D 2 Do you mean C^{11D}, vol. 2, fol. 19–19v.

23. For Cadillac's integration into the Guyon family, see Boutonnet, *Lamothe-Cadillac*, 17–46; Toujas, *Le destin extraordinaire du Gascon Lamothe Cadillac*, 15–19. The title "de Lamothe, Sieur de Cadillac" was likely inspired by tracts of land near his birthplace in France.

24. Denonville to Seignelay, July 1689, AN, Col., C^{11A}, vol. 10, fol. 342.

25. Cadillac to Seignelay, December 29, 1689, BnF, Collection Clairambault, vol. 882, fol. 143–144.

26. For Cadillac's introduction to Versailles during these months, see Boutonnet, *Lamothe-Cadillac*, 55–59.

27. For Cadillac's appointments, see Louis XIV to Frontenac, 1691, AN, Col., B, vol. 16, fol. 34–39v, and Frontenac to Pontchartrain, October 15, 1691, AN, Col., C^{11A}, vol. 11, fol. 222.

28. William J. Eccles's biography of Frontenac is still the best available and addresses these crucial years of the war, as well as his association with Cadillac. See the most recent version with an introduction by Peter Moogk, William J. Eccles, *Frontenac: The Courtier Governor* (Lincoln: University of Nebraska Press, 2003). For an overview of the activities of officials planning the invasion of New England and New York, see Louise Dechêne, *Le peuple, l'État et la guerre au Canada sous le Régime français* (Montreal: Boréal, 2008), 209–214.

29. Frontenac to Pontchartrain, December 15, 1692, AN, Col., C^{11A}, vol. 12, fol. 23.

30. For Cadillac's reconnaissance efforts, see Frontenac to Pontchartrain, December 15, 1692, AN, Col., C^{11A}, vol. 12, fol. 23; for his summons to Versailles, see Pontchartrain to Frontenac, AN, Col., B, vol. 16, fol. 103–104v.

31. See Cadillac, "Mémoire de l'Acadie, Nouvelle-Angleterre, Nouvelle-Hollande et Virginie par le Sieur de Cadillac," AN, Col., C^{11D}, vol. 10, fol. 15.

32. For an additional report, see Cadillac, "Mémoire du sieur de Lamothe Cadillac sur l'Acadie. Description de ce pays et de la Nouvelle-Angleterre. Projet d'une attaque contre la Nouvelle-York et Boston," AN, Col., C^{11D}, vol. 2, fol. 192–200. The adjoining maps are now housed in the BnF, Département des Cartes et plans, under the titles "Plan de Manathes ou Nouvelle Yorc [*sic*] Verifiée par le Sr. de la Motte (1693)" and "Carte de la Ville, Baye, et Environs de Baston par Jean Baptiste Louis Franquelin Hydrog. du Roy [*sic*], verifée par le Sr de la Motte (1693)."

33. Boutennet, *Lamothe-Cadillac*, 71.

34. There are a number of works that address Frontenac's strategy of *la petite guerre*, but no single monograph devoted to the subject. The best and most recent is Dechêne, *Le peuple, l'État et la guerre au Canada*, 153–286.

35. One finds this term throughout the files of the Marine during the eighteenth century, used both by officers presenting their own merits and administrators describing the quality of their personnel to superiors at Versailles. During Frontenac's administration, the *"zèle"* of particular officers is addressed in nearly every annual report sent to the Marine describing the affairs of New France. See AN, Col., C^{11A} generally.

36. For Cadillac's promotion to Michilimackinac, see Frontenac to Pontchartrain, October 25, 1694, AN, Col., C^{11A}, vol. 13, fol. 64.

37. For Louvigny's biography, see Yves Zoltvany, "Louis de La Porte de Louvigny," in *Dictionary of Canadian Biography Online*, http://www.biographi.ca.

38. The Iroquois Wars were the single greatest obstacle to the development of New France in the mid-seventeenth century, and commenced as early as 1609 when Samuel de Champlain, the celebrated "Father of New France," accompanied a Huron war party on a raid into Iroquois territory. Beginning in the 1640s, the Iroquois overran much of the *Pays d'en Haut* and posed a constant threat to the French settlements of the St. Lawrence valley until the Grand Settlement, or *La Grand Paix*, of 1701. The literature on the Iroquois Wars, therefore, is extensive. Perhaps the best overview remains Daniel Richter, *The Ordeal of the Longhouse: The Peoples of the Iroquois League in the Era of European Colonization* (Chapel Hill: University of North Carolina Press, 1992). For an equally important study on Iroquois policy during the war, see José Brandão, *"Your Fyre Shall Burn No More": Iroquois Policy toward New France and Its Native Allies to 1701* (Lincoln: University of Nebraska Press, 1997).

39. The role of Michilimackinac is treated extensively throughout Havard, *Empire et métissages*. See also Joseph L. Peyser and José António Brandão, eds., *At the Edge of Empire: Documents from Michilimackinac, 1671–1716* (East Lansing and Mackinac Island, Mich.: Michigan State University Press and Mackinac State Historic Parks, 2008). For an overview of French posts in the interior, see Arnaud Balvay, *L'Épée et la Plume: Amérindiens et soldats des troupes de la marine en Louisiane et au Pays d'en Haut, 1683–1763* (Quebec: Presses de l'Université Laval, 2006). For the geostrategic positioning of Michilimackinac vis-à-vis the peoples of the *Pays d'en Haut*, see Helen Hornbeck Tanner, ed., *Atlas of Great Lakes Indian History* (Norman: University of Oklahoma Press, 1987), 32–34.

40. Cadillac to Pontchartrain, BnF, Collection Clairambault, vol. 882, fol. 147v.

41. For Indian forms of political authority in the *Pays d'en Haut*, see White, *Middle Ground*, 45–60. More generally, see Cornelius Jaenen, *Friend and Foe: Aspects of French-Amerindian Cultural Contact in the Sixteenth and Seventeenth Centuries* (New York: Columbia University Press, 1976), 84–119. For a classic anthropological comparison of Algonquian and European notions of sovereignty, see Walter B. Miller, "Two Concepts of Authority," *American Anthropologist*, new series, 57, 2, Part 1 (1955): 271–289.

42. Cadillac to Pontchartrain (written at Michilimackinac in 1694 or 1695), BnF, Collection Clairambault, vol. 882, fol. 137–139.

43. For Cadillac's efforts to forestall these developments, see AN, Col., C^{11A}, vol. 13, fol. 219–228.

44. Cadillac to Pontchartrain (written at Michilimackinac in 1694 or 1695), BnF, Collection Clairambault.

45. Cadillac to Pontchartrain, August 3, 1695, AN, Col., C^{11E}, (Transcripts) vol. 14, pp. 15, 19.

46. Ibid., p. 12.

47. Historians estimate that within three months at Fort de Buade, Cadillac had sent nearly 30,000 livres back to France (this was only a portion of his net gains) when the annual salary of a *capitaine à pied* was only 1,080 livres. For Cadillac's requests for promotions, see Cadillac to Pontchartrain (written at Michilimackinac in 1694 or 1695), BnF, Collection Clairambault, vol. 882, fol. 145r-147v; Cadillac to Pontchartrain, October 20, 1697, AN, Col., C^{11E}, (Transcripts) vol. 14, pp. 37–41. I would like to thank James Prichard for his assistance in understanding the importance of Cadillac's requests for a promotion to this rank.

48. The most succinct treatment of the relationship between trade and diplomacy in French and Indian alliances during this period is Gilles Havard, *The Great Peace of Montreal: French-Native Diplomacy in the Seventeenth Century*, trans. Phyllis Aronoff and Howard Scott (Montreal and Kingston: McGill-Queen's University Press, 2001), 15–57. See also White, *Middle Ground*, 94–141. For Crown-subsidized gifts, see Catherine Desbarats, "The Cost of Early Canada's Native Alliances: Reality and Rhetoric of Scarcity," *William and Mary Quarterly*, 3rd series, 52 (October 1995): 609–630.

49. Although some of the greatest contemporary and historiographic critiques of Cadillac have centered upon his voracious self-interest, his involvement in the fur trade at Michilimackinac and Detroit was hardly anomalous. In periods when the metropole allowed the trade to flourish, officers regularly entered into contracts with Montreal *marchands-équipeurs*, using the fur trade to exit their positions with increased wealth. Louise Dechêne has written, for example, that "the commercial advancement of the corps of officers settled

in the colony, a major social phenomenon, was a fait accompli in the second quarter of the 18th century." See Louise Dechêne, *Habitants et marchands de Montréal au XVIIe siècle* (Paris: Plon, 1974), 182–183. For more detailed studies, see Gratien Allaire, "Officiers et marchands: les sociétés de commerce des fourrures, 1717–1760," *Revue d'histoire de l'Amérique française* 40 (Winter 1987): 409–428. For a biography of one such officer (who was stationed at Michilimackinac from 1747 to 1749), see Joseph L. Peyser, trans. and ed., *Jacques Legardeur de Saint-Pierre: Officer, Gentleman, Entrepreneur* (East Lansing: Michigan State University Press, 1996).

50. Déclaration du roi, May 21, 1696, AN, Col., B, vol. 19, fol. 118–121.

51. For metropolitan efforts to curb the trade, see William J. Eccles, *The Canadian Frontier, 1539–1760* (Albuquerque: University of New Mexico Press, 1969), 103–185; Yves Zoltvany, "New France and the West, 1701–1713," *Canadian Historical Review* 46 (1965): 301–322. For the relatively small number of Canadians who prosecuted the western trade, see Dechêne, *Habitants et marchands*, 221–222. For the most thorough analysis of voyageur and *coureur de bois* life in the *Pays d'en Haut*, see Carolyn Podruchny, *Making the Voyageur World: Travelers and Traders in the North American Fur Trade* (Lincoln: University of Nebraska Press, 2006).

52. Cadillac to Pontchartrain, October 20, 1697, AN, Col., C^{11E}, (Transcripts) vol. 14, p. 43.

53. Frontenac to Pontchartrain, October 15, 1697, AN, C^{11A}, (Transcripts) vol. 15, pp. 99–100.

54. Desbarats, "Cost of Early Canada's Native Alliances," 610.

55. James Pritchard, *In Search of Empire: The French in the Americas, 1670–1730* (Cambridge: Cambridge University Press, 2004), 157.

56. In Quebec, Cadillac was accused by Louis Durand and Joseph Moreau of unjustly confiscating their trade goods and personal effects and imprisoning them at Michilimackinac. The two men had received a trading permit from Governor Frontenac and entered into a contract with Cadillac's wife in Montreal to supply the post. See Boutonnet, *Lamothe-Cadillac*, 89–97.

57. Today "Bkejwanong" refers to the Anishinabe Indian reservation on Walpole Island, but in the seventeenth century the term designated a much wider area, encompassing the St. Clair River, Lake St. Clair, the Detroit River, and the various islands within these bodies of water. Compared to Michilimackinac, the region of Bkejwanong offered more abundant game, and better soil for Odawa horticultural practices. The region also held spiritual significance for these people. Moreover, at Bkejwanong, the Odawa would be better positioned to control access to the upper Great Lakes and take advantage of English trade networks in New York if the minister did not

lift his prohibition. For motivations behind the Odawa movement toward Detroit, see William Newbigging, "History of the French-Ottawa Alliance, 1613–1763" (Ph.D. diss., University of Toronto, 1995), 224–260.

58. Over the course of the eighteenth century this policy would develop into what scholars have termed a "French crescent" of posts along the Mississippi River valley and Great Lakes, creating a great arc of containment from New Orleans, through the continental interior, to Quebec. See William J. Eccles, "La Mer de l'Ouest: Outpost of Empire," in *Essays on New France* (Toronto: Oxford University Press, 1987), 97–98; John C. Rule, "Jérôme Phélypeaux, Comte de Pontchartrain, and the Establishment of Louisiana, 1696–1715," in *Frenchmen and French Ways in the Mississippi Valley*, ed. John Francis McDermott (Urbana and Chicago: University of Illinois Press, 1969).

59. For quotations, see Jérôme Maurepas to Vauban, May 16, 1698 AN, Archives Privées (hereafter cited as AP), 261 (Fonds Vauban), vol. 31, fol. 37; Jérôme Maurepas to Vauban, May 16, 1699, AN, Marine, B⁷, vol. 65, fol. 285. In addition to the famed *"faction bourgogne"* (comprising the Archbishop François de Salignac de La Mothe-Fénelon dit Fénelon, the Abbé Claude Fleury, and the Duke of Beauvillier, who were all charged with the education of the king's grandson, and likely heir, the Duke of Burgundy), Vauban became a vociferous critic of Louis's war efforts in Europe and began aggressively advocating colonial expansion as an alternative during the 1690s. For Vauban's influence upon colonial policy, see Louise Dechêne, *La Correspondance de Vauban relative au Canada* (Quebec: Ministère des Affaires Culturelles, 1968); Werner Gembruch, "Zwei Denkschriften Vaubans zur Kolonial- und Aussenpolitik Frankreichs aus den Jahren 1699 und 1700," *Historisches Zeitschfrift* 195 (1962): 297–330.

60. Cadillac claimed his settlement would help limit the export of western furs in two primary ways: first, the Indians would be busy resettling at his post for one to two years, detracting them from their ability to trap beaver. Second, unlike Michilimackinac, the regions surrounding Detroit were home to lighter fur-bearing animals—particularly fox and martin and their *menues pelleteries*, or smaller pelts. These furs were used to trim the robes of civil and religious officials in France and, unlike those of the northern beaver, remained in stable demand. See Cadillac to the Minister, AN, Marine, C⁷, carton 163, document 3, p. 3.

61. Ibid.

62. Ibid.

63. "Envoi du Mémoire de Lamothe Cadillac sur la fondation d'un poste au Détroit. Extrait du mémoire du Roi au Sieur chevalier de Champigny, Intendant de la Nouvelle France, Versailles, 27 Mai 1699," in *Découvertes et*

établissements des Français dans l'Ouest et dans le Sud de l'Amérique septentrionale, ed. Pierre Margry, 6 vols. (Paris: D. Jouaust, 1879–1888), 5:136–137.

64. For Callière's and Champigny's objections, see "Extrait du mémoire de Lamothe Cadillac avec les annotations de Champigny, 20 Octobre 1699," AN, Col., C^{11E}, vol. 17, fol. 101–103; "Mémoire de Callière pour répondre à celui de Lamothe-Cadillac," AN, Col., C^{11E}, vol. 14, fol. 53–54.

65. The disapproval of the Marquis de Denonville, former governor of New France who was then acting as an adviser to the minister of the Marine in France, likely played a role as well. See Boutonnet, *Lamothe-Cadillac*, 104.

66. Persistent rumors that the English governor of New York, Richard Coote, First Earl of Bellomont, was also developing plans to seize the western Great Lakes added more pointed pressure. For disputes over sovereignty in the Great Lakes region, see Pontchartrain to M. de Tallard and M. d'Herbault (ambassadors in England), January 28, 1700, AN, Marine, B^7, vol. 66, fol. 949.

67. "Memoire du Roi à Callière et Champigny," AN, Col., B, vol. 22, fol. 110–111. Pontchartrain was not invited to sit on the king's supreme *conseil d'en haut*, but Louis XIV reserved one day a week to confer with his ministers privately on their respective affairs in appointments known as *le travail du roi*, or *la liasse*. Tuesdays were reserved for the Marine, and it was likely during one of these sessions that the king granted final approval for Detroit. See Antoine, *Le Conseil du Roi*, 62; for Pontchartrain's role in the royal government, see Frostin, *Les Pontchartrain*, and Chapman, *Private Ambition*.

68. Norbert Elias, *The Civilizing Process: Sociogenetic and Psychogenetic Investigations* (Oxford: Blackwell, 1994).

69. See Roger Chartier, "Le monde comme representation," *Annales HSS* 44 (1989): 1505–1520; Arthur Herman, "The Language of Fidelity in Early Modern France," *Journal of Modern History* 67 (March 1995): 1–24; Jay M. Smith, "'No More Language Games': Words, Beliefs, and the Political Culture of Early Modern France," *American Historical Review* 102 (December 1997): 1413–1440. For a similar study of this dynamic in the Austrian Hapsburg court, see Christian Ehalt, *Die Ausdruckformen Absolutishcer Herrschaft: Der Wiener Hof im 17. Und 18. Jahrhundert* (Vienna: Verlag für Geschichte und Politik, 1980).

70. Miquelon, *New France*, 33–36. Miquelon is referring to Molière's 1672 play, *Les fourberies de Scapin*, a critical success in its own time.

71. Quoted in Boutennet, *Lamothe-Cadillac*, 328.

72. Anthony Pagden has similarly described Hernán Cortés's "massively overextended letters" sent to the Crown from Mexico as essays "intended not merely to inform, but to persuade"—each one an instantiation of his "rhetorical

strategies" for political success and thus a "petition for honors" on the basis of alleged efforts and expertise in the colonial domain. See Hernán Cortés, *Letters from Mexico*, trans. and ed. Anthony Pagden (New Haven, Conn.: Yale University Press, 2001). For quotations, see Pagden's comparison between the writings of Cortés and Bartolomé de Las Casas in his introduction to Las Casas, *A Short Account of the Destruction of the Indies*, trans. and ed. Nigel Griffin (New York: Penguin Books, 1992), xxxi–xxxii.

73. Cadillac to Pontchartrain, August 6, 1701, AN, Marine, C^7, carton 163, document 4, p. 1.

74. Report of Detroit, August 31, 1703, in Cadillac Papers, in *Collections and Researches of the Pioneer and Historical Society of the State of Michigan*, ed. Historical Society of the State of Michigan, 40 vols. (Lansing, Mich.: 1874–1929), 33:170.

75. Cadillac to Pontchartrain, November 14, 1704, AN, Col., C^{11E}, vol. 14, fol. 187.

76. Ibid., fol. 186v.

77. Ibid., fol. 175. For Cadillac's conflicts with the Montreal merchants and Governor Vaudreuil, see Yves Zoltvany, *Philippe de Rigaud de Vaudreuil, Governor of New France, 1703–1725* (Toronto: McClelland & Stewart, 1974), 54–56, 58, 65, 67, 72; for his bitter feuds with the Jesuits, see Delanglez, "Genesis and Building of Detroit," 75–104; Delanglez, "Cadillac at Detroit," 152–176, 233–256; Delanglez, "Cadillac," 155–188, 226–258. Before Delanglez's death, these articles were originally intended as a book on Cadillac's relationship with the Jesuits.

78. To travel via canoe from Detroit to the principal settlements of Montreal or Quebec demanded several weeks, while return trips paddling against the current were considerably more grueling. Ships sailing out from Quebec then required as much as two months to reach Rochefort, with passage back to Quebec averaging twice that long. Between Rochefort and the court stretched more than 300 miles of early modern roadways, and an average round-trip of fifteen days. Such journeys were not only time-consuming. They were also fraught with dangers particular to the early modern Atlantic world. Even in times of peace, the elements themselves (in the form of treacherous rapids, slippery portages, and Atlantic storms) posed tangible threats. And in an era of frequent imperial war, messengers traveling from the *Pays d'en Haut* to the colonial capital often fell victim to enemy war parties, and royal vessels were interdicted by privateers on the high seas. At a crucial juncture in the formation of policy, for example, Governor Vaudreuil learned that his memorandum to the minister outlining the dangers at Detroit had "fallen into the hands of corsairs." Figures taken from Banks, *Chasing Empire across the Sea*,

71. For Vaudreuil quotation, see Vaudreuil to Pontchartrain, November 3, 1710, AN, Col., C^{11A}, vol. 31, fol. 39–62v.

79. Clairambault d'Aigremont to Pontchartrain, November 14, 1708, AN, Col., C^{11A}, vol. 29, fol. 36–45.

80. For Louisiana's early stigmas, see Allain Mathé, *Not Worth a Straw: French Colonial Policy and the Early Years of Louisiana* (Lafayette: Center for Louisiana Studies, University of Southwestern Louisiana, ca. 1988).

81. Marcel Giraud, *A History of French Louisiana*, trans. Joseph C. Lambert, 5 vols. (Baton Rouge: Louisiana State University Press, 1974), 1:249–250.

82. For these accusations, see *Memoire pour Antoine de la Mothe Cadillac, chevalier de l'Ordre de Saint Loüis, cy-devant gouverneur pour le Roy de la Loüisiane, et François le Bart, trésorier de S. A. S. Madame la Princesse de Conty, premiere doüairiere, demandeurs, Contre Antoine Crozat, commandeur & grand trésorier de l'Ordre du roy, deffendeur* (Paris: D. Jollet, s.d.), 1–28. This document is available at the William L. Clements Library, Ann Arbor, Michigan.

"Protection" and "Unequal Alliance"

The French Conception of Sovereignty over Indians in New France

GILLES HAVARD

ON DECEMBER 18, 1728, IN ORDER TO SOLVE THE PROBLEM OF THE inheritances of Illinois women who had lost their French husbands after converting to Catholicism, and, more generally, to clarify the status of Catholic Indians and their relatives in the Illinois Country, the edict of Louisiana's Superior Council stipulated that the aboriginal relatives of such a widow "must not take the possessions acquired by the French," because they were not "deemed *régnicoles*" (that is, "citizens"). The edict specified that, "moreover, the King grants them only his *protection* and not the same benefits as to his *subjects*."[1] Illinois men living in their own villages therefore did not enjoy the same privileges as the French, and converted Illinois women were refused the same rights as the colonists even though they lived among them.[2]

In France, under the ancien régime, "citizens," in the legal sense of "naturals," or *régnicoles*, were not defined as equal individuals under the law, or participants in exercising national sovereignty, but as individual beneficiaries of rights, as opposed to aliens (*aubains*), who were struck with legal incapacities.[3] However, in the seventeenth century, the king wanted to extend this citizenship not only to the colonists in the Americas but also to converted aboriginals. This is the meaning of Article 17 of the charter for the Company of One Hundred Associates of 1627, under which "Savages who are brought to knowledge of faith, and make a profession of it, will be deemed and treated as natural French . . . without being required to obtain any letters of . . . naturalization (*lettres de naturalité*)."[4] These provisions were similarly implemented, several years later, in the Lesser Antilles, and reiterated in the act establishing the Company of the West Indies, created by Louis XIV and his minister, Jean-Baptiste Colbert, in 1664.[5]

Theoretically, Christianized Indians therefore did not become privileged foreigners, or "naturalized," but automatically obtained the status of *régnicole*, by virtue of a process that was also at work in the home country: French territorial conquests, especially under the reign of Louis XIV (the annexations of Alsace in 1648, of Artois and Roussillon in 1659, of Franche-Comté in 1678, etc.), were accompanied by incorporation mechanisms that included extending the status of *régnicole* to the new inhabitants. Jurists sometimes insisted on the need for these inhabitants to apply in order to obtain individual naturalization, and this prevailed in some places, but automaticity was the norm.[6]

Attribution of nationality (*naturalité*); practices of social control, disciplinary management, and submission of populations; administrative and religious structures; diplomatic methods; and so forth: New France was shaped by many conventions from the *"milieu de la France,"* to use a royal expression.[7] Moreover, for the Catholic Church and the monarchy, it was not merely a question of duplication: *New* France offered the utopian hope for a *renewed* France where, as the Jesuit Paul Le Jeune wrote, the "wicked customs of many places in old France" would disappear, and the virtues of Tridentine Christianity and absolutism would flourish. Far from the unruly nobles and contractual compromises of the kingdom (proliferation of local customs, exemptions and privileges granted, etc.), the monarchy hoped to carry out its project of social normalization and centralized administrative management in virgin territory. Consequently, New France came to be a laboratory, with the policy of *francisation* of Indians leading authorities to reify French identity and indirectly sketch a normative portrait of the good "citizen."[8]

However, the fantasies that developed around the American colonial field clashed with the realities that played out there, whether the demands of the fur trade,[9] the local relationships of force, or the disillusions and procrastinations in the assimilationist project. From the beginning of the seventeenth century through 1760, despite a *process* of conquest essentially being at work, a "Frontier" situation[10] existed in all regions of North America claimed by the king of France: neither the Indian *domiciliés* in the St. Lawrence valley, whose villages were occasionally characterized as "small republics,"[11] nor, certainly, the aboriginals of Acadia, the Pays d'en Haut (Great Lakes region), or the Mississippi valley were deprived of their sovereignty in this period. This is illustrated in the disillusioned musings of the intendant of Canada, Gilles Hocquart, who in a 1730 letter to the Court raised the topic of "smuggling" between the Indians in the Montreal region and the English:

> This colony would need a greater number of troops to impress more respect and more fear upon the Savages and thereby give them the need to submit to the laws that the King imposes on the French, and until it pleases His Majesty to approve these wishes, we will take advantage of every opportunity to lead the Savages, little by little, to where they should be. The past considerations we have given them may have been necessary, but it would be desirable today to be able to force them to become Citizens.[12]

Hocquart's frustration underscores the difficulties faced by colonial authorities, throughout the French regime, in subjugating Indians. The intendant recalled the extent to which French policy toward Indians nearly always relied on considerations (*ménagements*)—in other words, strategic accommodation and adaptations such as to the aboriginals' customs, especially how to resolve crimes and misdemeanors committed by them.[13] Hocquart's words echoed the 1728 Louisiana edict, which effectively conveyed the limits of the assimilationist policy. It also fit into a context of increased racialization of social relations and the concomitant growth, especially among the administrative elites, of a fear of mixing. The tension that existed between the discourse of subordination and local constraints led colonial authorities to cobble together new strategies of incorporation and define new sociopolitical norms based on old repertoires. That way, seeing the failure of citizenship assimilation, the monarchy had recourse to other rhetorical devices of integration: rather than classifying the Illinois Indians as "subjects," noted the 1728 edict, the "King . . . grants them . . . his *protection*."[14]

This article will not inquire into the question of the *actual* relationships between the Indians and the French—nor, for that matter, the understanding the aboriginals had of those relationships—so much as the status of the aboriginals as conceived by the French monarchy. By discussing the concept of "protection," I examine how the French authorities assigned a special place to Indians, outside the sphere of citizenship, by simultaneously drawing on the repertoire of international relations and the repertoire proper to relations between the king and the provinces—two repertoires that were far from always being explicitly distinct. Indeed, the conquest of North America and the staking of claims of "sovereignty" over the aboriginal peoples and their lands rely in part on a complex politico-legal language where official forms of authority are not restricted to the simple imposition of a single, uniform "sovereignty" on identical "subjects."[15]

"IT IS ALWAYS EXPANDING HIS SOVEREIGNTY"

Taking possession of territory was one of the most common legal and rhetorical devices used by the French to symbolically place the aboriginals under their authority.[16] Such acts constituted, in part, an adaptation of the usual mechanisms of sovereignty in the context of colonization and imperialist rivalries. One adviser to Louis XIII, concerned with the rights of France in the east of the kingdom, wrote in 1632 that, through his conquests, the king "will be able to extend the borders of France to the ends of the Earth."[17] The primary goal of taking possession of lands in the Americas, besides satisfying the monarch's pretensions to universal glory, was to establish France's territorial claims vis-à-vis rival colonial powers and to do so, as in Europe, through an argumentative game based on antecedence. Seventeenth-century jurists attempted to legitimize French claims on the eastern borders by drawing on purported ancient rights. In 1632, for example, an evocatively titled treatise was published, featuring the concept of "protection": *On the sovereignty of the King in Metz . . . and other neighboring cities and countries that were in the former kingdom of Austrasia* [a Frankish kingdom in the early Middle Ages] *or Lorraine. Against the claims of the Empire, of Spain and of Lorraine and against the inhabitants of Metz who do not consider the King as their protector.*[18] In a similar tone, in 1667, *Les justes prétentions du Roi sur l'Empire* (*The Just Claims of the King over the Empire*) was published, a historico-legal dissertation seeking to demonstrate that Louis XIV could, if he wished, annex all the German states considered to be "the heritage of the ancient legacy of French princes, having been the possessions of Charlemagne as King of France."[19] These claims, sprinkled with threats and military pressure, multiplied from 1678 to 1681 with the so-called policy of reunion. This involved arguing ancient legal rights in border areas of the kingdom and, on that basis, making "claims" on a series of seigneuries, cities, and villages. Lands that, in the past, had been held by vassals of France were sought, then "the owner of the fief was called to appear before the chamber [of reunion] to pledge faith and homage; indirectly, he was acknowledging the sovereignty of the King of France."[20] This policy sought to extend, discreetly, an indirect form of sovereignty: that of the king-suzerain.

Obviously, in the Americas it was not a question of restoring ancestral rights, but by using the same logic of extending sovereignty the king's agents, in 1660–1680—a period of direct affirmation of monarchic power over New France—expanded their acts of taking possession in the Pays d'en Haut. "It is always expanding his sovereignty," Colbert wrote, significantly, about these acts.[21] In 1671, in Sault Ste.-Marie, the delegate of Intendant

Jean Talon, Simon-François Daumont de Saint-Lusson, planted a cross and a cedar pole before the Indian delegates, who had come from various villages of the Great Lakes to attend this ceremony.[22] The king's coat of arms was then attached to the pole, and the interpreter, Nicolas Perrot, declared to the Indians in their languages: "I take possession of this land in the name of he whom we call our King; this land is his, and all those peoples who hear me are his subjects."[23] Talon, who then reported to the Court on this act of taking possession, spoke of aboriginal nations who "voluntarily submitted to the rule of His Majesty, whom they regard exclusively and as their sovereign protector."[24]

Thus a principle of French government found itself transposed onto the colonial stage, since, traditionally, the bodies of the kingdom voluntarily demonstrated their loyalty toward and affection for the monarch.[25] The consent of the aboriginal populations was in this case purely imaginary, but Talon's statement nonetheless had a performative value and, in this sense, partook of the mechanisms of power. Although they were not considered to be subjects in the sense of *régnicoles* here, Indians were in fact placed under a form of "domination" called "protection" ("their sovereign protector").

THE DISCOURSE OF "PROTECTION"

This concept of "protection," which is compatible with the idea of alliance, was distinct from that of suzerainty. According to Jean Bodin, traditionally considered to be the great French theoretician of sovereignty:

> the vassal owed faith, homage and succor to his lord. . . . But . . . the word protection carries no subjection of he who is under protection, nor any command from the protector toward his adherents, but only the honor and reverence of the adherents toward the protector, who has taken up the defense and protection, without otherwise diminishing the majesty of the adherents, over whom the protector has no power. . . . The adherents . . . are in no way subjects of Protectors. . . . A mere adherent . . . owes neither service, nor obeisance, nor homage to the protector.[26]

Far from being an affirmation of sovereignty, protection was understood as an unequal alliance, a greater power being able to take a secondary power under its wing upon request: "as protection is nothing but the consideration and alliance of two princes . . . , whereby one recognizes the other as superior."[27]

As Dutch philosopher Hugo Grotius said of the "Right of Protection," "This Term is used when one Prince or State takes another less powerful Prince or State under *Protection*, and engages in its Defence."[28] At that point, the two political entities are placed less in a feudal relationship than in an international relationship with treaties of alliance in place. Indeed, Bodin indicated that "sovereign Princes who in a treaty of alliance recognize a protector who is greater than themselves are not their subjects."[29] In other words, the "protected" princes are not subjects, nor indeed vassals, but "allies." By writing "sovereignty" ("It is always expanding his sovereignty"), Colbert did not intend to draw an equivalence between taking possession and claiming a jurisdiction (ability to dispense justice, legislate, etc.). The term had no real meaning except in relation to rivalries with England. With regard to the aboriginals, this purely symbolic sovereignty involved the preeminence of the protector over his "adherent." The Indians of the Pays d'en Haut, under the French imperial conception, were subordinate allies who had performed an act of political allegiance, while still retaining their sovereignty.

A similar, or related, rhetoric prevailed in the drafting of treaties signed between the French and the aboriginals. French authorities may not have negotiated any treaties of territorial cession with Indians,[30] but they did sign several alliance and peace agreements with them. The most noteworthy was signed in 1701 in Montreal on the occasion of a conference that brought together representatives—called "delegates" or "ambassadors"—of nearly forty aboriginal "nations."[31] It should be noted that the concept of a "treaty" is not without certain ambiguities. Does such an act fall exclusively within the "international" sphere? Certainly, as Richelet's *Dictionnaire* (1680) underscored, "treaty" means "Accord, agreements entered into by Kings, Princes and States for the interest of their subjects, for peace or for commerce." The term "treaty" seems to imply that the contracting parties are in possession of sovereignty. But such "accords" could also be reached, over the course of France's history, by the king-suzerain and his vassals. Collections of treaties from the eighteenth century include many accords reached in the late Middle Ages by the monarch and the kingdom's great vassals, which had been negotiated "in the same forms used for international relations in the modern sense."[32]

To establish the status of the aboriginals, monarchic rhetoric drew on two repertoires that were somewhat entangled. The first was the domestic politico-legal tradition in the kingdom, which since the Middle Ages had determined the relationships between the king and the thousands of bodies that made up the kingdom (provincial parliaments, provincial estates, seigneurial courts, municipal bodies, corporations, etc.). With the growth of the state, and the advances in royal administration, the period from the sixteenth to the eighteenth centuries was witness to the progressive strengthening of the link between the king and all of his subjects, while the "traditional feudal relationship of man to man, vassal to suzerain"[33] was on the wane—although this relationship never completely disappeared, and new life was occasionally breathed into it. In the seventeenth century, the king continued to be seen as the suzerain of suzerains: lord of his own domain (the "royal domain"), but more generally of all lands in the kingdom.[34]

The second repertoire was that of international law—that is, state-to-state relations. Of course the use of the term "international" for this period is debatable. "In a world where nations did not really exist," explains the historian Lucien Bély, "and where sovereignty most often belonged to a prince, it is problematic to speak of international relations already, even though the reality existed. Another phrase would need to be invented instead: inter-prince, or inter-sovereign, relations."[35] The king of France maintained diplomatic relations with the other European princes (the king of England, the king of Spain, etc.), but also with princes located beyond Europe (the king of Morocco, the Turkish emperor, the king of Siam, etc.). These international relations were gradually formalized, over the course of the sixteenth to the eighteenth centuries, by diplomatic visits, ambassadorial stays, international conferences, and the signing of treaties.[36] In other words, this was a period of emergence for the "international" rhetoric, which helped to draw a clearer distinction between domestic and foreign affairs, and was accompanied by an affirmation of the art of diplomacy.[37] But it is important to emphasize the fact that these two registers, "national" and "international," were not always rigorously differentiated in the seventeenth century.[38]

Consequently, in the act establishing the Company of the West Indies in 1664, the king granted the status of "natural" (or *régnicole*) to converted aboriginals and their descendants, while at the same time adopting the rhetoric of international law.[39] For the company, this meant establishing itself in the lands entrusted to it "either that said lands belong to us to be or to have previously been inhabited by the French, or that said company establish itself there, by hunting or subjugating the Savages or natives of the lands or the other nations of Europe that are not in our alliance, in order that, said Company having established strong Colonies in said Lands, it can govern them (Preamble)." In the context of war, the "Savages" were placed on an equal footing with the "other nations of Europe."[40] Moreover, the company was asked to "trade in peace and alliance in our name with the Kings and Princes of the Lands where it would like to establish its dwellings and commerce, and agree with them on conditions and treaties that will be approved by us;

in case of insult, declare war on them, attack them and defend itself by force of arms (Article 29)."[41] The king's representatives were able to sign treaties with the Indians. If no alliance was possible, war and subjugation would rule the day. In short, the king of France recognized the independence and even the sovereign nature of the peoples encountered, but this nonetheless did not mean that the treaties would be designed as among "equals."

Though the concepts of "protection" and "suzerainty" were distinct, they were nonetheless used in a quasi-concomitant way by the French. The treaties signed with the aboriginals often took a feudal point of view, whether explicitly or not, as the ones negotiated between the French and the Iroquois in 1665 and 1666 testify. In January 1667, Minister Hugues de Lionne wrote to Intendant Talon: "I have received your letter of October 13th along with the Treaty you made with the Iroquois. I will keep it as a document of some curiosity and much Wisdom; the King listened to it being read with great pleasure."[42] Lionne, who was a seasoned diplomat, well versed in negotiations with the Spanish, English, and Dutch, noted the exotic, extraordinary nature—"a document of some curiosity"—of this "treaty" with the Iroquois, which the French authorities readily likened to an act of obedience and submission. However, the official 1665 document sent to the Court bore all the hallmarks of an international treaty.[43] Peace was granted "in the name and on behalf of the Most Christian King by My Lord Alexandre de Prouville," the king's lieutenant-general in America who acted "by virtue of the power given him by his Majesty's letters patent dated 19 November 1663." These authorized him to "make, according to circumstances, peace or truce, either with the other nations of Europe established in said country, or with the barbarians [Indians]."[44]

Article 1 of the 1665 treaty decreed that the Huron and Algonquin allies (who were notably absent from the peace conference) were to be "subjects of said Lord King, or living under His Protection" (note the uncertainty of the "or"). Article 2, which offers some clarifications, shows the extreme ambiguity of the French lexicon:

> That said Hurons and Algonquins . . . may not in the future be disturbed in their Hunting by the four Iroquois Nations, or troubled in their Commerce while coming by trade routes to Montreal, to Trois-Rivières, to Quebec, or anywhere else . . . Said Lord King declaring here and now that he takes them all, not only under His Protection, but as his own Subjects, once they have given themselves to his Majesty in subjection and vassalage . . . there will be mutual friendship and assistance between all said Nations, who will unite as Brothers for their common defense, under the protection of said Lord King.[45]

The terms used by the king's representatives drew on a triple rhetoric: the rhetoric of subjection ("as his own Subjects"), the rhetoric of feudalism ("vassals," "Lord King"), and the rhetoric of protection, which was an international rhetoric.

This composite discourse reflects, in part, the complexity of certain territorial situations in Europe: enclaves located on the kingdom's borders, but falling under the Holy Roman Empire, were placed in a vassalage relationship with the king of France. The king had vassals there who owed him homage, but whose sovereignty he in no way disputed. For example, Charles of Ghent (1506–1555, alias Charles V), Lord of Artois and Flanders, owed homage to the king of France in this way. The king was Charles's suzerain, but still had no sovereignty over these two territories. An identical situation prevailed in an area of Lorraine (the *Barrois mouvant*), a buffer principality between France and the Holy Roman Empire: the Duke of Lorraine had been the vassal of the king of France there since the fourteenth century. In 1661, then again in 1699, he pledged allegiance ("faith and homage") to Louis XIV.[46] These ties of vassalage, rekindled by the oath of faith and homage being taken, could be used as arguments for legal legitimacy and to contribute to affirming the French state's sovereign power in certain territories.[47] It is also useful to distinguish between sovereignty, on the one hand, which theoretically involves the ability to govern and dispense justice in a given territory (these are the *droits régaliens*, or the rights and powers attached to the royal prerogative), and, on the other hand, suzerainty, in the sense of a relationship between men that compels the vassal, in exchange for the protection of his seigneur-suzerain, to faith and homage (which are feudal rights).[48] However, since the Middle Ages, a shift from suzerainty toward sovereignty was at work in the king's various "vassal" principalities.[49]

The cryptic colonial discourse in the 1665–1666 treaties later faded. Thus in the 1701 Great Peace of Montreal[50] the aboriginals were not considered to be "subjects," nor explicitly characterized as "vassals," but described as the "allies" and "children" of the governor, who enjoyed preeminence over them in the same way a "patron" or "protector" would.[51] The "father and children" metaphor was by no means an innovation at the time: since at least the 1670s, aboriginals had systematically been called "children" by the French governor in diplomatic talks. Incidentally, it should be noted that this metaphor was also used in the politics of attributing citizenship. Essentially, naturalization constituted an emotional act that resembled adoption. Sixteenth-century French jurist Jean Bacquet referred to letters of naturalization as letters of adoption, and naturalized individuals were often called "adopted children." Obviously, the letter of naturalization (as it existed in France) did not incorporate this metaphor into its text, but its preamble often evoked the idea of abandonment and orphanage, and the king's traditional role as father.[52] Thus naturalization was closely associated with the concept of patriarchy, which structured French-Indian relations in the eyes of the Crown. Furthermore, in the kingdom, it was conceived as an act of rebirth whose principle, by changing the "nature" of the subject, was similar to that of ennoblement. In both cases, the king erased a "*vice de naissance*" and granted a status that modified or reconstituted the nature of the applicant.[53] This mechanism was no doubt imposed with unusual force when it came to the "Savages," since the original goal of the colonial project had been to transform them, rather than simply incorporating them. But the metaphor survived the failure of the citizenship policy, and the Indians themselves made use of it, though without submitting to the authority of the French governor, whom they considered to be essentially a purveyor. In 1730, Governor Charles de la Boische, Marquis de Beauharnois, and Intendant Hocquart wrote:

> You are informed, Monseigneur, that all the nations of Canada regard the Governor-General as their father, who as a result in this capacity . . . should give them something to eat, to dress themselves with and to hunt, and if they have been right thus far to call the Governor-General by this name through the goodness and kindness with which they have been treated, one could also say that they have been treated as spoiled children, and that they will not mend their ways until we are in the position to inspire in them greater fear and respect.[54]

By associating the terms "children" and "allies," the French (as in the treaty of 1701) clarified their conception of relations with the Indians: they relied on the legal language of unequal alliance. For Grotius, in an "unequal alliance" the "inferior power could . . . enjoy sovereignty." The aboriginals were not completely denied sovereignty: they maintained a strong autonomy in the same way as the king's great vassals. But they were in fact placed under French patronage: "*Clients* are under the Protection of their *Patrons*," wrote Grotius, "So Nations, who are *inferior* by a Treaty of Alliance, are under the Protection of the People who are their *Superior* in Dignity. They are *under their protection, not under their Domination*."[55] For Bodin, "protection carries no subjection, but rather superiority and prerogative of honor."[56]

The Indian nations, whether they agreed to convert to Christianity or not, were officially placed under the "protection" of the king, who formed alliances and signed treaties with them. The officer of the *Troupes de la Marine*, Louis de La Porte de Louvigny, explained in 1717 that he had announced "the death of our great King [Louis XIV] . . . to all those nations of the [Great] lakes who must come down in the coming year to mourn the death of the King and ask his august successor for his protection."[57] As early as 1670, Intendant Talon spoke of the "8ta8actz [Ottawa, or more generally the aboriginals of the Great Lakes] that the King has taken under his protection."[58] In 1703, Governor Philippe de Rigaud, Marquis de Vaudreuil, assured the Onondagas (members of the League of Five Nations) of his "protection,"[59] and two years later declared to an Iroquois delegate, in a feudal vein: "I clothe you to give you a second proof of my friendship and assure you of my protection as long as you are faithful to me."[60] Indians were thus described as "allied nations" (or "Nations of Savages," "Allied Savages," etc.);[61] at the same time, it was a question of "governing":[62] governing in the sense of running a family, where the father supervises his children, and also to the extent that a power that tends toward coercion finds itself established. Moreover, the political morality of the seventeenth century, as inspired by principles of reason of state (raison d'état), was not bothered by the king using secret and violent approaches to governing. For example, in 1639 Gabriel Naudé explained that the tactic of the coup d'état, with its attendant artifice, deceit, and manipulation, should guide the prince's actions, especially in the context of the "New World."[63]

MEDIATION AS AN INSTRUMENT OF POWER

The king's instructions to Governor Pierre François de Rigaud, Marquis de Vaudreuil-Cavagnail, in 1755 stipulated that "the system of government of the Savages in Canada" should be based on "the sentiments of justice and Humanity that guide His Majesty." The French believed that they played "the role of protectors and peacemakers" among the aboriginal nations.[64] Although they lacked the military means to establish strict jurisdiction over Indians, these prerogatives (protection and peacemaking) were nonetheless conceived, in the seventeenth and eighteenth centuries, as being so many mechanisms of obedience. The strategy of *Pax Gallica*, which involved establishing peace among aboriginal groups and, ultimately, extending forms of domination over them, is in fact related to "silent war," to use Michel Foucault's expression.[65] This "peace-war" was built on concepts of arbitration and mediation, which were among the common levers of international power.

Arbitration and mediation were two of the most highly valued methods for settling a dispute between states in Europe.[66] Henri IV (1589–1610) increased arbitration throughout Europe by dispatching ambassadors, who engaged in peacemaking efforts with belligerent countries, at the express request of those countries.[67] Louis XIV intervened in the same way in northern and eastern Europe.[68] According to the historian Lucien Bély, this role as intermediary and mediator "allowed a domination to be established that dared not admit its existence or that concealed itself beneath flattering features."[69] On this question, François de Callières, a famous negotiator from the time of Louis XIV and the brother of the signatory of the Great Peace of Montreal of 1701, Louis-Hector, had this to say:[70] "It is . . . in the interest of a great Prince to employ Negotiators to offer his mediation in the quarrels that arise between Sovereigns, and to bring them peace through the authority of his intervention, nothing is more suitable for extending the reputation of his power, and to make all the Nations respect him."[71]

The approach proposed by Intendant Jacques Duchesneau in 1681 was thus inspired by European diplomatic practices:

> Our interests are to keep these peoples [aboriginals] united, to learn of all their disputes, no matter how small, to watch carefully that none of them are settled without our mediation and to make ourselves their arbiters and protectors in all matters, and engage them thereby in great dependency, and through the kindness with which we will treat them, flattering them, giving them presents, sending them on visits.[72]

The governor of New France, through his power and ability to control information, intended to set himself up as arbiter of international relations.[73] This arbitration—thrown into particularly sharp relief in the negotiations of the Great Peace of Montreal[74]—while relying on "kindness" and "flattery," was the means that they hoped would, in time, establish an effective form of domination over the aboriginals. To work toward mediation, officers were placed in the posts in the Pays d'en Haut starting in the 1680s. These diplomats in Indian lands, veritable political intermediaries, gave their hosts many gifts while simultaneously intervening in their domestic affairs, which was more difficult and less common in Europe.[75] Unlike the French embassies in Morocco, Persia, Turkey, or Siam (all remote embassies), the French agents on Indian territory made an effort to chip away at local sovereignty by playing the role not only of ambassador but also—they proclaimed—of "protector" and arbiter. A parallel could be drawn with the policy of "reunions" of Louis XIV, who, on the eastern border of the kingdom, sought to transform a claimed situation of suzerainty into one of full sovereignty.[76]

On the subject of treaties of unequal alliance, Grotius wrote:

In the mean Time it is true, that it often happens, that if he who is superior in the League, be much more powerful than the Rest, he by Degrees usurps a sovereignty, properly so called, over them, especially if the League be perpetual, and that he has a Right to plant Garrisons in their Towns . . . then those who had been Allies become Subjects, or at least there is made a Partition of the Sovereignty.[77]

Officially, the French agreed to a "Partition of the Sovereignty" with their aboriginal partners, who were placed under their "protection." By virtue of their vaunted superiority, the French claimed the right to interfere in aboriginal affairs and, in the margins of their empire, "fabricated" international law to some extent to ensure the symbolic subjugation of the Indian "nations."

A FLEXIBLE SOVEREIGNTY

This politico-diplomatic discourse was juxtaposed with a rhetoric that drew on existing contractual forms within the kingdom and that in fact relied on the flexibility of the nature of sovereignty. The monarchic French state in the seventeenth century had nothing to do with a unified state as seen in the modern day, with a clearly delimited territory and inhabitants who are all subject to the same laws everywhere. Instead, there was a great variety of systems, tied to the past history of the kingdom, which had been built up gradually since the Middle Ages on a basis of territorial dispersion of feudal powers. In the seventeenth century, a veritable mosaic of administrative districts still enjoyed their own legal traditions. The outlying provinces, in particular, were tied to the Crown by a special treaty that accorded them a certain number of favors, especially in matters of taxation. The so-called conquered provinces, or "border provinces," maintained their privileges for a long time.[78] The province of Artois, for example, which was incorporated into France in 1659 (in the Treaty of the Pyrenees), "retained most of its status and previous institutions, especially its provincial estates, taxation privileges, legal council, urban charters and customs."[79] Similarly, the cities of the Spanish Netherlands conquered by Louis XIV (Douai, Lille, and so forth) had all their privileges recognized, including the right to govern themselves.[80] Provence, through the *Assemblée des communautés* and Parliament of Aix, was also able to resist affirmation of the monarchic order through the seventeenth and eighteenth centuries. The work by the Abbé de Coriolis, *Traité sur l'administration du comté de provence* (*Treatise on the Administration of the County of Provence*; 1786–1788), illustrates the idea of a "non-subordinate co-State" of the kingdom.[81] As for Dauphiné (incorporated into France in 1349), it usually asserted itself as a monarchy, separate from the kingdom. General Attorney Vidaud de La Tour explained in the eighteenth century that "Dauphiné is a distinct and separate state from the kingdom, inseparably attached to the kingdom, but governed by its own laws and customs."[82] Although the king was sovereign in Dauphiné (where he bore the title of "Dauphin"), this province was theoretically located outside the kingdom.[83]

In fact, the Indian nations that were not affected by the policy of naturalization, but were simply placed under the king's protection, were also considered, much like certain French provinces or cities, to be independent, even "separate," bodies. Governor Vaudreuil, in a 1711 letter to his New York counterpart, wrote, regarding the aboriginal allies in New France: "These nations are ours through the friendship they have always felt toward the French nation, but they are not sufficiently subordinate for us to make them change their customs and mores."[84] These "nations," in other words, were under a minimal form of domination, but they had not given up their cultural traditions, and certainly not their political autonomy.[85] Vaudreuil's discourse made it quite clear what absolutism was in France itself: an aspiration to unending unification, constrained by the "real" country.[86]

In certain contexts, the French authorities even adopted a discourse that distinctly recognized Indian independence. To the English, who asserted their sovereignty over Iroquoia and denied the French the right to build forts there, a memorialist responded as follows in 1727:

> We do not know by what virtue the English can view the Iroquois as their Subjects. There is no savage Nation that France or England can Treat in this way; all the savages, and the Iroquois in particular, who are superior to all the others, currently have the spirit of independence and Their Liberties at heart, that they could be but extremely outraged if one were to dare let them know that they were viewed as Subjects. They maintain they are their masters and so they are. . . . It must be admitted . . . that there is no Savage Nation in North America that could be considered other than on a footing of friendship and equality.[87]

Obviously, it was that much easier for this author to recognize the Indians' independence when his intention here was to counter British pretensions. His discourse is nonetheless revealing of the French conception of relations with the Indians, which also took international, or "infra-international," forms and which cannot be reduced to a mere policy of subjection.

TWO FORMS OF SOVEREIGNTY

Two very different types of sovereignty can therefore be identified in New France. One was "sovereignty-subjection," which sought to transform the aboriginals into true subjects; it was aimed primarily at Christianized Indians from the Illinois Country and the Indian missions established in the St. Lawrence valley. The other was a type of infra-sovereignty that could be called "suzerainty-protection." Colonial authorities, in that way, developed two statuses for Indians, which were intended to meet absolutist and colonialist ideals of domination and integration as well as more universalist ideals of religious and cultural unification. First was the status of subject, in the sense of "natural," a status that illustrates the inclusive nature of citizenship under the ancien régime.[88] A legal category, it was open to men and women, to peasants and nobles, to children and adults, to foreigners living on French soil and, therefore, to colonized peoples who, once converted, could automatically enjoy this status. Of course this was not without its problems in concrete terms, as the Louisiana edict of 1728 attests, since it was undermined by the vagaries of *francisation*.

The second possible status was that of an ally placed under the protection of the king, with whom the French would negotiate using a model inspired by contractual practices in the kingdom and international diplomacy. Here, the French monarch positioned himself more as "king-suzerain" than "king-magistrate." Above all else, he demanded a feudal-style allegiance of the aboriginal populations. These peoples were not subjected to his law, but to a colonial form of suzerainty. Such a status accounts for real relationships less imperfectly; moreover, it is in part built and theorized on the foundations of colonial empiricism. If the Illinois, according to the 1728 edict, were not considered to be true subjects of the king, they were nonetheless placed under his "protection." The plasticity of the concept of sovereignty, coupled with specific forms of preeminence in the international order—including "protection"—allowed the French imperial system to incorporate Indians in other ways than through the status of "natural-subject" (*sujet-naturel*).

This second discourse, which was aimed primarily at the most "peripheral" Indian populations, was not completely invented in situ, but it did become that much more mobilized as the failures of subjection and *francisation* became manifest. When cultural and legal assimilation proved difficult, it seemed more realistic to subject Indians to discreet forms of political integration. Overseas, in the space of North American colonization, the monarchy "cobbled together" an original vision of sovereignty outside the sphere of citizenship. The "Savage nations" did not fully belong to the international European family of states, but were perceived as political entities that were sufficiently organized for treaties to be negotiated with them. Their chiefs were welcomed in Montreal (and New Orleans) as ambassadors; moreover, they were often designated as such in official documents.

No contradiction exists between the idea of forming an alliance relationship with a country or a people and the introduction of elements of subordination into this alliance. Diplomatic practices of protection and mediation should not be confused with subjection proper, although these usages all have the shared objective of establishing power. Moreover, the logic of *clientélisation*, which belongs to mediation, becomes radicalized in contact with Indian peoples—just as certain mechanisms of monarchic normalization became further entrenched or, rather, renewed. The French policy toward Indians, seen through the lens of the legal and diplomatic realities of the "Old World," presents a remarkable paradox: the aspirations to unification were at once more virulent in the Americas than in the home country—the colonial crucible bolstered the royalty's unification project, as illustrated by the policy of *francisation*—and, given the politico-military weight and the independence of the Indians, more hindered. It is perhaps not surprising to see that the very moment when the economic and political importance of alliances with the Indians of the Pays d'en Haut was affirmed, in the 1680s, was also the point when the "civilizing" utopia in Canada declined.[89] Less out of step with the real reports than the dry rhetoric of subjugation, the discourse of protection and unequal alliance nonetheless allowed the king to symbolically formalize a relationship of domination.

NOTES

This article has been translated from French by Matthew Kayahara (text) and Robert Englebert (notes). It reprises certain passages, in modified form, from a previous article entitled " 'Les forcer à devenir cytoyens': État, Sauvages et citoyenneté en Nouvelle-France (XVIIᵉ-XVIIIᵉ siècle)," *Annales. Histoire, Sciences Sociales* 64 (September–October 2009): 985–1018.

1. Arrêt du conseil supérieur de la Louisiane, December 18, 1728, Archives nationales de France, Colonies (hereafter cited as AN, Col.), A, vol. 23, fol. 102 (emphasis added).

2. The inheritances of widows of Frenchmen who died without children were assigned to the Domain of the Company. Their goods were put under the protection of legal guardians, who allocated two-thirds of the revenues to children and heirs. One-third was allocated to the widow, at least "as long as she stays among the French, regardless of whether she remarries or not, but the instant she returns to the savages to live according to their ways the pension will cease to be paid." See Extrait de la lettre de Mr la Chaise, AN, Col., F³, vol. 24, fol. 142–143; Questions à décider concernant les alliances matrimoniales des françois avec les sauvages, 1729, AN, Col., F³, vol. 24, fol. 144–147. The writ of 1728, despite being ratified by Versailles (see Guillaume Aubert, "'The Blood of France': Race and Purity of Blood in the French Atlantic World," *William and Mary Quarterly*, 3rd series, 56 [July 2004]: 471), appears to have never been applied and put into practice. See Cécile Vidal, "Les implantations françaises au pays des Illinois au XVIIIe siècle, 1699–1765" (PhD diss., École des hautes études en sciences sociales, Paris, 1995), 498. Depriving aboriginal women of their inheritance rights ran counter to the interests of the colonists with whom they could remarry. In form and substance, Indian converts were considered the king's subjects, with all of the inheritance rights assumed therein. These debates are proof that the status of aboriginals, constantly rethought and amended, was not self-evident.

3. On French policy regarding naturalization under the ancien régime, see Peter Sahlins, *Unnaturally French: Foreign Citizens in the Old Regime and After* (Ithaca, N.Y.: Cornell University Press, 2004); Peter Sahlins, "La nationalité avant la lettre: les pratiques de naturalisation en France sous l'Ancien Régime," *Annales. Histoire, Sciences Sociales* 55 (September–October 2000): 1083–1084; Yves Durand, *L'ordre du monde: idéal politique et valeurs sociales en France du XVIe au XVIIIe siècle* (Paris: Sedes, 2001), 14–20.

4. Robert Shore Milnes, ed., *Édits, ordonnances royaux, déclarations et arrêts du Conseil d'État du roi, concernant le Canada*, 2 vols. (Québec: P. E. Desbarats, 1803–1806), 1:7; Articles accordés par le cardinal de Richelieu à la Compagnie de la Nouvelle-France dite des Cent-Associés, AN, Col., C¹¹ᴬ, vol. 1, fol. 79–84.

5. See Gérard Lafleur, *Les Caraïbes des Petites Antilles* (Paris: Karthala, 1992), 29; Milnes, *Édits, ordonnances royaux*, 1:30, 37, 366.

6. Peter Sahlins, *Frontières et identités nationales: la France et l'Espagne dans les Pyrénées depuis le XVIIe siècle* (Paris: Belin, 1996), 130–131; Sahlins, *Unnaturally French*, 164, 193–195. Unlike in France, citizenship in New France

ultimately rested on one intangible criterion: religion. In a context where evangelization was used as the main justification for the colonial project, Indians had to convert in order to become French. See Saliha Belmessous, "Être français en Nouvelle-France: identité française et identité coloniale aux dix-septième et dix-huitième siècles," *French Historical Studies* 27 (Summer 2004): 512–513.

7. Mémoire du roi pour servir d'instruction à Talon, March 27, 1665, in *Rapport de l'archiviste de la province de Québec*, ed. Pierre-Georges Roy, 42 vols. (Quebec: Imprimeur du roi, 1921–1963), 11:9.

8. I already demonstrated that the Indian assimilation experience contributed to the redefinition of the concept of naturalization by rendering it more interdependent with culture. In the context of strong otherness that questioned—or crystallized—French identity, baptism and political loyalty were not enough to make individuals actual *régnicoles*; full conversion to the new model of Frenchness now seemed required. It is also possible that the colonial project of *francisation* of the "Savages" subverted certain traditional principles related to the ancien régime monarchy, and thus participated in the advent of a more unitary and centralized State. See Havard, " 'Les forcer à devenir cytoyens.' "

9. Alain Beaulieu, *Convertir les fils de Caïn: Jésuites et Amérindiens nomades en Nouvelle-France, 1632–1642* (Quebec: Nuit Blanche, 1994), 139–140.

10. See the definition of Gregory H. Nobles, *American Frontiers: Cultural Encounters and Continental Conquest* (New York: Hill & Wang, 1997), xii.

11. See Marc Jetten, *Enclaves amérindiennes: les "réductions" du Canada, 1637–1701* (Sillery, Q.C.: Éditions du Septentrion, 1994), 7.

12. Hocquart au ministre, Quebec, October 10, 1730, AN, Col., C^{11A}, vol. 53, fol. 217rv. In a letter from that same year, Governor Charles de la Boische, Marquis de Beauharnois, and Intendant Gilles Hocquart wrote similarly: "The Savages would have become much more useful to the colony if it had been possible to enslave them bit by bit, they would have become good citizens and the better part of them would have seemingly embraced Christianity." Beauharnois et Hocquart au ministre, Québec, October 15, 1730, AN, Col., C^{11A}, vol. 52, fol. 33v–34r. Thus citizenship here is uniquely perceived as the imposition of certain constraints on "Savages" who were reluctant to be part of the colonial project.

13. On the difficulties of applying French justice to cases involving Indians, see Jan Grabowski, "Crime and Punishment: French Justice and Amerindians in New France," *European Review of Native American Studies* 7, no. 1 (1993): 20–28; Denis Vaugeois, ed., *Les Hurons de Lorette* (Sillery, Q.C.: Éditions du Septentrion, 1996); Denys Delâge and Étienne Gilbert, "Les Amérindiens face à la justice coloniale française dans le gouvernement de Québec,

1663–1759: 1—Les crimes capitaux et leurs châtiments," *Recherches améri-ndiennes au Québec* 33, no. 3 (2004): 79–90; Richard White, *The Middle Ground: Indians, Empires and Republics in the Great Lakes Region* (New York: Cambridge University Press), 75–93; Gilles Havard, *Empire et métissages: Indiens et Français dans le Pays d'en Haut, 1660–1715* (Sillery, Q.C. and Paris: Éditions du Septentrion and Presses de l'Université de Paris-Sorbonne, 2003), 457–472.

14. Arrêt du conseil supérieur de la Louisiane, December 18, 1728, AN, Col., A, vol. 23, fol. 102 (emphasis added).

15. The concept of sovereignty was defined theoretically by French jurists who sought to legitimate and reinforce the king's authority in the kingdom at the end of the sixteenth and start of the seventeenth centuries. Jean Bodin defines sovereignty as the "absolute and perpetual power of a Republic," that is, a state. Jean Bodin, *Les six livres de la République* (Paris: Jacques Du Puys, 1576), 122. See also Robert Descimon and Alain Guéry, "Un État des temps modernes?," in *Histoire de la France*, ed. Jacques Le Goff, Vol. 4, *La longue durée de l'État* (Paris: Seuil, 2000), 261, 292. In *De la souveraineté du Roy* (1632), Cardin Le Bret noted that sovereignty served to "reduce everything to being under one individual; it is no more divisible than a point in geometry." Cited in Descimon and Guéry, "Un État des temps modernes?," 254; Joël Cornette, *La monarchie entre Renaissance et Révolution, 1515–1789: histoire de la France politique* (Paris: Seuil, 2000), 145; Fanny Cosandey and Robert Descimon, *L'absolutisme en France: histoire et historiographie* (Paris: Seuil, 2002), 295. Monarchical authority is meant to be "absolute" and indivisible. Since the Middle Ages, application of the law in society had been considered central in the definition of supreme political authority: thus sovereignty appeared fundamentally as the capacity to render justice in the heart of a given territory. Put another way, the propensity of individuals and groups within a territory to call upon the sovereign (as a last resort), or to his representatives, in order to obtain recognition of their rights or settle disputes, conveyed the existence of a form of sovereignty. See Lucien Bély, *Les relations internationales en Europe, XVIIe-XVIIIe siècles*, 4th ed. (Paris: Presses universitaires de France, 2007), 53. However, legislative power was also increasingly evoked. Jean Bodin sees legislative power as an essential criterion of sovereignty, "the power to make and break the law." Descimon and Guéry, "Un État des temps modernes?," 256, 262. In 1608, Charles Loyseau defined "acts of cases of sovereignty" (sovereignty held by the king) in the following manner: "Make laws, create officers, mediate war and peace, to be the last resort for justice and to issue new currency." Cited in Joël Cornette, *Le roi de guerre: essai sur la souveraineté dans la France du Grand Siècle* (Paris: Payot & Rivages, 1993), 120.

This having been laid out, the singular aspiration of the king had to take into account the great political complexity of the kingdom, tied essentially to its judicial pluralism, as well as to the confusion between the "national" and the "international." This situation was accompanied by sovereignty stacking or sharing, the importance of which has to be measured in order to understand the official status of Indians in New France.

16. See Patricia Seed, *Ceremonies of Possession in Europe's Conquest of the New World, 1492–1640* (Cambridge: Cambridge University Press, 1995); Havard, *Empire et métissages*, 259–263; Colbert à Talon, St Germain en Laye, April 5, 1667, AN, Col., C[11A], vol. 2, fol. 294; Pierre Margry, ed., *Découvertes et établissements des Français dans l'Ouest et dans le Sud de l'Amérique septentrionale*, 6 vols. (Paris: D. Jouaust, 1879–1888), 1:82.

17. Jacques de Cassan, cited in Cornette, *Le roi de guerre*, 140.

18. The original French title reads as follows: *De la souveraineté du Roy à Metz . . . et autres villes et pays circonvoisins qui étaient à l'ancien royaume d'Austrasie ou Lorraine. Contre les prétentions de l'Empire, de l'Espagne et de la Lorraine et contre les habitants de Metz qui ne tiennent le Roy pour leur protecteur.* See Cornette, *Le roi de guerre*, 139–140, 380 note 94.

19. Cited in Cornette, *Le roi de guerre*, 139, 142.

20. Bély, *Les relations internationales en Europe*, 277; Lucien Bély, *L'art de la paix en Europe: naissance de la diplomatie moderne, XVIe-XVIIIe siècle* (Paris: Presses universitaires de France, 2007), 363–364; Cornette, *Le roi de guerre*, 144–145.

21. Margry, *Découvertes et établissements*, 1:77.

22. Reuben Gold Thwaites, ed., *The Jesuit Relations and Allied Documents: Travels and Explorations of the Jesuit Missionaries in New France, 1610–1791*, 73 vols. (Cleveland: Burrows Brothers, 1896–1903), 55:106–108.

23. Claude-Charles le Roy de Bacqueville de la Potherie, *Histoire de l'Amérique septentrionale*, 4 vols. (Paris: J.-L. Nion et F. Didot, 1722), 2:129–30; Thwaites, *Jesuit Relations*, 55:108–114.

24. Margry, *Découvertes et établissements*, 1:93.

25. Seed, *Ceremonies of Possession*, 56–62; Cosandey and Descimon, *L'absolutisme en France*, 122.

26. Bodin, *Les six livres de la République*, 101, 103.

27. Ibid., 104.

28. Hugo Grotius, *Le droit de la guerre et de la paix*, trans. Jean Barbeyrac, 2 vols. (Amsterdam: Pierre de Coup, 1724), 1:158, note 7. This excerpt is taken from the English version. See Hugo Grotius, *The Rights of War and Peace in Three Books*, 3 vols. (London: printed for W. Innys et al., 1738), 1:93, note 7 (emphasis added).

29. Bodin, *Les six livres de la République*, 105. See also Bély, *Les Relations internationales en Europe*, 120.

30. Colonists individually negotiated land purchases with Indians, most notably in the Illinois Country. See Gilles Havard and Cécile Vidal, *Histoire de l'Amérique française*, 3rd ed. (Paris: Flammarion, 2008), 316–317.

31. AN, Col., C[11A], vol. 19, fol. 41; Gilles Havard, *The Great Peace of Montreal of 1701: French-Native Diplomacy in the Seventeenth Century*, trans. Phyllis Aronoff and Howard Scott (Montreal and Kingston: McGill-Queen's University Press, 2001), 111–159.

32. Monique Constant, "Les traités: validité, publicité," in *L'invention de la diplomatie: Moyen Âge-Temps modernes*, ed. Lucien Bély (Paris: Presses universitaires de France, 1998), 237.

33. Bély, *Les relations internationales en Europe*, 53.

34. Pierre Goubert and Daniel Roche, *Les Français et l'Ancien Régime*, 2 vols., 2nd ed. (Paris: Armand Colin, 1991), 1:206–207.

35. Lucien Bély, *Louis XIV: le plus grand roi du monde* (Paris: J.-P. Gisserot, 2005), 78.

36. Bély, *Les relations internationales en Europe*, 340.

37. Bély, *L'art de la paix en Europe*, 673.

38. Ibid., 12–13; Claire Gantet, *Guerre, paix et construction des États, 1618–1714: nouvelle histoire des relations internationales* (Paris: Seuil, 2003), 169–170.

39. From the sixteenth century, royal commissions accorded French explorers and monopoly holders the power to make war and negotiate peace treaties with the peoples they encountered. See "Commission délivrée à Roberval (15 janvier 1541)," in Jacques Cartier, *Relations*, ed. Michel Bideaux (Montreal: Presses de l'Université de Montréal, 1986), 247–249. See also Grotius, *Le droit de la guerre et de la paix*, 2:480, 485.

40. See Michel Morin, *L'usurpation de la souveraineté autochtone: le cas des peuples de la Nouvelle-France et des colonies anglaises* (Montreal: Boréal, 1997), 70–71.

41. Milnes, *Édits, ordonnances royaux*, 1:30–31, 36. See also Michel Morin, "'Manger avec la même micoine dans la même gamelle': à propos des traités conclus avec les Amérindiens," *Revue générale de Droit* 33 (2003): 100; Morin, *L'usurpation de la souveraineté autochtone*, 70–71; Milnes, *Édits, ordonnances royaux*, 1:362–363.

42. Lionne à Talon, January 7, 1667, AN, Col., F[3], fol. 335, cited in Morin, "'Manger avec la même micoine dans la même gamelle,'" 116.

43. Ibid., 112.

44. Morin, *L'usurpation de la souveraineté autochtone*, 112–115; Morin, "'Manger avec la même micoine dans la même gamelle,'" 112–113, 116; Articles de paix demandée par six ambassadeurs Iroquois (décembre 1665), Bibliothèque

nationale de France (hereafter cited as BnF), Baluze 196, fol. 72–3; AN, Col., C[11A], vol. 2, fol. 187–190; AN, Col., F[3], vol. 3, fol. 335; Colbert à Talon, St Germain en Laye, April 5, 1667, in Roy, *Rapport de l'archiviste de la province de Québec*, 11:70.

45. Articles de paix demandée par six ambassadeurs Iroquois (décembre 1665), BnF, Baluze 196, fol. 72–3; Morin, *L'usurpation de la souveraineté autochtone*, 88.

46. See Bély, *L'art de la paix en Europe*, 12–13; Daniel Nordman, *Frontières de France: de l'espace au territoire, XVIe-XVIIIe siècle* (Paris: Gallimard, 1998), 196–197.

47. See Cornette, *Le roi de guerre*, 140.

48. Jacques Le Goff, "Le Moyen Âge," in Le Goff, *Histoire de la France*, 112–113.

49. Ibid., 114.

50. Havard, *Great Peace of Montreal*, 30, 136, 155, 210.

51. See Antoine Furetière, *Dictionnaire universel contenant généralement tous les mots françois, tant vieux que modernes, et les termes de toutes les sciences et des arts*, 3 vols. (La Haye: Pierre Husson et al., 1690), 3: "Protection."

52. See Sahlins, *Unnaturally French*, 73–74, 126.

53. Descimon and Guéry, "Un État des temps modernes?," 387–388; Sahlins, *Unnaturally French*, 1, 65, 116, 130; Sahlins "La nationalité avant la lettre," 1107.

54. Beauharnois et Hocquart au ministre, Québec, October 15, 1730, AN, Col., C[11A], vol. 52, fol. 33v–34r. For more on the interpretation of the metaphor of the father and his children, see Denys Delâge, "L'alliance franco-amérindienne, 1660–1701," *Recherches amérindiennes au Québec* 19, no. 1 (1989): 3–15; Havard, *Empire et métissages*, 360–373; Gilles Havard, " 'Coupper un membre à son enfant': la vision politique du 'père' dans l'alliance franco-amérindienne au Canada," in *Les Français à la découverte des premières nations en Nouvelle-France*, ed. Florence Leschevin d'Ere and Georges Viard (Langres, France: Société historique et archéologique de Langres, 2004), 147–162.

55. Grotius, *Le droit de la guerre et de la paix*, 1:107, 157–160 (emphasis added).

56. Bodin, *Les six livres de la République*, 105–106.

57. Louvigny au comte de Toulouse, Québec, October 1, 1717, AN, Col., C[11A], vol. 37, fol. 325v.

58. Talon au ministre Colbert, September 20, 1670, in Roy, *Rapport de l'archiviste de la province de Québec*, 11:118.

59. AN, Col., C[11A], vol. 21, f. 60.

60. AN, Col., C[11A], vol. 22, f. 280. See also Mémoire touchant le droit françois sur les nations iroquoises, September 12, 1712, AN, Col., C[11A], vol. 33, fol. 284.

61. Louis XIV à Duchesneau, April 30, 1681, AN, Col., C[11A], vol. 5, fol. 344–345; Memoire du Roy pour les sieurs de Frontenac et de Champigny, Versailles, May 26, 1696, AN, Col., B, vol. 19, fol. 85; Mémoire instructif des intentions de sa majesté pour le Canada, 1716, AN, Col., C[11A], vol. 36, fol. 44.

62. Relation de ce qui s'est passé de plus remarquable en Canada depuis le départ des vaisseaux de 1695 jusques au commencement de novembre 1696, AN, Col., C[11A], vol. 14, fol. 40. See also *Dictionnaire de l'Académie française* (Paris: Imprimeur ordinaire du roi, 1694), "Gouverner."

63. Gabriel Naudé, *Science des Princes, ou Considérations politiques sur les coups-d'état* (Rome: 1639). See also Louis Marin, "Pour une théorie baroque de l'action politique, Lecture des *Considérations politiques sur les coups d'État* de Gabriel Naudé," in *Considérations politiques sur les coups d'État* (Paris: Éditions de Paris, 1988), 74–78, 87–88, 121, 143–144; Pierre Charron, *De la sagesse* (Paris: 1671), 440, 444; Durand, *L'ordre du monde*, 83–88.

64. Instructions du Roy pour Vaudreuil de Cavaignal, AN, Col., C[11A], vol. 100, fol. 50–51, cited in Maxime Gohier, *Onontio le médiateur: la gestion des conflits amérindiens en Nouvelle-France, 1603–1717* (Sillery, Q.C.: Éditions du Septentrion, 2008), 229.

65. Michel Foucault, *Il faut défendre la société* (Paris: Gallimard/Seuil, 1997), 16. See also Guillaume Boccara, *Guerre et ethnogenèse mapuche dans le Chili colonial: l'invention du soi* (Paris: L'Harmattan, 1998), 177–267.

66. See Gohier, *Onontio le médiateur*, 24–41.

67. Kinga Maria Kantorska, "Les médiations françaises auprès des Couronnes du Nord au XVIIe siècle: les tentatives d'arbitrage," in Bély, *L'invention de la diplomatie*, 231–232; Gohier, *Onontio le médiateur*, 40.

68. Bély, *L'art de la paix en Europe*, 324–325.

69. Ibid., 327.

70. Gilles Havard, "D'un Callières l'autre ou comment le protocole diplomatique louis-quatorzien s'adaptait aux Amérindiens," in *Mémoires de Nouvelle-France: De France en Nouvelle-France*, ed. Philippe Joutard and Thomas Wien (Rennes: Presses universitaires de Rennes, 2005), 199–208.

71. François de Callières, *De la manière de négocier avec les souverains, de l'utilité des négociations, du choix des ambassadeurs & des envoyez, et des qualitez necessaires pour réüssir dans ces emplois* (Amsterdam: 1716), 18; Kantorska, "Les médiations françaises," 231–234.

72. Memoire de Duchesneau au ministre Colbert, Québec, November 13, 1681, AN, Col., C[11A], vol. 5, fol. 308rv.

73. Mémoire de Talon au Roy, Québec, November 2, 1671, in *Collections de manuscrits contenant lettres, mémoires et autres documents historiques relatifs*

à la Nouvelle-France, ed. Jean Blanchet, 4 vols. (Quebec: A. Côté & Cie, 1883–1885), 1:214.

74. Havard, *Great Peace of Montreal*, 98, 155; Bacqueville de la Potherie, *Histoire de l'Amérique septentionale*, 4:241.

75. See Bély, *L'art de la paix en Europe*, 311; Havard, *Empire et métissages*, 404–414. For a comparison with the Spanish experience in the Americas, see Guillaume Boccara, "Structure, histoire, pouvoir: penser les frontières améric-aines," in *Pour une histoire souterraine des Amériques: jeux de mémoires—Enjeux d'identités*, ed. Anath Ariel de Vidas (Paris: L'Harmattan, 2008), 15–44.

76. Bély, *Les relations internationales en Europe*, 277; Bély, *L'art de la paix en Europe*, 363–364; Cornette, *Le roi de guerre*, 144–145.

77. Grotius, *Le droit de la guerre et de la paix*, 1:164–165.

78. Jean Bérenger, "Provinces conquises, Provinces-frontières," in *Dictionnaire de l'Ancien Régime: royaume de France, XVIe-XVIIIe siècle*, ed. Lucien Bély (Paris: Presses universitaires de France, 1996), 1037; Constant, "Les traités"; Durand, *L'ordre du monde*, 13; Goubert and Roche, *Les Français et l'Ancien Régime*, 1:258.

79. Alain Lottin, "Artois," in Bély, *Dictionnaire de l'Ancien Régime*, 91.

80. Olivier Chaline, *Le règne de Louis XIV* (Paris: Flammarion, 2005), 459.

81. François-Xavier Emmanuelli, "Provence," in Bély, *Dictionnaire de l'Ancien Régime*, 1035.

82. Cited in Sylvain Soleil, "Centralisation et décentralisation à la française: histoire, modèles et théorie," conférence anniversaire, 15 ans, ressources con-sultant finances, June 29, 2006, http://www.ressources-consultants.eu/IMG/pdf/Memoire116.pdf; Vital Chomel, "Dauphiné," in Bély, *Dictionnaire de l'Ancien Régime*, 387.

83. Pierre Goubert, *Mazarin* (Paris: Fayard, 1990), 66.

84. Lettre de Vaudreuil a Mr Nicolson, January 14, 1711, AN, Col., C^{11A}, vol. 31, fol. 112v.

85. See Cornelius Jaenen, "French Sovereignty and Native Nationhood during the French Regime," in *Sweet Promises: A Reader on Indian-White Relations in Canada*, ed. James R. Miller (Toronto: University of Toronto Press, 1991), 30.

86. Cornette, *La monarchie entre Renaissance et Révolution*, 246.

87. Réponse au mémoire de sa Majesté britannique au sujet du fort de Niagara, AN., Col., C^{11E}, vol. 3, fol. 201–208. The Iroquois were considered British subjects since the Treaty of Utrecht in 1713. Yet when referring to a rival power, the colonial discourse demonstrated that the Indians had not been subjugated or put down. For example, in 1748 the French required the Iro-quois to sign an "act of independence" to deny British sovereignty. Thus there are inherent contradictions in the colonial discourse, and it is through those

contradictions that one can best see proof of Indian sovereignty. AN, Col., C¹¹ᴬ, vol. 91, fol. 251–254.

88. Sahlins, *Unnaturally French*, 11.

89. For more on the end of the civilizing program, see Saliha Belmessous, "Assimilation and Racialism in Seventeenth- and Eighteenth-Century French Colonial Policy," *American Historical Review* 110 (April 2005): 337. On the geopolitical significance of the *Pays d'en Haut*, see Havard, *Empire et métissages*, 91–95.

The French and the Natchez
A Failed Encounter

ARNAUD BALVAY

THE NATCHEZ LIVED IN SEVERAL VILLAGES COVERING A ZONE ABOUT forty miles long on the east bank of the Mississippi River, near present-day Natchez, Mississippi. At the end of the seventeenth century, they constituted the most powerful indigenous nation of the area. Yet they are essentially forgotten today, especially in France, where they are basically absent from the limited collective memories of the French colonial experience in the present-day southern United States. Some know the Natchez through François-René de Chateaubriand's 1826 novel, *Les Natchez*, although they are probably only a handful.[1] This oblivion is rather counterintuitive, for few other indigenous groups have aroused as rich and detailed ethnographic observations as the Natchez.

The "ordered" worship, sacred mounds, human sacrifices, tattooed warriors, absolute-looking monarch, and class-based society of the Natchez greatly fascinated early eighteenth-century French settlers in Louisiana. Some of these colonists wrote detailed memoirs about the Natchez, and many of these have been preserved in the French national archives. In the twentieth century, several American anthropologists aimed to describe and analyze the social organization of the Natchez based on the division between the nobility and the commoners. Some of the works published by these anthropologists attempted to explain the famous "Natchez paradox."[2] American historians also studied the Natchez society, notably through their relations with the French.[3] The aim of this essay is to sum up that history since the first French-Natchez meeting in 1682 until 1736, evoke the 1729 Natchez rebellion during which more than 200 French people were killed, and finally explain the reasons for the uprising.

THE BEGINNING

The first meeting between the French and the Natchez took place in March 1682, when the expedition of René-Robert Cavelier, Sieur de la Salle, voyaged down the Mississippi River. The French explorer and his companions visited the Grand Village and were welcomed by the chief. Cavelier de la Salle's associate, Henri de Tonty, described and evaluated Natchez territory: "Their lands support maize, all kinds of fruit, olive trees and vineyards. One can see large grasslands, big forests, all kinds of livestock; fishing and hunting are their occupations and their wealth."[4] Nicolas de la Salle, who was part of the expedition of Cavelier de la Salle, noted that the Natchez's huts "look like a dome; with large canes which support them to the top. They are fifteen feet tall, do not have any windows, but a square door which is four feet tall."[5] The Natchez impressed the French during this first visit. Part of this rested in the military strength of the Natchez. Tonty commented on how the Natchez were able to amass a force of more than 3,000 armed warriors. According to their own criteria, the French thought of the Natchez as more "civilized"[6] than the other Native Americans they had encountered and developed relationships with farther north: "They are very different from our savages from Canada in their housing, clothing, morals, inclinations, and customs . . . their chiefs have all the authority . . . they have their servants and their officers who follow them and serve them everywhere. They present the favors and gifts at their goodwill. . . . In a word, one finds there commonly some men."[7] Cavelier de la Salle and the Grand Village chief smoked the calumet during this first visit, and the explorer came away with a favorable impression of the relationship that had been forged. During the official French appropriation of Louisiana on April 9, 1682, Cavelier de la Salle declared that the Natchez, as well as other Amerindian nations met during his journey, consented to recognize French supremacy and were allies.[8] Despite the declaration, the alliance was young and seemingly fragile, because only days later, during the French ascent of the Mississippi, the Natchez turned extremely hostile and forced the French to leave the region.[9]

Between 1699 and 1702, when Pierre Le Moyne, Sieur d'Iberville, led three successive expeditions to establish the colony of Louisiana, the Natchez received him particularly well. They even agreed to welcome missionary François de Montigny, who sought to evangelize them. To explain this warm reception, it is necessary to note that the Natchez were at war with the Chickasaws. English traders from Carolina had supplied the Chickasaws with firearms, which made alliance with the French very attractive. The

Natchez hoped to be able to better resist the Chickasaw attacks thanks to the alliance with the French, for, at the very minimum, there would have to be some commercial exchanges, and the Natchez thought they would obtain firearms.

THE DISCOVERY OF THE NATCHEZ NATION

In the Natchez, the French encountered a nation "less barbaric" than the other Amerindian nations—according to the criteria of the time. The French began to note details about the Natchez's morals and habits, and it was from this moment that they became fascinated with the Natchez and their social organization. One of the prominent authors writing about this nation was Antoine-Simon Le Page du Pratz,[10] who lived among the Natchez and described their sociopolitical system in detail. Divided into nine villages, the Natchez society was a very hierarchical theocracy with, on the one hand, the "nobility," made up of "Suns" (or leaders), "Noblemen," and "Considered"; and, on the other hand, the common people, called "Stinkards," although "it was not decent to pronounce this word in front of them."[11] According to eighteenth-century French observers, the Great Chief or Great Sun had absolute power over his nation.[12] He had the power of life and death over his subjects, who paid him tribute. His life was structured according to a well-established set of protocols, and all his subjects owed him respect. Master carpenter André Pénicaut wrote that "his servants do not approach him out of respect; when they talk to him, they stand four feet away from him. . . . When he gets up, all his relatives or some old 'considered' men approach his bed and, raising their arms, they make horrible screams. So they salute him without him deigning to look at them."[13] Furthermore, when a Sun died, humans were sacrificed to accompany him in the afterlife. The rules of marriage and succession were extremely complex. Indeed, Suns could not marry commoners; their male children dropped a notch in the hierarchy and thus became merely "Nobles," whereas the females kept their Sun status. The power of the Great Sun was passed on to the son of his sister. For several decades, anthropologists have attempted to understand how this system worked, and in doing so have at times employed the Natchez paradox.[14]

THE FIRST SUSTAINED CONTACTS AND TENSIONS

In 1700, missionary Jean-François Buisson de Saint-Cosme settled among the Natchez and lived with them for six years.[15] This priest was quickly discouraged in his attempt to convert the nation to Catholicism. Saint-Cosme argued that Natchez social structure and organization made conversion extremely difficult and noted that there was little he could do to convince them to abandon their faith because they were completely subjected to their leader, who was considered a descendant of the celestial sun and thus a demigod.[16]

Following Saint-Cosme's death in 1706,[17] the French neglected to maintain relations with the Natchez because they were preoccupied with their own survival in Mobile, farther south.[18] The colonists received practically no help from metropolitan France, which was mired in the long War of the Spanish Succession (1701–1714), and depended almost completely on the generosity of the nearby Amerindians. Resources became so scarce that Governor Jean-Baptiste Le Moyne, Sieur de Bienville, was even obliged to send volunteers to go live in the native villages so that there would be fewer mouths to feed in the colony.[19]

Seeing Louisiana's weakened position, English traders visited the Amerindian nations of the region and tried to convince them to join their side. In 1708, English captain Thomas Welch managed to hold a meeting at the Yazous, where he had also gathered the Natchez and the Taensas, and tried to persuade them to join the British cause. Five years later, when the French finally established a trading post among the Natchez, the chief of the expedition, Captain de La Loire, found three English traders and an officer named Hugues. They were from Carolina and had come to the Natchez to engage them to wage war against other Amerindian nations in order to collect slaves.[20] According to Pénicaut, the Natchez had already seized eleven Chaouachas slaves.[21] Soon after, La Loire received the order to arrest Hugues. La Loire questioned him and learned that the British officer planned to travel down the Mississippi River to meet the Colapissas. The French officer then decided to leave the Natchez with Pénicaut and go downstream to wait for Hugues and seize him as he did not dare arrest him "in the Natchez village because the Natives would have opposed it."[22] This sentence by Pénicaut is particularly important for it shows that the English had already established a foothold among the Natchez. The governor of Carolina had commissioned Hugues to prepare Natchez territory for British westward expansion.[23] British presence in Natchez territory certainly threatened French-Natchez relations. Yet the French observed that two clans had developed within the Natchez nation: one pro-English and the other pro-French. This caused considerable tension, both within the Natchez nation and between the Natchez and the French.

This tension led to a short conflict in 1716. The governor of Louisiana, Antoine Laumet dit de Lamothe, Sieur de Cadillac, had passed through Natchez territory the previous year on his way to the Illinois Country in order to search out suitable locations for developing mines. Discovering none, he retraced his steps toward Mobile, but he neglected to smoke the peace pipe with the Natchez in order to maintain their alliance. This refusal to renew the friendship between the Natchez and the French was interpreted as a declaration of war. Not long after, news reached Mobile that the Natchez had killed four French travelers and plundered the trading post in their territory.

As a result, Cadillac asked Bienville, who was then *lieutenant du roi* and commandant of the Louisiana troops, to punish the Natchez. Bienville departed with thirty-four men, but this was hardly a real threat to the Natchez. Estimates of the Natchez warriors numbered between 800 and 1,500.[24] Upon arriving close to Natchez territory, Bienville deceived the Natchez by asking their leaders to come to his small and well-entrenched camp under the pretext of negotiating an alliance. Once the Suns arrived, Bienville arrested them and held them hostage until their subjects brought Bienville the heads of those who had killed the French traders. Natchez from the pro-English villages were brought in and executed, which only strengthened the anti-French clan. However, almost immediately following the incident, a peace was struck. According to the terms of the peace treaty, the Natchez supplied all the material to build a fortification for the French, Fort Rosalie. Although the fort was officially justified as a way to improve relations between the French and the Natchez, the fort's prime aim was in fact to protect trade and prevent the intrusion of British traders.

This first Natchez "war" in 1716 underscored the changes that had been taking place within Natchez society and the effects of contact with the French and British. Imperial competition had created a rift among the Natchez that ultimately called into question the supposed omnipotence of the chief—the Great Sun. Despite being pro-French, the chief was unable to prevent his subjects from the White Apple village, who were pro-British, from attacking the French. According to Saint-Cosme's account of Natchez society, this type of defiance would have been unthinkable only years earlier. Faced with the growing influence of defiant pro-British factions within Natchez society, Bienville's expedition came just at the right moment for the chief because it allowed the Great Sun to get rid of opposition leaders.

THE FRENCH COLONIZATION OF NATCHEZ TERRITORY

The great fortune and misfortune of the Natchez was that they lived on magnificent and extremely fertile land. French colonization of the Mississippi valley began in earnest when John Law launched his famous Company of the West and several land concessions were established at Natchez. During the 1720s, 4,000 colonists landed in Louisiana, and Natchez country rapidly became the center of colonization efforts.[25] Colonists settled down mostly in the outskirts of the Natchez villages. They were generally well received, and they easily acquired lands abandoned by the natives after crop rotation or given to them against payment.[26] The colonists then embarked on an extensive agricultural program, steered by the East India Company, which demanded, first and foremost, the cultivation of tobacco and indigo cash crops. As they were short of manpower to exploit these large lands, the colonists very quickly required the hands of enslaved workers. Numerous slaves came to Louisiana, mainly from Senegal, and were transported to French colonial land concessions in the Natchez territory. The two most important concessions were Sainte-Catherine and Terre Blanche (White Earth). Founded by the commissary-general of Louisiana, Marc-Antoine Hubert, Sainte-Catherine boasted numerous slaves, cattle, and even a mill. Terre Blanche belonged to the secretary of state for war, Claude le Blanc.

At first, French settlers and soldiers at Fort Rosalie appear to have been on friendly terms with the Natchez. Le Page du Pratz described how some French colonists worked with the Natchez to prepare and sow their fields.[27] Other French colonial accounts echoed Le Page du Pratz and depicted the reciprocal relationship between the Natchez and newly established French settlers. For example, Jean-François-Benjamin Dumont de Montigny wrote that the Natchez worked as hunters, pickaxed the lands, or brought some firewood, poultry, maize, or bear oil to the colonists who, in exchange, gave them goods.[28] However, these amicable relationships were short-lived. While early settlement saw a great deal of cooperation between the French and the Natchez, the ever-increasing number of colonists soon provoked new tensions.

THE TENSIONS OF 1722

As tensions increased with the Natchez, the strength of Fort Rosalie's garrison decreased to about twenty soldiers by staff shortage. The French dependence on the Natchez, particularly in regard to food and labor, abated as African slaves were brought to Natchez.[29] These various factors explain why some Natchez from the pro-English White Apple village suddenly attacked the Sainte-Catherine concession in 1722. In February, the concession's director complained of stolen cattle and slaughtered horses.[30] Tensions continued to escalate and, months later, boiled over, leading to a second "war" with the Natchez. French-native relations in North America had largely been built upon a foundation of trade—imperial goods, food, pelts, and so forth. Like many other nations with which the French dealt, the Natchez were eager for manufactured products. Many Natchez gradually became indebted to the French settlers and soldiers, leading to regular quarrels. In 1722, a quarrel between a French sergeant and his Natchez debtor degenerated. The wife of a sergeant Fontaine called in reinforcements from Fort Rosalie, and the French soldiers killed the Amerindian, a resident of the Natchez pro-English village. The White Apple village's leader, according to the French witnesses, had only been waiting for an excuse to take revenge for the death of his relative, one of the former pro-English leaders executed by Bienville during the first Natchez "war" in 1716. In response to the incident at Fort Rosalie in 1722, the White Apple village's leader and his men began harassing the concession of Sainte-Catherine. Not long after hostilities began, this group of pro-English Natchez ambushed the manager of the concession, a Mr. Guénot, and shot him to death. Immediately, pro-French Natchez jumped in to play the mediator between the French and their pro-English fellow countrymen. The brother of the Great Sun, the powerful war chief named the Tattooed Serpent, made several trips between the concession, Fort Rosalie, and the "rebel" villages in order to reassure the French of Great Sun's loyalty. Moreover, the pro-French Natchez sought to convince the French that the Great Sun's power still extended to all the Natchez villages and that he had the power to make the "rebels" fall back into line. The sequence of these events exposed the dualism that existed among the Natchez and proved how much this cleavage had profoundly shaken both the social organization and cohesion of the nation since 1716.

THE 1723 EXPEDITION

Once again, in 1723 Bienville was sent to resolve the problem for the French. In 1716, Bienville had a small force and had to rely primarily on trickery to accomplish his goal. This time he was able to assemble a much larger expedition because he could rely on French colonists and the troops sent by the Company of the Indies. Bienville did not set out to attack the entire Natchez nation, but rather to destroy the "rebel" villages. He went directly to the village of White Apple, where his expeditionary force razed deserted houses and proceeded to arrest and enslave a number of men and women. Having made this punitive expedition, however, Bienville soon realized that the culprits he sought were elsewhere. Indeed, he discovered that the alleged harassment of the Sainte-Catherine concession was in fact a ruse—the product of Frenchmen from the concession who had killed the cattle for food and then arranged things to look like the Natchez were responsible for slaughtering the cattle and plundering the concession. Embarrassed, Bienville wrote in his report:

> Being informed that the savages of the Apple and the Noyeux villages did not quite commit the evil that one imputes them to have done to the concession of Sainte-Catherine, the enlisted men of this concession having had a lot of share . . . and even more the French gave occasion to all the disorders that these savages could cause by the mistreatments they could do to them beating them and shackling them on simple refusals to give them what they had.[31]

Realizing that he had been deceived, Bienville moved quickly to conclude a peace with the Tattooed Serpent and to restore good relations between the French and Natchez. In an attempt to redress the balance of power, the peace treaty outlined that Fort Rosalie's commandant would henceforth do everything he could to see proper justice done to the Natchez in cases of altercations with the settlers. Bienville also took the opportunity to ask for the heads of "the most rebellious" pro-English leaders. The Great Sun and his brother granted this request in an attempt to strengthen their declining power.[32]

The Natchez's attitude toward the French following the tensions of 1722 proves that Bienville's expedition constituted a real breach in the French and Natchez relationships. Indeed, the Natchez saw the French incursion as an injustice, highlighted by the fact that numerous settlers took part in the expedition. Le Page du Pratz wrote that the Natchez rarely came to visit him after 1723. Even his good friend the Tattooed Serpent, who was a faithful supporter of the French, went to Fort Rosalie only when summoned by the commandant. When Le Page du Pratz questioned him to ascertain the reason for his resentment, the Tattooed Serpent seemed to be embarrassed and asked if the French "have two hearts, a good one today, and tomorrow a bad one?" He added that his fellow countrymen did not know what to think of the French, "who after having begun the war, granted a peace, and themselves offered it; and then at the time we were quiet, believing ourselves to be at peace, people come to kill us without saying a word."[33] When Le Page du Pratz asked him to explain further, the Tattooed Serpent embarked on a long discourse in which he told of the Natchez bitterness:

> Why did the French come into our country? We did not seek them: they asked us for land, because their country was too little for all the men that were in it. We told them they might take land where they pleased, there was enough for them and for us; that it was good the same sun should enlighten us both, and that we would walk as friends on the same path; and that we would give them of our provisions, assist them to build, and to labor in their fields. We have done so; is not this true? What occasion then had we for Frenchmen? Before they came, did we not live better than we do now, seeing we deprive ourselves of a part of our corn, our game, and fish, to give a part to them? In what respect, then, had we occasioned for them? Was it for their guns? The bows and arrows which we used, were sufficient to make us live well. Was it for their white, blue, and red blankets? We can do well enough with buffalo skins, which are warmer; our women wrought feather-blankets for the winter, and mulberry-mantles for the summer; which indeed were not so beautiful; but our women were more laborious and less vain than they are now. In fine, before the arrival of the French, we lived like men who can be satisfied with what they have; whereas at this day we are like slaves, who are not suffered to do as they please.[34]

The settlers' greed for Natchez land and the problem of indebtedness to French settlers and soldiers only added to the rancor of the Natchez, who increasingly felt like intruders in their own territory. Natchez chiefs, such as the Tattooed Serpent, felt this humiliation all the more as their authority, once nearly beyond reproach, declined and was regularly questioned. Social reorganization of Natchez society in the wake of European contact represented a fall from grace for Natchez chiefs that must have been difficult to endure. And yet Tattooed Serpent's discourse to Le Page du Pratz rendered a sentiment that many Natchez felt, as they became increasingly aware of the decay of their society, which was hastened by illness and exacerbated by their dependence on the French.

THE LAST ACT

The Tattooed Serpent died in 1725, followed by the Great Sun three years later. These two losses were irreparable for the French because these two leaders had been the mainstays of the French-Natchez alliance. But the French did not seem to realize what they had lost. The pro-French Natchez were the only ones to perceive that the political balance was shifting within their nation.

In 1728, the Great Chief was replaced by a man named, curiously enough, Saint-Cosme, just like the missionary who had attempted to convert the Natchez years earlier. According to Le Page du Pratz, this Natchez leader was rather young and inexperienced.[35] One year after taking power, on the morning of November 28, 1729, the Natchez went in small groups to all of the French houses as well as to the fort. At a given signal, they killed almost everyone, sparing only the women, children, and slaves, and plundered all the houses around Natchez before departing.[36] The news of the destruction of the Natchez post arrived in New Orleans on December 2, and immediately caused a panic among the French inhabitants, who feared that the entire colony of Louisiana could fall victim to the Amerindian nations. The arrival of local Native Americans offering their services to help avenge the French only increased feelings of paranoia.[37] In light of the attack at Natchez, the French were very uneasy about a prospective joint Amerindian-French response, convinced that local natives were only coming to spy and plot future surprise attacks. The slightest movement provoked fear of the apocalypse.

The rumor of a general Amerindian plot quickly took shape, and the French organized a relatively weak defense. The attack at Natchez gave rise to another fear, even more terrifying to the colonists than that of an Amerindian attack, the possibility of the slaves and Amerindians uniting in order to exterminate them. To counter both of these potential scenarios, Louisiana governor Étienne Périer found nothing better to do than to engage New Orleans's slaves to massacre a small neighboring nation, the Chaouachas. In his letter to the secretary of state for the navy, the governor justified his actions, writing that "the fear got such the upper hand that [even the] Chaouachas, who were a nation of thirty men living south of New Orleans, shook our inhabitants, which made me decide to have them destroyed by our negroes."[38] Périer did not seem to be aware of the injustice he had committed and seemed convinced that this action had kept the other small nations at bay.[39]

In January 1730, a first expedition was led against the Natchez. A French army led by Henri de Loubois stopped at the Tonicas' village to wait for Choctaw warriors led by a French officer named Le Sueur, but the Choctaws attacked the Natchez directly and removed the women and the children, who were kept prisoners. Learning of this attack, Loubois laid siege to the Natchez forts, but the Natchez succeeded in escaping and took refuge on the west bank of the Mississippi.

Reinforcements arrived from France at the end of the year, and Governor Périer personally led a second expedition in early 1731. Once the Natchez forts were located, the French laid a traditional siege, and the Natchez quickly surrendered under the pressure of sustained French bombardment. The Grand Sun Saint-Cosme, as well as most of the families, were then sent to New Orleans and were subsequently shipped to Saint-Domingue to be sold as slaves. Nevertheless, hundreds of Natchez succeeded in escaping and continued to harass the French settlers and soldiers. Several skirmishes with intermittent attempts at restoring the peace took place until 1736. By 1736, the Natchez had taken refuge among the Chickasaws, which led to two conflicts between the French and the Chickasaws. In the 1740s, the Natchez went to live among the Creeks and the Cherokees. However, by then the Natchez nation no longer existed as an independent political entity.

THE CAUSES OF THE NATCHEZ REVOLT

At the time, the Natchez revolt was placed in the framework of a general Indian plot, as mentioned earlier. Yet several facts dispute this version. First of all, when Governor Périer wrote to Versailles to transmit the news of the destruction of the Natchez post, he mentioned no such plot. He mentioned the plot in later correspondence, but without providing any proof.[40] Yet many French authors in the eighteenth and nineteenth centuries adopted the plot theory. Those who wrote on this subject some years later again used this story and embellished it with more and more details of how the plot had been planned and why it had not been carried out.[41] However, the leader of the colonial militia, a Mr. du Laye, formally disputed this theory, writing:

> some people want that this Plot was general . . . and that the Choctaws should have struck on New Orleans at the same time as the Natchez, but the latter struck too early.
>
> Those who are of this feeling do not know the colony nor the savages, and do not know all that took place since the beginning of this affair. The Choctaws

are enemies and for a very long time, of the Natchez. . . . They did not know anything at all, because they learnt of this massacre by way of the French. The Natchez kept this affair very secret; they did not want to communicate it to any nation for fear of being betrayed.[42]

In Paris, the Company of the Indies was in no way convinced by the plot theory either. The general controller, who was in charge of the company, let it be known to Périer and wrote him:

> as you do not give any proof of the general conspiracy that you claim to have been formed by all the nations at the prompting of the English, I found it quite difficult to persuade myself. . . . I believe on the contrary that if it had any foundation, the Choctaws would not have marched at M. Le Sueur's first word for the service of the French as they did and which I am most pleased of.[43]

Another alternative interpretation comes from a document that pointed to the massacre as the result of a British plot. An anonymous author wrote of how he had been charged by Cardinal Fleury, Louis XV's main secretary of state, to get some tobacco worthy of Virginia's, which was considered at the time to be of the highest quality. Fostering a French tobacco industry had become a pressing concern because each year France was spending more than six million livres to buy tobacco from England. Unfortunately, the tobacco produced in Louisiana was disappointing and was hardly any better than that produced in France. The Company of the Indies asked its agent in London to buy tobacco and to send a spy to Virginia in order to bring back various kinds of seeds. The spy succeeded in his mission and brought back "small packages of Virginia's earth which produced these different sorts of seeds so that by the degustation of these different earths and the chemical analysis that we would do of it, we could choose Louisiana's lands which are the most similar to the quality of Virginia's soils." He also submitted a report on how to cultivate the tobacco. The company gave him the 6,000 livres of reward that it had promised him "provided that he would go to Louisiana with proportioned wages and that in concert with the governors and the main employees of the Company, he would endeavor to have the same seeds he had to bring there cultivated by our colonists." The company subsequently founded a tobacco farm in Natchez country, but soon after the anonymous author learned "that the British had debauched the Natchez and destroyed the first cultures of these seeds."[44] According to this anonymous account, the massacre could only have been the result of a clever plot hatched by the British to preserve the English seizure of the

French tobacco market. This story is incredible, but no more so than the other conspiracy theory involving a general Indian plot. Another author, without providing any information regarding the spy's mission, wrote that "all the various views that the 'savages' have expressed since this affair make you know enough that the English have fomented and set the savage nations against the French because of the feeling of jealousy that they have conceived regarding the tobacco plantations in the said place, as we are in the habit of drawing them from their plantations for the most part of what is consumed in France."[45]

In France, members of the Company of the Indies and the royal court were remarkably well informed regarding events in Louisiana and accused Fort Rosalie's commandant, d'Etcheparre (also called Chépart or Chopart), as being responsible for the Natchez revolt. Eighteenth-century writers ultimately retained this theory and incorporated it into the written histories of Louisiana and the Natchez revolt. They all systematically accused d'Etcheparre of being at the origin of the uprising.[46] He was depicted as a tyrannical commandant who tortured French settlers and Native Americans alike with his oppressive policies. According to these authors, the Natchez had decided to rebel only after the commandant had given them an order to evacuate the openly pro-English White Apple village. The commandant's motivation for evacuating the village was supposedly in order to establish his own personal concession. It was deemed that the commandant's actions pushed the Natchez to attack the French in response for being expelled from their village and territory. It is important to underscore the fact that the authors who promoted this interpretation had a good understanding of the Natchez's motivations and thought the Natchez rebelled because they had no other option. Dumont de Montigny, for example, wrote:

> God, who is just, abandoned this post [Natchez] because his chief had reached the most supreme degree of arrogance so that we could not talk to him anymore. He threatened to exterminate the savages, he mistreated the inhabitants, despised the officer, punished the soldier wildly, deserted the service and only considered to fill his purse and to construct a magnificent house in his spirit and that it would not cost him a lot, imitating by his actions Baltazar, King of Babylon, who by his arrogance incurred the wrath of God and the warrant of his condemnation and the loss of his kingdom, such was indeed that of Sr De chepare.[47]

A letter from Raymond Amyault, Sieur d'Auseville, argues that the governor of Louisiana was involved in the effort to set up a new concession and that d'Etcheparre did not act unilaterally.[48] According to d'Ausseville, Périer spread the conspiracy theory in order to distract people from focusing on d'Etcheparre's mistreatment of the Natchez and to keep his own name from being implicated in the controversy surrounding the revolt. In particular, Périer was trying to avoid judgment for not having recalled d'Etcheparre earlier. However, this hypothesis is not very well-founded. There is no proof of the Périer-d'Etcheparre association, beyond the accusations found in d'Ausseville's letter and one manuscript written by an anonymous author. These accusations were likely the product of an old dispute between the governor and the authors of the letter and manuscript.

Finally, there is a responsibility that virtually no one has established in the eighteenth century, that of the Company of the Indies. Over the years, the Natchez had become the center of attention for the company, which expected a lot from its investment in tobacco production. In 1726, the company gave instructions to Périer and recommended that he go to Natchez and examine "if he thought it was dangerous to leave these villages where they are and [if it was not the case] he would make a present to the leaders to determine them to go away."[49] Regardless of whether the governor gave the order to evacuate the Natchez village or was involved in the decisions surrounding the revolt, it is quite clear that the Company of the Indies's colonizing interests in Natchez were largely responsible for the unfortunate outcome of the French-Natchez interactions.

Commandant d'Etcheparre likely tyrannized the Natchez, but it can hardly be said that his predecessors had been more humane in their treatment of the local natives. It is necessary to add the important colonization of Natchez and the presence of numerous French colonists as a good motivation for the Natchez to rebel. French settlers lived in a culturally French way among fellow countrymen even if they were also in relations with the natives. Being superior in force, the colonists did not hesitate to mistreat the Indians. Le Page du Pratz mentions the supposed words of an old chief during the preparation of the revolt. Obviously, Le Page du Pratz did not attend this meeting, but his words translate well what the Natchez felt:

> We have a long time been aware that the neighborhood of the French brings a greater harm than benefit to us. . . . Before the French came amongst us, we were men, content with what we had, and that was sufficient: with boldness we walked every road, because we were then our own masters: but now we go groping, afraid of meeting thorns, we walk like slaves, which we shall soon be, since the French already treat us as if we were such. When they are sufficiently strong, they will no longer exercise politics. For the smallest fault of our young people,

they will tie them to a post, and whip them as they do their black slaves. Have they not already done so to one of our young men; and is not death preferable to slavery?[50]

NOTES

The author thanks Benn E. Williams from the Center for French Colonial Studies for his assistance in writing this article. All translations from French are from the author unless otherwise noted.

1. See François-René de Chateaubriand, *Les Natchez: roman indien par le Vicomte de Châteaubriand*, 3 vols. (Paris: E. Droz, 1826).

2. The so-called paradox concerns the Natchez kinship system. If all men and women of the upper castes had to marry members of the commoner caste, some anthropologists concluded that in ten generations the population of commoners would disappear unless replenished by adoptions or conquests. The paradox was first elaborated by C. W. M. Hart, "A Reconsideration of Natchez Social Structure," *American Anthropologist* 45 (July–September 1943): 379–386. See also Jeffrey P. Brain, "The Natchez 'Paradox,'" *Ethnology* 10 (April 1971): 215–222; Carol Mason, "Natchez Class Structure," *Ethnohistory* 11 (Spring 1964): 120–133; Douglas R. White, George P. Murdock, and Richard Scaglion, "Natchez Class and Rank Reconsidered," *Ethnology* 10 (October 1971): 369–388. For a good summary of the debate, see Patricia Galloway and Jason Baird Jackson, "Natchez and Neighboring Groups," in *Handbook of North American Indians*, ed. William C. Sturtevant, 17 vols. (Washington, D.C.: Smithsonian Institution, 1978–2008), 14:598–615.

3. Andrew C. Albrecht, "Indian-French Relations at Natchez," *American Anthropologist*, New Series 48 (July–September 1946): 321–354; Patricia D. Woods, "The French and the Natchez Indians in Louisiana: 1700–1731," in *The Louisiana Purchase Bicentennial Series in Louisiana History*, vol. 1: *The French Experience in Louisiana*, ed. Glenn R. Conrad (Lafayette: University of Southwestern Louisiana, 1995), 278–295; Jim Barnett, *The Natchez Indians* (Natchez, Miss.: Department of Archives and History Popular Report, 1998).

4. H. de Tonty, "Relation de la Louisianne et du Mississippi par le chevalier de Tonti," in Jean-Frédéric Bernard, *Recueil des voyages au Nord contenant divers mémoires très utiles au commerce et à la navigation*, 10 vols. (Amsterdam: 1715–1738), 5:127.

5. Nicolas de la Salle, "Récit de Nicolas de la Salle," in *Découvertes et établissements des Français dans l'Ouest et dans le Sud de l'Amérique septentrionale*, ed. Pierre

Margry, 6 vols. (Paris: D. Jouaust, 1879–1888), 1:558. Nicolas de la Salle was not related to Cavelier de la Salle. He later became a commissary in Louisiana.

6. For eighteenth-century Frenchmen, there were several "civilization markers": the settled way of life, the aptitude for work, subordination, and religious beliefs. See Arnaud Balvay, *L'épée et la plume: Amérindiens et soldats des Troupes de la Marine en Louisiane et au Pays d'en Haut, 1683–1763* (Quebec: Presses de l'Université Laval, 2006), 105–111.

7. Zénobe Membré, "Relation," in Chrestien Le Clercq, *Premier établissement de la foy dans la Nouvelle-France* (Paris: Amable Auroy, 1690), 258–259. In his *Dictionnaire*, published in 1690, Antoine Furetière wrote that "man distinguishes himself . . . according to his morals and his natural qualities. The Spaniards asked themselves if Indians were men, if we had to baptize them." Antoine Furetière, *Dictionnaire universel contenant généralement tous les mots françois, tant vieux que modernes, et les termes de toutes les sciences et des arts*, 3 vols. (La Haye: Pierre Husson et al., 1690). Membré used the word "man" in that meaning.

8. Jacques Métairie, "Procès-verbal de la prise de possession de la Louisiane," April 9, 1682, Archives nationales de France, Colonies (hereafter cited as AN, Col.), C^{13C}, vol. 3, fol. 28v.

9. Historians do not precisely know why the Natchez turned so hostile. There are several hypotheses: la Salle possibly irritated the Natchez by giving them Quinipissas' scalps, ignoring that the Quinipissas were their allies. It is also possible that the Natchez feared to be the target of slave catchers. Barnett, *Natchez Indians*, 29–32.

10. For more information about Le Page du Pratz, see Gordon Sayre, *Les Sauvages Américains: Representations of Native Americans in the French & English Colonial Literature* (Chapel Hill: University of North Carolina Press, 1997); Gordon Sayre, "Plotting the Natchez Massacre: Le Page du Pratz, Dumont de Montigny, Chateaubriand," *Early American Literature* 37 (2002): 381–413; Patricia K. Galloway, "Rhetoric of Difference: Le Page du Pratz on African Management in Eighteenth-Century Louisiana," *French Colonial History* 3 (2003): 1–15; Patricia K. Galloway, "Natchez Matrilineal Kinship: Du Pratz and the Woman's Touch," in *Practicing Ethnohistory: Mining Archives, Hearing Testimony, Constructing Narrative* (Lincoln: University of Nebraska Press, 2006), 97–108; Patricia K. Galloway, "Savage Medicine: Du Pratz and Eighteenth-century French Medical Practice," in *France in the New World: Proceedings of the 22nd Annual Meeting of the French Colonial Historical Society*, ed. David Buisseret (East Lansing: Michigan State University Press, 1998), 107–118; Shannon L. Dawdy, "Enlightenment from the Ground: Le Page du Pratz' *Histoire de la Louisiane*," *French Colonial History* 3 (2003): 17–34.

11. "Journal de d'Iberville," in Margry, *Découvertes et établissements*, 4:179; André Pénicaut, "Relation," in Margry, *Découvertes et établissements*, 5:441; Antoine-Simon Le Page du Pratz, *Histoire de la Louisiane*, 3 vols. (Paris: Bure, Delaguette et Lambert, 1758), 2:392–394.

12. Marc Villiers du Terrage, "Extrait d'un Journal de voyage en Louisiane du Père Paul du Ru (1700)," *Journal de la Société des Américanistes* 17 (1925): 126; Pénicaut, "Relation," 5:449–450; Le Page du Pratz, *Histoire de la Louisiane*, 3:54.

13. Pénicaut, "Relation," 5:450.

14. See note 2.

15. He replaced Father de Montigny, who gave up trying to convert the Natives.

16. Buisson de S[ain]t-Cosme, from Natchez, January 8, 1706, Séminaire de Québec, Lettres R, no. 40, fol. 2.

17. He was killed by some Chitimachas. Bienville to the Secretary of State, Fort de la Louisiane, February 20, 1707, AN, Col., C¹³A, vol. 1, fol. 11; Jean-Baptiste Bénard de la Harpe, *Journal historique de l'établissement des Français à la Louisiane* (Paris–New Orleans: Bossange-Boimare, 1831), 101.

18. They only went back to the Natchez villages in 1713.

19. See, for example, la Salle to the Secretary of State, Fort Louis de la Mobile, June 20, 1710, AN, Col., C¹³A, vol. 2, fol. 519; D'Artaguiette to the Secretary of State, Fort Louis de la Mobile, June 20, 1710, AN, Col., C¹³A, vol. 2, fol. 550. None of them tells who these natives were.

20. On the Indian slave trade in the Southeast, see Robbie F. Ethridge and Sheri M. Shuck-Hall, *Mapping the Mississippian Shatter Zone: The Colonial Indian Slave Trade and Regional Instability in the American South* (Lincoln: University of Nebraska Press, 2009); Allan Gallay, *The Indian Slave Trade: The Rise of the English Empire in the American South, 1670–1717* (New Haven, Conn.: Yale University Press, 2003); Daniel H. Usner, *Indians, Settlers, and Slaves in a Frontier Exchange Economy: The Lower Mississippi Valley before 1783* (Chapel Hill: University of North Carolina Press, 1992); David J. Libby, *Slavery and Frontier Mississippi, 1720–1835* (Jackson: University Press of Mississippi, 2008); George Edward Milne, "Rising Suns, Fallen Forts, and Impudent Immigrants: Race, Power, and War in the Lower Mississippi Valley" (Ph.D. diss., University of Oklahoma, 2006).

21. Pénicaut, "Relation," 5:506–507.

22. Ibid., 5:507. Pénicaut and de La Loire arrested Hugues, who was taken to Mobile. Bienville received the British officer very courteously and then enjoined him to go back to Carolina. Hugues was killed soon after by Native Americans as he was between Pensacola and Carolina.

23. Verner W. Crane, *The Southern Frontier, 1670–1732* (Tuscaloosa: University of Alabama Press, 2004), 105.

24. "Mémoire en forme de journal de ce qui s'est passé dans la première expédition que Mr de Bienville fit aux Natchez en 1716 pour forcer cette nation à lui faire satisfaction de cinq François qu'elle avait fait assassiner," AN, Col., C¹³ᴬ, vol. 4, fol. 787.

25. The Grand Village of the Natchez (also called "Les Natchez") was the center of the colonization because of the presence of Fort Rosalie nearby.

26. Jean-François-Benjamin Dumont de Montigny, *Mémoires historiques sur la Louisiane, contenant ce qui y est arrivé de plus mémorable depuis l'année 1687 jusqu'à present*, 2 vols. (Paris: Bauche, 1753), 2:93–94.

27. Le Page du Pratz, *Histoire de la Louisiane*, 1:193.

28. Dumont de Montigny, *Mémoires historiques sur la Louisiane*, 2:64.

29. Daniel H. Usner, *American Indians in the Lower Mississippi Valley: Social and Economic Histories* (Lincoln: University of Nebraska Press, 1998), 24.

30. "Relation de la guerre des sauvages Natchez," Received with M. de la Chaise's of 6th September 1723, AN, Col., 04DFC 31, fol. 1–2.

31. "Conseil de guerre assemblé par ordre de Monsieur de Bienville Commandant général de cette Province de la Louisiane composé de mondit sieur de Bienville, de Monsieur Pailhoux major général et de messieurs le blanc Berneval, Renault d'auterive, de desliette et de Tchepart Capitaines d'infanterie en l'hotel de mondit Sieur de Bienville pour deliberér s'il convient dans la situation ou sont les choses de continuer a faire la guerre aux villages de la pomme et des Voyas ou s'il est plus avantageux de leur acorder la paix a des conditions," AN, Col., C¹³ᴬ, vol. 7, fol. 173v-174.

32. Ibid.

33. Le Page du Pratz, *Histoire de la Louisiane*, 1:203.

34. Ibid., 1:203–205.

35. Ibid., 3:242.

36. Many authors wrote the story of that assault. See, for example, Dumont de Montigny, *Mémoires historiques sur la Louisiane*, 2:141–146; Le Page du Pratz, *Histoire de la Louisiane*, 3:255–258. See also Périer to the Secretary of State, New Orleans, March 18, 1730, attached to the letter sent on April 10, 1730, AN, Col., C¹³ᴬ, vol. 12, fol. 37–38v.

37. These natives were mostly the ones that the French called "*les Petites nations*" (small nations), such as the Chaouachas, Ossogoulas, Oumas, or Tapoussas.

38. Périer to the Secretary of State, New Orleans, March 18, 1730, AN, Col., C¹³ᴬ, vol. 12, fol. 39v.

39. Périer to the Secretary of State, New Orleans, March 18, 1730, AN, Col., C¹³ᴬ, vol. 12, fol. 40.

40. Writing to the secretary of state on December 5, 1729, Périer does not mention any plot. Périer to the Secretary of State, New Orleans, December 5, 1729,

AN, Col., C^{13A}, vol. 12, fol. 33–35v. He first mentions a plot in the detailed narrative of the massacre that he sends to the secretary of state in April 1730. Périer to the Secretary of State, New Orleans, March 18, 1730, attached to the letter sent on April 10, 1730, AN, Col., C^{13A}, vol. 12, fol. 38–38v.

41. See, for example, Pierre François Xavier de Charlevoix, *Histoire et description de la Nouvelle France, avec le journal historique d'un voyage fait par ordre du roi dans l'Amérique septentrionale*, 4 vols. (Paris: Rollin, 1744), 4:255–260; Jean Bernard Bossu, *Nouveaux voyages dans l'Amérique septentrionale* (Paris: Veuve Duchesne, 1778), 263–264; Abbé Guillaume Thomas François Raynal, *Histoire philosophique et politique des établissements et du commerce des Européens dans les deux Indes*, 10 vols. (Geneva: Jean-Léonard Pellet, 1780–1781), 6:118–189; Father Mathurin le Petit, "Letter from Father le Petit, Missionary, to Father d'Avaugour, Procurator of the Missions in North America. At New Orleans, the 12th of July, 1730," in *The Jesuit Relations and Allied Documents: Travels and Explorations of the Jesuit Missionaries in New France, 1610–1791*, ed. Reuben Gold Thwaites, 73 vols. (Cleveland: Burrows Brothers, 1896–1903), 68:161. In his novel *Les Natchez*, Chateaubriand also adopted the plot theory.

42. "Relation du massacre des françois aux Natchez et de la guerre contre ces Sauvages" [By officer De Laye], June 1, 1730, AN, Col., 04DFC 38, fol. 66–67.

43. The contrôleur général to Périer, Paris, November 1, 1730, AN, Col., C^{13A}, vol. 12, fol. 339–339v.

44. "Mémoire sur le tabac a faire venir a la Louisianne," AN, Col., C^{13A}, vol. 10, fol. 135–136.

45. "Relation de ce qui s'est passé de plus remarquable sur le massacre, que la nation sauvage des Natchez a fait de la Garnison du Poste et des habitans de l'Etablissement, que la Compagnie des Indes avoit formée auprès de la dite nation, pour la culture des Tabacs, et de la maniere dont on s'y est pris pour leur faire la Guerre, a Commencer du 28 9bre 1729 jusques au 2 fevrier 1730," Newberry Library, Ayer, MS 293, vol. 4, fol. 387.

46. Bossu, *Nouveaux voyages dans l'Amérique septentrionale*, 1:54–55; Dumont de Montigny, *Mémoires historiques sur la Louisiane*, 2:128–129; Le Page du Pratz, *Histoire de la Louisiane*, 3:231–233; "Letter from Father Vivier of the Society of Jesus to a Father of the same Society, Among the Illinois, November 17, 1750," in Thwaites, *Jesuit Relations*, 69:215.

47. "Memoire de L. D. [Dumont de Montigny] officier Ingenieur contenant Les Evenemens qui se sont passés à la Louisiane depuis 1715 jusqu'a present ainsi que ses remarques sur les mœurs, usages et forces des diverses nations de L'Amerique Septentrionale et de ses productions," Newberry Library, Ayer, MS 257, fol. 216.

48. Raymond Amyault, sieur d'Auseville to the Secretary of State, New Orleans, January 20, 1732, AN, Col., C^{13A}, vol. 14, fol. 264.

49. "Mémoire de la Compagnie des Indes servant d'instruction pour M. Perier nouvellement pourveu du commandement général de la Louisiane, September 30, 1726," AN, Col., C^{13B}, vol. 1, fol. 90v.

50. Le Page du Pratz, *Histoire de la Louisiane*, 3:238–239.

From Subjects to Citizens

Two Pierres and the French Influence on the Transformation of the Illinois Country

JOHN REDA

FOR NEARLY A CENTURY THE HANDFUL OF FRENCH VILLAGES IN THE Mississippi valley known collectively as the Illinois Country lay at the center of an imperial arc that stretched from the mouth of the St. Lawrence River to the Gulf of Mexico. But in 1763, "with the scratch of a pen," the Mississippi River became an international boundary dividing the Illinois Country in two.[1] The former French colony was split suddenly between the Spanish and British empires, and both powers struggled to establish and maintain sovereignty. Neither succeeded. Yet a number of French colonials such as Pierre Chouteau and Pierre Menard also struggled—and eventually prospered—in the shifting imperial landscape of the Illinois Country.

This essay analyzes the significance of the careers of these two Pierres. Both were instrumental in shaping an American transformation of the Illinois Country that was unlike the earlier failed European attempts to rule the area from distant capitals and that avoided much of the violence that characterized the American incorporation of the rest of the trans-Appalachian West. Both came to the Illinois Country as young men and built commercial fortunes against a backdrop of dramatic political, economic, and social changes. Like many French colonials, both men's deep involvement in the fur trade included close ties to the Indian and métis peoples of the Illinois Country. Unlike most, however, Chouteau and Menard were able to maintain their relationships and livelihoods under successive sovereigns by identifying the points at which their private interests intersected with imperial imperatives.

This usually involved pursuing trade and land by peaceful, if sometimes coercive, means, for the transformation of the Illinois Country, while not without violence, was largely a commercial affair.[2] As the balance of military power between white settlers and Indians precluded a military conquest, it was left to men such as Chouteau and Menard to turn a profit while simultaneously working to keep the peace between the empires they served and the Indian peoples with whom they did business. In doing so the two Pierres made the most of their own transformations: from subjects to citizens.

THE TWO PIERRES AND THE DEVELOPMENT OF THEIR INDIVIDUAL NETWORKS

Pierre Chouteau was born in New Orleans in 1758, the son of Marie Chouteau and Pierre Laclède. After being abandoned by her husband, René Chouteau, in 1755, Marie met Pierre Laclède, newly arrived from France, and had four children with him, although they never married. Their union lasted until Laclède's death in 1778. In 1763, Laclède and Auguste Chouteau, Marie's only child from her marriage, traveled up the Mississippi River to the Illinois Country after Laclède and his partner, Gilbert Maxent, secured an exclusive grant for the colony's Indian trade. Marie and the rest of the family soon followed, joining Laclède and the teen-aged Auguste in the town of St. Louis, which Laclède had founded in 1764. While awaiting the arrival of Spanish officials, St. Louis was administered in its first years by holdovers from the French colonial era.[3]

In 1770, Captain Pedro Piernas became the first lieutenant governor of what the Spanish called Upper Louisiana. Pierre Chouteau, barely in his teens, helped Piernas conduct the first formal survey of St. Louis's town lots in 1771. As the town's founders, Laclède and the Chouteaus were interested parties in the survey and were relieved when Piernas granted formal title to all of their original landholdings. The family had suffered a financial blow in 1765 when the Spanish Crown revoked Laclède's Indian trade grant, forcing Pierre and his older brother Auguste to move quickly to secure trading licenses from the lieutenant governor. By the time of Laclède's death, the Chouteaus were well established in the Missouri River trade with the Osage, the colony's largest and most formidable nation. Pierre, who conducted most of the trading while brother Auguste handled the supply end of the business, spent several years wintering with the Osage and almost certainly fathered at least one child with an Osage wife.[4]

The Osage had long enjoyed good trade relations with the French of the Illinois Country and were determined, under the Spanish regime, to maintain their access to European goods, particularly firearms. For their part, Spanish officials wanted nothing more than to maintain peace with the Osage and to share in the profits of the colony's Indian trade. There were problems, however. Spain's involvement in the American Revolution led directly to shortages of trade goods in New Orleans by the late 1770s, threatening the peace and prosperity of Upper Louisiana. The Chouteaus' expanding family connections provided an answer. In 1786, Auguste Chouteau married Marie Thérèse Cerré, the daughter of Gabriel Cerré, a local merchant with close ties to Canadian suppliers of Indian trade goods. Additionally, Auguste and Pierre's three sisters each married men with trade connections on both sides of the Mississippi, giving the Chouteaus further access to British goods coming down from Canada. Local Spanish officials proved willing to temporarily sanction this trade, despite its obvious violation of prevailing mercantilist policies. When this proved unacceptable to their superiors, they simply chose to ignore the illegal importation of such goods into Upper Louisiana since the alternative would have meant an open rupture with the Osage.[5]

The American Revolution thus crippled Spain's Indian trade in Upper Louisiana by creating conditions that led to the redirecting of fur exports through Canada, strengthening the positions of British trade companies—and also those of the rapidly expanding Chouteau trade network. During the 1780s and 1790s, a succession of Spanish governors and lieutenant governors dealt with sporadic Osage aggression by turning to Pierre and his brother to keep the violence to a minimum and to share in the profits generated by the largely illegal trade being conducted.[6] In 1787, Pierre traveled up the Mississippi River from New Orleans with incoming lieutenant governor Manuel Perez and made good use of the travel time to convince him that the Chouteau brothers were the only men in the colony able to control the impetuous Osage. Henceforth Pierre made the escort of incoming officials to St. Louis something of a tradition.[7]

Pierre and his brother provided the Osage with the trade goods they required to maintain their regional dominance amid threats from hostile Indian nations. Osage aggression toward settlers and traders in Upper Louisiana was primarily a function of trade goods shortages that weakened the Osage position relative to tribes supplied by the British or by the Spanish in Santa Fe. Osage loyalty to Pierre Chouteau—and his to them—became a form of mutual extortion. Pierre would do what was necessary to provide the Osage with goods as long as their leaders worked to minimize violence against white settlers and traders. In 1800 testimony to the Chouteaus' success, Lieutenant Governor Carlos Delassus wrote to his superior that "since Don Augusto and Pedro [Pierre] Chouteau have had the privilege of trading with the Osage nation . . . it is agreed that that nation has greatly lessened its raids against the rest of us, and they can really be said to be nothing in comparison to what they were before."[8] The result through the beginning of the nineteenth century was a growing trade network for Pierre and his family, and relative peace—and a piece of the action—for imperial Spain and its colonial officials.

During the years Pierre Chouteau was building a successful commercial and diplomatic career on the west side of the Illinois Country, Pierre Menard was doing the same on the east side. Born near Montreal in 1766, Menard's father was a French soldier who came to Canada to fight against the British in the Seven Years' War and stayed to fight them again during the American Revolution. Menard likewise cast his fate with the United States when he immigrated to the town of Vincennes in the American Northwest Territory sometime in the mid-1780s. He entered the fur trade and by 1789 was respected enough to be chosen to travel east to meet with George Washington in an effort to coordinate the defense of the western frontier against Indian attacks from the Maumee Confederacy. To that end Menard teamed with William Clark in 1792 in a military expedition to bring supplies to the Illinois Country. Later that year Menard moved from Vincennes to the largest town in the Illinois Country, Kaskaskia, and formed a partnership with François Vallé Sr., a wealthy merchant living on the west side of the Mississippi River in Ste. Geneviève. In 1795, Governor Arthur St. Clair named Menard an officer in the local militia. Following the formation of Indiana Territory in 1800, Menard moved quickly to establish a relationship with incoming governor William Henry Harrison.[9]

From the moment he arrived in the Illinois Country, Menard began forming friendships with the Native Americans and métis peoples he encountered in the fur trade. One of his closest friends was the métis Louis Lorimier, who had been instrumental in persuading large numbers of Shawnee and Delaware to move across the Mississippi River from the Northwest Territory to Upper Louisiana during the 1790s.[10] Menard's growing reputation for fairness and kindness to Indians was balanced by his desire to gain influence with the American officials charged with organizing the western territories. Like Pierre Chouteau, Menard became adept at pursuing commercial advantage within the confines of the prevailing imperial policies. Lacking formal education, but eminently practical and a shrewd judge of men, Menard stood out from most of the French living in the Illinois Country in his willing engagement with the political and military institutions being formed in the territory.[11] As such, Menard was well positioned for the rapid changes that followed the purchase of Louisiana by the United States in 1803.

THE LOUISIANA PURCHASE

Following the Louisiana Purchase, the transfer of Upper Louisiana to the United States took place in St. Louis in March 1804.[12] Among those attending the ceremonies were Meriwether Lewis and William Clark, who spent the winter of 1803–1804 camped with the Corps of Discovery across the Mississippi River near the town of Cahokia in what is today Madison County, Illinois.[13] That winter, Lewis and Clark made Pierre Chouteau's home their unofficial St. Louis headquarters, and the Chouteau brothers and Menard provided a great deal of assistance in securing the supplies, maps, and boatmen needed for the explorers' momentous journey up the Missouri River. Twenty years earlier, the Chouteaus had provided goods to a desperately undersupplied George Rogers Clark (William Clark's older brother) during the occupation of the Illinois Country during the American Revolution.[14]

The friendships that Pierre Chouteau and Menard developed with Lewis, Clark, and other American officials had much to do with establishing trust and respect between the incoming Americans and the established inhabitants of Upper Louisiana, including the Osage. Chouteau's efforts included an offer—accepted by Lewis—to recruit a delegation of Osage leaders to travel with him to Washington to meet with President Thomas Jefferson. He also lent $600 (American dollars) to Captain Amos Stoddard, the American appointed to administer the new territory, in order to pay for a party the captain had hosted to celebrate the American takeover. Chouteau also provided Stoddard with an inventory of Spanish properties in the area. In turn, Meriwether Lewis, while the governor of the Louisiana Territory later in the decade, entrusted Chouteau with blank documents for bonds, oaths, and trading licenses to be used in an expedition along the upper Missouri River and to be handed off to Pierre Menard when Chouteau returned to St. Louis.[15]

A few days ahead of the departure of the Lewis and Clark expedition into the West, Pierre Chouteau headed east with the Osage delegation, where in Washington they met with President Jefferson. While at the capital, Chouteau was appointed Indian agent for all nations north of the Arkansas River. On his way back to St. Louis, Chouteau joined William Henry Harrison as he traveled up the Mississippi River to assume his duties as acting governor. In a moment of great imperial symbolism, Chouteau and Harrison passed departing Spanish Lieutenant Governor Delassus on his way down the Mississippi River to New Orleans.[16] Although pleased with his new appointment, Chouteau's job as an Indian agent would not be easy. The cordiality of the meeting between Jefferson and the Osage delegation could not mask the fact that the president's message of assimilation was at odds with the Osage desire to remain independent. Chouteau also knew that the acquisition of Indian lands was a top priority of the administration. In a letter to Jefferson shortly after his return from Washington, Chouteau declared, "Believe me, monsieur, that I have nothing more at heart than to fulfill exactly the duties of the mission with which the government has charged me."[17]

While in St. Louis, Governor Harrison held a conference with Sac and Fox representatives, ostensibly to settle a case involving the murder of four settlers on the Cuivre River in present-day Missouri. During the conference, however, Harrison proposed a large land cession that Pierre Chouteau supported by providing a large number of gifts to the Indians. The resulting treaty netted the United States several million acres, including the area containing the Dubuque lead mines (in which Auguste Chouteau owned a part interest). Although the treaty helped cement relations between the Chouteaus and Harrison, it later became a source of friction between the Sac and Fox, on the one hand, and the United States, on the other. Pierre had shown that he was attuned to the realities of American expansionism, but had seemingly forgotten that the Chouteau family's success was based on what was at the least reciprocal, if not equitable, dealings with the Osage and other Indian nations. Harrison had failed to observe the customary treaty protocols, the most important being the need to negotiate only with representatives authorized to sell land—which the Indians present were not. This lesson was not lost on Chouteau, who in the future would be more careful about his participation in land cession treaties.[18]

Meanwhile, Pierre Menard also allied himself with Harrison, who was unquestionably the most powerful U.S. official in the West. Harrison appointed Menard to a judgeship, named him a militia officer, and, most important, selected him as one of the five members of Indiana Territory's first executive council. When the United States created land commissions to adjudicate the hundreds of unconfirmed land claims in the territory, the governor authorized Menard to take depositions and examine witnesses, even as he waited for dozens of his own claims to be adjudicated. Menard's reputation for good relations with local Indians led Harrison to rely on him to use the local militia to protect friendly Indians from attacks by those Indians hostile to U.S. interests. But Menard broke with the governor in 1807 when Indiana's politics began to be plagued by partisan clashes over slavery and the rulings of the land commissions, both of which involved many of Menard's friends and neighbors. Menard resigned from the executive council, citing the "private circumstances of my family," and thereafter remained aloof from politics until the creation of the Illinois Territory in 1809.[19] Although Menard was himself a slave owner and land speculator, he was concerned with maintaining his credibility with the territory's Indian and French inhabitants, who had no direct stake in partisan politics.

THE BIRTH OF AN INFLUENTIAL PARTNERSHIP

It was during the years following the Louisiana Purchase that the lives of the two Pierres became directly intertwined. Pierre Chouteau's first wife died in 1794, and the following year he married Brigitte Saucier of Kaskaskia. In 1804, Pierre Menard's first wife died, and two years later he married Brigitte's sister, Angélique. The two men were now brothers-in-law, and this kinship connection was later strengthened by the marriage of Chouteau's son from his first marriage to Menard's daughter.[20] To no one's surprise, Chouteau and Menard were soon involved in a joint business venture.

In 1807, Manuel Lisa, a prominent St. Louis fur trader, led a group of trappers on a profitable trading expedition to the upper Missouri River into areas reconnoitered by Lewis and Clark just a few years previously. Lisa's success led directly to the formation of the St. Louis Missouri Fur Company in 1809. The company included Pierre Chouteau, Pierre Menard, Lisa, William Clark, Reuben Lewis (the brother of Meriwether Lewis), and Benjamin Wilkinson, the son of General James Wilkinson.[21] The controversial Wilkinson had replaced acting governor William Henry Harrison as governor of Upper Louisiana in 1805 and had been, like Perez and Harrison, the recipient of one of Pierre Chouteau's personal escorts up the Mississippi River en route to St. Louis. The two became political allies, although Chouteau quickly distanced himself from Wilkinson when rumors reached the territory of the general's likely complicity in Aaron Burr's allegedly treasonous plot for a western empire.[22] In 1809, President Jefferson appointed Meriwether Lewis to replace the suspect Wilkinson as the territory's governor and at the same time named William Clark as the U.S. Indian agent for all nations west of the Mississippi, except for the Osage, who remained Pierre

Chouteau's responsibility. As the Missouri Fur Company readied itself for its first foray up the Missouri River, Governor Lewis offered the company $7,000 to escort the Mandan chief Shahaka back to his home in present-day North Dakota. Shahaka had traveled to Washington in 1806, when Pierre Chouteau led a second Indian delegation out east to meet with President Jefferson. The first attempt to return the chief to his people had failed after Sioux warriors attacked the escort delegation, forcing it to retreat to St. Louis. Caught in a diplomatic bind, Governor Lewis turned to the Missouri Fur Company to ensure Shahaka's safe return, and named Pierre Chouteau to head a force of 125 militiamen to accompany the expedition.[23]

As it turned out, Shahaka's return was the only thing that went as planned on the trip. After returning the Mandan chief to his people, the military escort headed by Pierre Chouteau returned to St. Louis while the traders, including Pierre Menard, continued up the Missouri River and spent the winter of 1809–1810 hunting and trapping in the midst of hostile nations. Menard and his partners based their decision to venture into this dangerous country on the belief that the size of the expedition and the large amount of goods it carried would be sufficient to persuade the Indians they encountered to engage in peaceful trade.[24] They were mistaken. A letter written by Menard to Chouteau told the story:

> Dear Sir and Brother-in-law—I had hoped to write you more favorably than I am now able to do. A party of our hunters was defeated by the Blackfeet on the 12th [April]. There were two men killed, all their beaver stolen, many of their traps lost, and the ammunition of several of them, and also seven of our horses. . . . This unhappy mishap causes us considerable loss, but I do not propose on that account to lose heart. The resources of this country in beaver fur are immense. It is true that we shall accomplish nothing this spring, but I trust we shall next Autumn.[25]

Despite his optimistic appraisal of the situation, subsequent attacks by the Blackfeet forced Menard and most of the remaining members of the expedition to abandon the upper Missouri River country a few weeks later.[26] Menard, true to his word, was not discouraged by the setback and in later years led or financed expeditions into parts of the West where few Americans had previously traveled. Menard's motivation for pursuing these subsequent ventures was a combination of prospects for personal profit and the expansion of U.S. interests, even if his diplomatic mandate was sometimes more presumed than actual.[27]

Back in St. Louis, Pierre Chouteau and Meriwether Lewis were censured by the incoming Madison administration for mixing private and public business and for organizing the second Shahaka expedition without possessing the authority to do so. William Eustis, the new secretary of war, went as far as to state that "as the Agency of Mr Chouteau is become vacant by his accepting the command of the Detachment it is in contemplation to appoint a suitable character to supply his place."[28] Chouteau's son, Pierre Jr., replied to Eustis in his father's absence:

> My father interested himself in this new Company, and did not think it any dereliction of his duty since he was authorized to do so by the example of General Clark . . . the Governor [Lewis] thought it apropos to nominate my father Commander of this Expedition, so far as it would be Military;—that is to say, until the moment when the Mandane Chief should have arrived in his Nation . . . and the influence my Father has enjoyed over the nations of the Missouri during so long a period, seem to justify the Governor's choice. My father accepted this proposition with joy, in the view of being useful to the Government. . . . What would be his grief if he knew that you disapprove his conduct!—but I flatter myself that when it shall be fully known to you—(and I pray you to take all possible information on the subject)—you will do justice to his zeal and to his blind obedience to the orders of his superiors.[29]

After his return to St. Louis, Pierre Chouteau wrote a series of letters to Eustis further describing the context for his involvement in the Shahaka expedition as well as the details of his working relationship with Governor Lewis. Acting governor Frederick Bates also wrote Eustis, stating, "It is to be greatly feared that the character of Mr. Chouteau has not been entirely understood in Washington. I do not fear to hazard the assertion that he possesses a respectability and weight in this country, beyond any other person employed in the transaction of Indian business.—And this reputation . . . has, on all proper occasions been thrown into the American Scale." Secretary Eustis eventually responded favorably to the various entreaties in Chouteau's defense, marking the end of a rocky period in Chouteau's relationship with federal officials.[30]

Chouteau's problems with federal officials had actually begun in 1806 when the secretary of war criticized him for spending too much on presents for the Indians and for continuing to trade with the Osage while serving as a U.S. Indian agent.[31] Having come of age under a Spanish regime that cared little about mixing personal business with imperial diplomacy, Chouteau did not immediately realize that American ideology demanded a different standard. One of his missteps involved a land cession treaty that William

Clark negotiated in 1808. A delegation of Osage leaders who had not attended the treaty council renounced the deal, and Governor Lewis subsequently modified the treaty and charged Pierre Chouteau with presenting it to the Osage for approval. The new treaty included a larger annual annuity as well as the promise of a blacksmith, a mill, and agricultural implements. During the final negotiations a clause was added—either at the request of the Osage or by Chouteau himself—reaffirming the gift of a large tract of land that had been given to Pierre by the tribe in the early 1790s. To American officials and to some American settlers living in the territory, this smacked of favoritism if not corruption. To Chouteau and the Osage, it was part of the process by which trust and loyalty were built. This was explicitly detailed in a letter from twelve Osage chiefs to Pierre that accompanied the gifted land in 1792:

> Brother:
>
> As thou hast, since a long time, fed our wives and our children; and that thou have always been good for us, and that thou has always assisted us with thy advice . . . take thou on the river a la Mine, the quantity of land which may suit thee. . . . This land is ours; we do give it to thee; and no one can take it from thee, neither today nor ever. . . . Thou askest a paper from us, and our marks. Here it is. If our children do trouble thine, they have but to show the paper; and if some nation disturbs thee, we are ready to defend thee.[32]

Over the following seventeen years the Osage found no reason to disavow their gift to Pierre Chouteau. They still saw him as a trustworthy middleman helping them to stay in the good graces of the current imperial regime. However, Pierre was no longer a middleman, but rather an official agent of the current imperial regime.

The reprimands that federal officials delivered to Pierre Chouteau during the years between 1806 and 1809 underscore the inherent challenge that Chouteau faced in trying to remain in good standing with both the federal government and the Osage nation. While the Osage placed great value on continuity and long-standing relationships, Pierre Chouteau, as a U.S. Indian agent, needed to respond to the shifts in policy dictated both by territorial officials such as Governor Lewis and by the transition from one presidential administration to another. Unlike Pierre Menard, who could easily sacrifice his local offices for a number of years in order to avoid the perils of political factionalism, Pierre Chouteau's role as a federally appointed official placed him firmly at the intersection of territorial and national politics, making it far trickier to preserve his usefulness to the federal government without compromising his relationship with the Osage or sacrificing his own commercial interests.

By 1811, however, the widespread belief that a war was likely between the United States, Great Britain, and their respective Indian allies presented both Pierre Chouteau and Pierre Menard with new opportunities to demonstrate their usefulness to their various political and commercial constituencies. Growing violence between white settlers and Indians combined with rising tensions between the United States and Great Britain to create a general state of alarm in the Illinois Country. Menard had returned to politics after Illinois became a separate territory in 1809, and was elected president of Illinois's executive council in 1812. In this capacity he lobbied the federal government to increase its military presence in the West, in anticipation of hostilities.[33] Both Chouteau and Menard held appointments as militia officers, and when war broke out both also worked to recruit Indian allies to help defend the frontier against Great Britain and its own Indian allies. Menard served under Colonel Henry Dodge and recruited friendly Shawnee to serve as guides and scouts. At the request of acting governor Bates, Chouteau enlisted a force of 260 Osage warriors to help defend the frontier. To his chagrin, however, Governor Howard arrived in St. Louis and overruled Bates, deciding that an armed force of Osage passing through the vicinity was too risky. Chouteau received orders to disband the Osage contingent after already having marched 360 miles and called upon his considerable diplomatic skills to reconcile the Osage to the inconvenience and insult they experienced.[34]

At the 1815 Portage des Sioux treaty council that ended the War of 1812 in the Old Northwest, both Pierre Chouteau and Pierre Menard played important roles behind the scenes. Their widespread reputations as loyal Americans who were not associated with the rise of indiscriminate Indian-hating allowed them to maneuver between Indian and U.S. government camps in negotiations over the restructuring of the West. Over the next several years both men helped in the diplomacy that led to a series of Indian treaties.[35] Complicating the situation were the voluntary migrations of eastern Indians across the Mississippi River into Missouri. Although federal officials ostensibly supported these migrants, their presence even in passing was as unwelcome to white settlers in Missouri and Illinois as was that of the Indians already residing there. The demands of white settlers for access to *all* Indian lands created an explosive situation that threatened the recently negotiated peace and clashed with the official federal policy calling for white settlers to refrain from squatting on lands to which Indians still held title.[36]

Chouteau and Menard intervened repeatedly on behalf of the area's

Indian peoples. In one case Illinois officials wrote to Washington describing "the wretched and starving condition of the Kaskaskia Indians," who were "now dependent on the bounty of Colo Menard," while remaining "in danger from the hostile tribes, but still more from our own Citizens, who neither can nor will discriminate between friends and foes."[37] In another, Menard paid for the ferry passages of 1,300 Delaware and their 1,500 horses across the Mississippi River and helped arrange for a supply of beef, flour, corn, and salt to provision the group during their 1820 journey. In 1826, when guides assigned by the federal government abandoned a group of Shawnee and Seneca migrants from Ohio in the wilds of southern Illinois, Menard encouraged the near-starving Indians to camp for the winter near his home in Kaskaskia. Menard also intervened in the early 1820s in the case of a Shawnee man beaten and driven from his eastern Missouri farm by a white man who wanted to appropriate the land and its improvements. Despite the overwhelming evidence presented, Missouri officials blocked local efforts to prosecute the offender, and the injustice stood. In an effort to help prevent such incidents from becoming widespread, Menard assisted the Shawnee and Delaware of eastern Missouri in successful negotiations with the federal government to trade their lands near Cape Girardeau for a larger tract of land farther west.[38] Pierre Chouteau also worked during the postwar years to minimize violence between local Indians and both incoming settlers and Indian nations. One of his most delicate missions involved supervising the survey of Osage lands that had been acquired by the United States in the disputed treaty of 1808. Pierre Chouteau also joined with his brother Auguste, along with the governors of Illinois and Missouri, to end—if only for a few years—a war between the Osage and Cherokee.[39]

THE TWO PIERRES' STAKES

While Menard's and Chouteau's actions did not have much of an effect either on official U.S. policy or on the behavior of settlers moving into the region, the two did manage to improve the situations of thousands of Indians during these years. Their actions, however, should not be characterized as purely altruistic. Both men continued to acquire lands for themselves while also controlling a significant portion of the lucrative Indian fur trade.

At the same time that the two Pierres were working in both official and unofficial capacities on behalf of the Illinois Country's Indians, they were also involved in the political development of their respective communities.

Menard returned to politics when Illinois became a territory in 1809, and he lobbied Washington to expedite the settlement of disputed land claims, to secure overdue compensation for men who had served in the War of 1812, and for judicial reform. This helped make Menard popular with all of Illinois's political constituencies and led to his election as the state's first lieutenant governor. The members of the Illinois statehood convention even drafted a special clause exempting Menard from the state constitution's thirty-year citizenship requirement.[40] Likewise, Pierre Chouteau held office in Missouri as a justice of the peace, as a member of the St. Louis Board of Trustees, and as a state senator. Chouteau also continued as the U.S. Indian agent for the Osage until 1818, when he was dismissed by Secretary of War John Calhoun and later replaced by his son, Paul Liguest Chouteau.[41]

The postwar years were also profitable for the two Pierres. When the land commissions in both territories finally finished their work, both Chouteau and Menard found themselves holding confirmed titles to vast holdings that rapidly increased in value as a flood of white settlers poured into Illinois and Missouri. Both men also continued to push their trade ventures ever deeper to the north and west as British traders were finally forced to retreat from American territory. In 1817, Menard formed a new partnership with the descendants of his old partner, François Vallé Sr., which dominated the Indian trade in the Ozark mountain region until the early 1830s.[42] By the time Illinois and Missouri reached statehood in 1818 and 1821, respectively, the next generation of Chouteau's and Menard's intertwined families had already begun to expand their commercial empires into what many perceived as the seemingly boundless American future.

During the 1820s, the two Pierres began slowing down—a little—to enjoy the fruits of their labors. Each received numerous honors from their local communities, and during the Marquis de Lafayette's 1825 tour of the United States, Chouteau and Menard took turns playing host to the Revolutionary War hero during his stay in the area.[43] The two men and their families played key roles in the expansion of U.S. trade into the West and continued to be held in high esteem by the Indians who knew them, despite their frequent involvement in the land cessions and subsequent removals of Indian peoples that characterized the period. President John Quincy Adams named Menard as one of three commissioners charged with negotiating with Indians living along the route of a proposed road leading from St. Louis to Santa Fe in 1825. In 1828–1829, Menard helped to negotiate three treaties that netted the United States over four million acres, many of which were a part of the disputed 1804 cessions negotiated by Pierre Chouteau and William Henry Harrison. In the late 1820s and early 1830s, Presidents Adams and Jackson as well as Illinois governor John Reynolds all called upon Menard to undertake the thankless job of mediating the removal of groups of Indians residing in various corners of the Illinois Country. Menard might have been describing his own legacy when, in 1833, he wrote to his old friend William Clark, proffering his resignation: "'the poor remnant' . . . of those who once covered the greatest portion of our quarter of the Globe, are more indebted to your active and humane exertions, for the comparative happiness which they have in prospect, than to any other individual within my knowledge."[44] Over the course of his long career, Menard had served in one capacity or another under each of the first seven American presidential administrations, from George Washington to Andrew Jackson.

The next generation of the Chouteau-Menard clan began to emerge in the 1820s, with impressive results. Chouteau's sons A. P. Chouteau, Pierre Chouteau Jr., and François Chouteau (whose wife was Menard's daughter Berenice) were all involved in the expansion of the fur trade into the steam age and to the Rocky Mountains and beyond. Although the financier John Jacob Astor's American Fur Company came to dominate the fur trade in the 1820s, the Chouteau and Menard families were able to survive and prosper to the extent that in 1834, Pierre Menard and A. P. Chouteau traveled together to New York City, where they successfully negotiated the purchase of the western division of Astor's company.[45]

Perhaps more important, the Chouteau and Menard offspring maintained their families' reputations for fair dealings with their Indian trading partners. Pierre Jr., Auguste Pierre, and Paul Liguest Chouteau became deeply involved in Indian removals, but they fought to ensure, as much as possible, that those involved were not cheated or abused. François and Berenice Chouteau established the first trading post among the Kansas and Shawnee at the site of present-day Kansas City and were successful despite their refusal to supply liquor to their Indian customers. This was in keeping with the family's long record (with some lapses) of restraint in the use of liquor in the Indian trade. In another example of Indians holding these families in high regard, Pierre sent his nephew Michel Menard to trade with the Shawnee in what is now Arkansas. Michel rose to become a Shawnee chief before moving on to Texas, where he served as a member of the convention that declared Texan independence.[46]

These two Pierres were remarkable men. Born the subjects of distant monarchs, they died in the 1840s as citizens of a country whose presidents they had met and served faithfully. Their stories are not the typical eighteenth- and nineteenth-century tales of violent conquest and manifest destiny. Their stories are in fact distinctly French, arguments for the idea that while the French empire in North America may have been vanquished in the 1760s, its influence reached deep into the next century. Pierre Chouteau and Pierre Menard influenced the transformation of the Illinois Country through a mixture of adaptation and cultural persistence. They embraced the changes that republican government brought, although not without a few missteps; but they also stuck to the French imperial formula of accommodation and respect in their relations with the Indians of the Illinois Country. By doing so, both men proved indispensable to the two groups—Indians and whites—locked in a decades-long struggle for the Illinois Country, and ultimately for the lands farther west.

CONCLUSION

The transformation of the Illinois Country from a land dominated militarily by Indians during successive European regimes to a land militarily, economically, and culturally dominated by an American empire that denied its imperial ambitions while relentlessly pursuing them is a familiar story. Familiar, unless we ask why this particular transformation lacked the endemic violence that accompanied the American takeovers of the Ohio valley (including Kentucky, Ohio, and Indiana), the Old Southwest (including Tennessee, Georgia, Alabama, and Mississippi), and most of the trans-Mississippi West. The answer involves our two Pierres. By positioning themselves, along with other French and métis residents of the Illinois Country, between white settlers and Indians, they helped engineer a transformation that was less a conquest than a slow transition. As French Creoles they were, of course, whites, but whites whose close ties to Indians gave them credibility with both groups.

The aim here is not to romanticize these men. Chouteau and Menard were businessmen and slaveholders whose benevolence toward Indians was more paternalistic than egalitarian.[47] Their racial views were milder but not substantively different than those of other whites of their day. What was different about these two Pierres and about the French in general was the pragmatism of their approach to Indian-white relations. Living as a minority in the Illinois Country from the late seventeenth century, the French prospered not through conquest—with some exceptions—but through commerce. Long-established Indian trade networks incorporated European goods when they were introduced, and as demand increased, so did the profits of those able to supply the coveted goods. But the dangers to white settlers also increased if goods were withheld or not available. Chouteau and Menard recognized this dynamic and flouted Spanish and British mercantilist trade restrictions while building a family-based trade network that provided access to European goods and markets via the Mississippi River through New Orleans and via the St. Lawrence River through Montreal and Quebec. The Indian fur trade was the platform upon which Chouteau and Menard acquired influence and working capital, but it was land that made them and their descendents truly rich.

And land was at the heart of the American takeover. Where earlier regimes had rewarded those who could conduct trade with the Indians of the Illinois Country without provoking violence, the Americans wanted much more: trade, peace, sovereignty—and land. For men such as Chouteau and Menard, the stakes were thus raised, and the challenges grew tougher. As citizens, they were offered a direct stake in the empire they would now be helping to build, but there were rules to be followed and a ruthless equation to be acknowledged. Peace and prosperity would attract ever-growing numbers of settlers whose past experiences were marked by violence and indiscriminate Indian-hating. Nothing if not pragmatic, Chouteau, Menard, and their families moved quickly to turn their fur trade profits into claims on lands they helped the United States acquire from their Indian trading partners. Neither man thought it possible to change this equation. But both men realized that if placed in positions of responsibility and discretion, they could make the transformation less a debacle than those that took place elsewhere.

The record of the Chouteau-Menard clan speaks loudly about the effort they made and the relative success they achieved. Correspondence with federal officials included demands for better-quality goods, annuities to be paid on time, blacksmiths to be posted, and mills to be built where promised.[48] They exercised relative restraint in the use of liquor in the Indian trade. They assisted tribes who had moved west in the 1780s and 1790s and who now had to move again. And not all of these migrations were tragic tales of degradation. There were nations who were able to steer clear of white settlers for several generations and who shrewdly bargained for good lands as they moved west. In the middle of many of these relatively benign relocations could be found Pierre Chouteau, Pierre Menard, or one of their offspring.[49]

If the appropriation of Indian lands was, in the long run, inevitable, it did not take place all at once or in the same manner in all places. In the Illinois Country, a group of mostly French entrepreneurs navigated the twists and turns of imperial politics and succeeded in putting their stamp on the changes taking place during their lifetimes. Relying on family ties and a century-long tradition of good relations with Indian and métis peoples, they built fortunes that were quintessentially American—parlaying commercial profits into vast real estate holdings—but did so in a way that tells a story outside the usual American narrative of violent and ruthless conquest.[50] If the results were, in the end, the same, there is still much to be said for the distinction in methods.

NOTES

1. This trope is the source of the title and brilliantly developed in the introduction to Colin G. Calloway's *The Scratch of a Pen: 1763 and the Transformation of North America* (New York: Oxford University Press, 2006), where he credits Francis Parkman for its origin. Francis Parkman, *Montcalm and Wolfe: The French and Indian War* (Boston: 1884; repr., New York: Da Capo Press, 1995), 535.

2. Prominent among the recent works exploring the commercial dimension of the changes taking place throughout the Old Northwest in the late eighteenth and early nineteenth centuries is Jay Gitlin, *The Bourgeois Frontier: French Towns, French Traders, and American Expansion* (New Haven, Conn.: Yale University Press, 2010). Gitlin argues that French commercial families in the region played crucial roles in both the transition to U.S. sovereignty in what he calls the "Creole Corridor" and in the broader expansion of American interests into the trans-Mississippi West. Also useful are Susan Sleeper-Smith, *Indian Women and French Men: Rethinking Cultural Encounter in the Western Great Lakes* (Amherst: University of Massachusetts Press, 2001); and Robert Englebert, "Merchant Representatives and the French River World, 1763–1803," *Michigan Historical Review* 34 (Spring 2008): 63–82.

3. William E. Foley and C. David Rice, *The First Chouteaus: River Barons of Early St. Louis* (Urbana: University of Illinois Press, 1983), 3–4, 14.

4. Ibid., 8, 15–21; Shirley Christian, *Before Lewis and Clark: The Story of the Chouteaus, the French Dynasty That Ruled America's Frontier* (New York: Farrar, Straus and Giroux, 2004), 87–88; A. P. Nasitir, ed., *Before Lewis and Clark: Documents Illustrating the History of the Missouri, 1785–1804*, 2 vols. (St. Louis: 1952; repr., Lincoln: University of Nebraska Press, 1990), 1:62–63.

5. Christian, *Before Lewis and Clark*, 49–50; Foley and Rice, *First Chouteaus*, 21, 26, 36–38, 45, 73.

6. The complexities of the fur trade in this region and of the St. Louis–New Orleans and St. Louis–Montreal networks are best explained in David Lavender, *The Fist in the Wilderness* (New York: 1964; repr., Lincoln: University of Nebraska Press, 1998); and Richard Oglesby, *Manuel Lisa and the*

Opening of the Missouri Fur Trade (Norman: University of Oklahoma Press, 1963). The Spanish lieutenant governors at St. Louis were Pedro Joseph Piernas (May 1770–May 1775), Fernando de Leyba (May 1775–June 1778), Francisco Cruzat (September 1780–November 1787), Manuel Pérez (November 1787–July 1792), Zenon Trudeau (July 1792–August 1799), and Carlos Dehault Delassus (August 1799–March 1804). Trudeau and Delassus were actually French, the former born in New Orleans, the latter born in France. Both joined the Spanish army as young men. Bonnie Stepenoff, *From French Community to Missouri Town: Ste. Genevieve in the Nineteenth Century* (Columbia: University of Missouri Press, 2006).

7. Christian, *Before Lewis and Clark*, 53; Foley and Rice, *First Chouteaus*, 40, 90–91.

8. Christian, *Before Lewis and Clark*, 64–66; Carlos Delassus to Casa Calvo, November 29, 1800, in Nasitir, *Before Lewis and Clark*, 2:622–624.

9. Arthur Clinton Boggess, *The Settlement of Illinois, 1778–1830* (Chicago: Chicago Historical Society, 1908), 113; Christian, *Before Lewis and Clark*, 341; Richard E. Oglesby, "Pierre Menard," in *French Fur Traders & Voyageurs in the American West*, ed. Leroy R. Hafen (Spokane, Wash.: 1965; repr., Lincoln: University of Nebraska Press, 1997), 217–218; Landon Y. Jones, *William Clark and the Shaping of the West* (New York: Hill and Wang, 2004), 66; Edward G. Mason, ed., *Early Chicago and Illinois* (Chicago: Fergus Printing, 1890), 144–145. An appointment as a militia officer was a sign of great respect during this period, as militias were largely responsible for the defense of frontier communities.

10. Tanis C. Thorne, *The Many Hands of My Relations: French and Indians on the Lower Missouri* (Columbia: University of Missouri Press, 1996), 80–81. Louis Lorimier's race remains a matter of debate, as some historians believe his mother to be of French descent and some of Indian descent. The French military engineer Nicholas de Finiels toured Upper Louisiana in the early 1800s and met Lorimier, who he described as the "son of a white man and a Shawnee woman." Nicholas de Finiels, *An Account of Upper Louisiana*, ed. Carl J. Ekberg and William E. Foley (Columbia: University of Missouri Press, 1989), 35.

11. Boggess, *Settlement of Illinois*, 208; Oglesby, "Pierre Menard," 218–219, 223–225.

12. The ceremonies on March 9 and 10, 1803, marking the transfer of Upper Louisiana from Spain to France and then from France to the United States are recounted in detail in Floyd C. Shoemaker, "The Louisiana Purchase, 1803, and the Transfer of Upper Louisiana to the United States, 1804," *Missouri Historical Review* 48 (October 1953): 10–15. Included in Captain

Amos Stoddard's address at the transfer ceremony was the phrase, "you are divested of the character of Subjects, and clothed with that of citizens." Amos Stoddard, "Papers of Captain Amos Stoddard," Missouri Historical Society, *Glimpses of the Past* 2 (1935): 78–122.

13. Robert E. Hartley, *Lewis and Clark in the Illinois Country: The Little-Told Story* (Westminster, Colo.: Sniktau Publications, 2002), 97.

14. Christian, *Before Lewis and Clark*, 6–18, Foley and Rice, *First Chouteaus*, 27, 90; Financial Records of the Lewis and Clark Expedition, August 5, 1807, in *Letters of the Lewis and Clark Expedition with Related Documents 1783–1854*, ed. Donald Jackson, 2 vols. (Urbana: University of Illinois Press, 1978), 2:419–431.

15. Foley and Rice, *First Chouteaus*, 90–94; Meriwether Lewis to William Clark, February 18, 1804, in Jackson, *Letters of the Lewis and Clark Expedition*, 1:167–168; William Clark to William Croghan, May 2, 1804, in Jackson, *Letters of the Lewis and Clark Expedition*, 1:178–179; Governor Lewis to Pierre Chouteau, June 8, 1809, in *The Territorial Papers of the United States*, ed. Clarence Carter, 27 vols. (Washington, D.C.: U.S. Government Printing Office, 1934–1975), 14:348–352.

16. Christian, *Before Lewis and Clark*, 114–118; Foley and Rice, *First Chouteaus*, 91.

17. Foley and Rice, *First Chouteaus*, 105–111; Missouri Historical Society (hereafter cited as MHS), Chouteau Collection, Pierre Chouteau to Thomas Jefferson, October 12, 1804, Pierre Chouteau Sr. Letterbook, Box 7.

18. Robert M. Owens, *Mr. Jefferson's Hammer: William Henry Harrison and the Origins of American Indian Policy* (Norman: University of Oklahoma Pres, 2007), 86–91; Foley and Rice, *First Chouteaus*, 112–113. Located on these lands were lead mines sold to Auguste Chouteau by Julien Dubuque, despite Dubuque's having only been granted by local Indians something they conceived as closer to a lease on the mines than ownership of the land itself. One of those opposed to this treaty was the young Sac warrior Blackhawk, who in 1832, by leading a group of Indians from Iowa back into Illinois onto lands signed away in 1804, triggered the short war that bears his name.

19. J. P. Dunn Jr., *Indiana: A Redemption from Slavery* (Boston: Houghton, Mifflin, 1899), 326; Solon Buck, *Illinois in 1818*, 2nd ed. (Urbana: University of Illinois Press, 1967), 191; Mason, *Early Chicago*, 146; Logan Esarey, ed., *Messages and Letters of William Henry Harrison* (Indianapolis: Indiana Historical Commission, 1922), 20, 23, 182, 196–197, 213–214; Pierre Menard to William Henry Harrison, September 19, 1807, in Esarey, *Messages and Letters*, 256.

20. Oglesby, "Pierre Menard," 218–219; Christian, *Before Lewis and Clark*, 89, 98. Brigitte and Angélique Saucier were members of a family long prominent on both sides of the Mississippi.

21. Oglesby, *Manuel Lisa*, 63–75; Foley and Rice, *First Chouteaus*, 127, 144–145.

22. The most thorough account of Aaron Burr's alleged plots in the West remains Thomas Abernethy's *The Burr Conspiracy* (New York: Oxford University Press, 1954), although Nancy Isenberg's *Fallen Founder: The Life of Aaron Burr* (New York: Viking Penguin, 2007) provides a broader context for Burr's activities in the West.

23. Christian, *Before Lewis and Clark*, 147–151, 163–168; Governor Lewis to Pierre Chouteau, June 8, 1809, in Carter, *Territorial Papers*, 14:348–352.

24. Oglesby, *Manuel Lisa*, 65–97.

25. Pierre Menard to Pierre Chouteau, April 21, 1809, in Hiram Chittenden, *The American Fur Trade of the Far West: A History of the Pioneer Trading Posts and Early Fur Companies of the Missouri Valley and the Rocky Mountains and of the Overland Commerce with Santa Fe*, 3 vols. (New York: 1902; repr., Stanford, Calif.: Academic Reprints, 1954), 3:893–898.

26. Oglesby, *Manuel Lisa*, 75–97; Oglesby, "Pierre Menard," 220–221.

27. Scattered throughout Pierre Menard's business correspondence are suggestions and directives to associates and relatives, the purpose of which often seems to be the improvement of the relationship between Indians and the federal government. One example would be a letter to his son Peter in 1821 asking him to remind the Indians in Peter's vicinity that their annuity payment (from a treaty with the United States) was going to be paid "in three months." Lincoln Presidential Library (Springfield, Ill.), Pierre Menard Collection, Pierre Menard to Peter Menard, May 5, 1821, Box 2, Folder 20.

28. The Secretary of War to Meriwether Lewis, July 15, 1809, in Carter, *Territorial Papers*, 14:285–286.

29. Pierre Chouteau Jr. to the Secretary of War, September 1, 1809, in ibid., 14:312–319.

30. Pierre Chouteau to the Secretary of War, December 14, 1809, in ibid., 14:343–348; MHS, Chouteau Collection, Pierre Chouteau to the Secretary of War, January 10, 1810, Pierre Chouteau Sr. Letterbook, Box 7; MHS, Chouteau Collection, Pierre Chouteau to the Secretary of War, April 12, 1810, Pierre Chouteau Sr. Letterbook, Box 7; Frederick Bates to William Eustis, September 28, 1809, in *The Life and Papers of Frederick Bates*, ed. Thomas Marshall (St. Louis: 1926; repr., New York: Arno Press, 1975), 86–92; Foley and Rice, *First Chouteaus*, 147; Jones, *William Clark*, 180–181. The result for Lewis was financial disgrace, as his superiors refused to honor his expenditures for the expedition, forcing him into insolvency. He quickly left St. Louis and headed to Washington to plead his case, but tragically he took his own life during the trip. Lewis died believing that Thomas Jefferson had given him the authority to take any actions necessary to ensure Shahaka's return,

Jefferson having written saying he was "uneasy" about having not heard from Lewis about "measures for restoring him to his country . . . an object which presses on our justice & our honour." Jefferson, however, was out of office by March 1809. The President to Governor Lewis, August 24, 1808, in Carter, *Territorial Papers*, 14:221–222.

31. The Secretary of War to Pierre Chouteau, May 12, 1806, in Carter, *Territorial Papers*, 13:510.

32. Governor Lewis to Pierre Chouteau, October 3, 1808, in ibid., 14: 229–231; Pierre Chouteau explained the Osage gift in a letter to the president, MHS, Chouteau Collection, Pierre Chouteau to Thomas Jefferson, December 10, 1808, Pierre Chouteau Sr. Letterbook, Box 7; Jay Buckley, *William Clark: Indian Diplomat* (Norman: University of Oklahoma Press, 2008), 73–78; Christian, *Before Lewis and Clark*, 160–162. Officials removed the provision reaffirming the Osage gift of land to Pierre Chouteau from the final version of the treaty, and it took Chouteau more than thirty years to gain title to the land in question.

33. Petition to Congress by the Territorial Legislature, November 30, 1812, in Carter, *Territorial Papers*, 16:271–272; Pierre Chouteau to the Secretary of War, March 5, 1813, in ibid., 14:639–640; Clarence Alvord, *The Illinois Country, 1673–1818* (Springfield: Illinois Centennial Commission, 1920), 430–432.

34. A Proclamation by Nathaniel Pope, April 28, 1809, in Carter, *Territorial Papers*, 17:620–622; William E. Foley, *The Genesis of Missouri: From Wilderness Outpost to Statehood* (Columbia: University of Missouri Press, 1989), 231; Mason, *Early Chicago and Illinois*, 146; Foley and Rice, *First Chouteaus*, 143, 149–151; Pierre Chouteau to the Secretary of War, May 20, 1813, in Carter, *Territorial Papers*, 14:671–673.

35. Stan Hoig, *The Chouteaus: First Family of the Fur Trade* (Albuquerque: University of New Mexico Press, 2008), 47; Thorne, *Many Hands*, 150.

36. For a full discussion of the voluntary migrations of eastern Indians into the Illinois Country, see John P. Bowes, *Exiles and Pioneers: Eastern Indians in the Trans-Mississippi West* (New York: Cambridge University Press, 2007).

37. Governor Edwards to Delegate Stephenson, October 18, 1814, in Carter, *Territorial Papers*, 17:33–35; Secretary Pope to Delegate Stephenson, October 20, 1814, in ibid., 17:35–36.

38. Bowes, *Exiles and Pioneers*, 41, 49; Stephen Warren, *The Shawnees and Their Neighbors, 1795–1870* (Urbana: University of Illinois Press, 2009), 81; John Mack Faragher, "'More Motley than Mackinaw': From Ethnic Mixing to Ethnic Cleansing on the Frontier of the Lower Missouri, 1783–1833," in *Contact Points: American Frontiers from the Mohawk Valley to the Mississippi,*

1750–1830, ed. Andrew Cayton and Frederika Teute (Chapel Hill: University of North Carolina Press, 1998), 321–322.

39. Thorne, *Many Hands*, 150; Foley and Rice, *First Chouteaus*, 157–158; Buckley, *William Clark*, 131.

40. Memorial to Congress from the Legislative Assembly, in Carter, *Territorial Papers*, 16:402–405; Petition to Congress by the Legislative Assembly, December 18, 1815, in ibid., 17:263–268; Memorial to Congress by the Legislative Assembly, January 2, 1816, in ibid., 17:273–275; Memorial to Congress by the Legislative Assembly, January 9, 1816, in ibid., 17:279; Memorial to the President by the Legislative Assembly, January 11, 1816, in ibid., 17:280–281; Memorial to Congress by the Legislative Assembly, February 13, 1816, in ibid., 17:299–300; Buck, *Illinois in 1818*, 203, 206, 286.

41. Foley and Rice, *First Chouteaus*, 158–159, 195–197.

42. Foley, *Genesis of Missouri*, 246; Foley and Rice, *First Chouteaus*, 179–180; Christian, *Before Lewis and Clark*, 348; Oglesby, "Pierre Menard," 227; Edwin C. McReynolds, *Missouri: A History of the Crossroads State* (Norman: University of Oklahoma Press, 1962), 103; Hoig, *Chouteaus*, 103, 136.

43. Hoig, *Chouteaus*, 163–164; Oglesby, "Pierre Menard," 226.

44. Menard in 1828–1829 helped secure four million acres for the United States, including much of the disputed land from the 1804 treaty that Chouteau and Harrison had negotiated. Christian, *Before Lewis and Clark*, 341–342; James E. Davis, *Frontier Illinois* (Bloomington: Indiana University Press, 1998), 193; Oglesby, "Pierre Menard," 225–226; McReynolds, *Missouri*, 103; Warren, *Shawnees*, 89–90; Buckley, *William Clark*, 202; William Foley, *Wilderness Journey: The Life of William Clark* (Columbia: University of Missouri Press, 2004), 259.

45. Excellent accounts of the many commercial activities involving the Chouteau and Menard offspring can be found in Hoig, *Chouteaus*; and Christian, *Before Lewis and Clark*. The breakup and sale of John Jacob Astor's American Fur Company is best described in Lavender, *Fist in the Wilderness*, 410–417; and Chittenden, *American Fur Trade*, 1:363–365.

46. Edward Mason, *Early Chicago*, 146–147. Pierre Chouteau, Pierre Menard, and their families undoubtedly included liquor in their supply of goods for the Indian trade, but their record is one of comparative restraint. François Chouteau wrote his father-in-law, Pierre Menard, on September 7, 1832, complaining, "The Loup tribe drinks a lot at the present and often many die. Not a day passes that at least 30 gallons of whiskey is not brought to the village. In five years from now, I presume that they will be almost destroyed if they keep on at that pace." Dorothy Marra, *Cher Oncle, Cher Papa: The Letters of Francois and Berenice Chouteau*, trans. Marie-Laure Pal, ed. David Boutros

(Kansas City: University of Missouri and Western History Manuscript Division, 2001), 103–104. François's half-brother, Pierre Chouteau Jr., was at the same time engaged in smuggling liquor to the upper Missouri country as part of a fierce competition with British companies.

47. Dunn, *Indiana*, 304; Buck, *Illinois in 1818*, 188, 217; Jones, *William Clark*, 319; Christian, *Before Lewis and Clark*, 237–247.

48. MHS, Chouteau Collection, Pierre Chouteau to Secretary of War Dearborn, October 1, 1805, Pierre Chouteau Sr. Letterbook, Box 7.

49. Numerous documents, including many cited earlier, demonstrating the attempts made by Chouteau, Menard, and their families on behalf of Indians can be found in Carter, *Territorial Papers*, chiefly in volumes 13, 14, 16, and 17.

50. For an extended discussion of the contrasts drawn by many nineteenth-century American writers between French and American actions and attitudes on the frontier, see Edward Watts, *In This Remote Country: French Colonial Culture in the Anglo-American Imagination, 1780–1860* (Chapel Hill: University of North Carolina Press, 2006). Watts argues that these contrasts were drawn as part of an alternative vision of American imperialism whose proponents hoped would more closely resemble French colonial practices. Richard White's *The Middle Ground: Indians, Empires, and Republics in the Great Lakes Region, 1650–1815* (Cambridge: Cambridge University Press, 1991) remains an excellent starting point for any discussion about French-Indian relations during this period.

Blue Beads, Vermilion, and Scalpers

The Social Economy of the 1810–1812 Astorian Overland Expedition's French Canadian Voyageurs

NICOLE ST-ONGE

TRACKING HIRED PERSONNEL INVOLVED IN THE NORTH AMERICAN fur trade economy in all their peregrinations is always problematic. Seeking to understand the underlying motives of voyageurs' social and economic behaviors poses even greater research challenges. While voyageurs constituted a vital class of workers, from the very beginning of European colonization efforts in North America until well into the nineteenth century, they are a difficult group to trace. Using the volume of recorded pelts being loaded onto boats at the port of Montreal between 1768 and 1776, researchers have calculated that a yearly average of 1,400 men would have been needed to move the furs out of the interior.[1] This manpower requirement continued to grow into the nineteenth century. Voyageur specialist Carolyn Podruchny has argued that by 1816 the Montreal-based North West Company (NWC) alone had at least 2,000 voyageurs in its employ.[2] To these NWC numbers must be added the voyageurs working for the Hudson's Bay Company (HBC), the American Fur Company, and myriad other smaller trading concerns. In the 1810 hiring season—the year that Pacific Fur Company (PFC) voyageurs were engaged for the Astorian expeditions by land and by sea—478 new contracts for men engaged in the fur trade were signed in front of Montreal notaries. And added to this total are those voyageurs who signed at Trois-Rivières and Sorel, east of Montreal, or in front of notaries in rural parishes of the St. Lawrence valley, as well as those already working in the interior on multiyear contracts. Fur trading was a vast, far-flung enterprise, employing hundreds, if not thousands, of French Canadian employees year after year.[3]

The fur trade was a key sector of various North American colonial economies prior to the mid-nineteenth century. It was also a crucial source of employment for the French Canadian population residing in the St. Lawrence valley, especially the Montreal area. Yet studying fur trade companies has always been difficult. The problem is, in part, a question of scale—how should one approach the study of an extensive, continent-wide, multigenerational enterprise involving both European immigrants and native populations? Key issues in examining the most numerous actors involved in fur trading, the voyageurs and *engagés*, stem from their lowly status (they were often perceived as not meriting attention), their mobility (the sheer logistical and practical problems of tracking voyageurs and their métis descendants through space, time, and multitudes of archival holdings can be daunting), and their lack of education. As most French Canadian men or their children residing in the interior were illiterate, they left few written traces of themselves. Some authors have taken up the challenge—most notably in recent years, Podruchny's magisterial *Making the Voyageur World: Travelers and Traders in the North American Fur Trade*; Tanis Thorne's research on French and Indian relations on the Lower Missouri; and Heather Devine's award-winning study, *The People Who Own Themselves: Aboriginal Ethnogenesis in a Canadian Family 1660–1900*.[4] But much work remains to be done in filling out and substantiating the vast canvas that they have painted.

This essay examines a group of voyageurs hired by agents of the newly formed PFC in Montreal and Michilimackinac in the spring and summer of 1810.[5] The overland expedition's destination was distant Fort Astoria, at the mouth of the Columbia River, in present-day Oregon.[6] The expedition departed from Montreal in early July 1810 and arrived, fragmented, at Fort Astoria between January and May 1812. It is argued here that the economic behaviors displayed by the men during the eighteen-month expedition reflect not only the realities experienced during the trek itself but also the histories of the individuals who signed up for the Columbia-bound expedition and, ultimately, their ambitions following the end of their five-year contracts. Voyageur behavior that at first glance may seem financially irresponsible or obsessively parsimonious reflected not only individual personalities and attitudes but also postexpedition goals and projects.

The overland Astorian expedition is exceptionally well documented. Few, if any, nineteenth-century expeditions have such a rich combination of surviving journals and account books. Five key sources were used to track the Astoria overland men. First and foremost were the two overland employee ledger and account books that were kept primarily by the expedition clerk John Reed and occasionally by expedition leader Wilson Price Hunt.[7] These contain careful entries of all the activities on the men's accounts with the PFC—when, where, and what they withdrew in cash or trade items from their accounts during the journey. From this, raw data patterns of economic behavior can be detected and inferences of social activities made. To provide context and flesh out the information provided by this admittedly dry source, this study used various editions of three journals kept by members of the expedition or by fellow travelers.[8] A fourth journal about the earlier Great Lakes section of the journey offers only a few clues as to the activities and attitudes of the hired men.[9] Journals and memoirs written by contemporaries of the overland expedition, such as those by Alexander Ross and Gabriel Franchere, who did not participate in the trek but had talked at length with the players involved, were also consulted.[10] Also examined were the descriptions of later chroniclers such as Washington Irving, whose research for a history of Astoria commissioned by John Jacob Astor involved correspondence and conversations with surviving members of both the land and sea expeditions to the west coast.[11] Other sources were used to better understand these French Canadian voyageurs within the St. Lawrence valley, including two large online demographic and archival databases, the *Projet de Recherche en Démographie Historique* (PRDH) hosted by the University of Montreal, and the *Voyageur Contracts Database Project* available online. Both allowed a thorough search for information on the individuals involved in the trek prior to their departure on the expedition, and, for some, after their return.[12] All these sources enabled a focused study of a clearly delineated group of fur trade employees from the time of their hiring in Montreal or Michilimackinac to the end of their five-year contracts, and provided a greater understanding of their social and economic behaviors. The analysis and interpretation of these behaviors shed further light on the overall voyageur world in the opening decades of the nineteenth century.

HIRING DIFFICULTIES

In the first days of July 1810, a *canot de maître* containing up to sixteen men left the docks at Lachine in Montreal for Michilimackinac. Their eventual destination was the soon-to-be-established Fort Astoria. Their departure from Montreal came late in the inland navigation season. Montreal fur trade merchants normally sent their brigades westward as early as possible—usually by mid-May—to allow men and supplies destined for distant forts safe arrival before the freeze-up.[13] But problems in recruitment, acquiring sufficient supplies, the relative inexperience of expedition leaders, and hostility from well-established competitors such as the NWC plagued overland Astorian expedition organizers William Price Hunt and Donald Mackenzie as they attempted to assemble their brigade.

Various authors have commented on the difficulties faced by Hunt and Mackenzie in hiring sufficient men of quality in Montreal, Michilimackinac, and St. Louis. However, the thirteen Astorian voyageurs recruited in Montreal for the overland expedition seem to fit, at first glance, the typical voyageur mold. Notarized contracts were located for ten of these thirteen men. All signed on to the expedition in front of prominent Montreal notary John Gerbrand Beek.[14] Although the merchant company is not listed on the contracts, PFC shareholder Alexander McKay is listed as the merchant representative. All the contracts located for both the land and sea expeditions to Astoria were signed between May 14 and June 24, 1810, in Beek's Montreal office.[15] Seven of the land expedition's men were hired as *milieu*, or middlemen, the lowest position in both the canoes and the fur trade hierarchy. Of the other three, Jean Baptiste Perrault, then a resident of Saint-François-du-Lac, was hired as a clerk; Pierre Picotte of Rivière-du-Loup-en-Haut (Louiseville) was the canoe's *gouvernail*, or steersman; and Joseph Robillard, hailing from Sainte-Anne-Bout-de-l'Isle (Sainte-Anne-de-Bellevue), was the expedition's guide to Michilimackinac. Robillard was the only one of the men hired who had a "going and coming" contract, earning a flat rate of 500 Lower Canada livres, equivalent to 83.83 colonial Spanish dollars, for the round-trip to the Great Lakes post and back to Montreal in one season. All the other men were hired as winterers contracted to work year-round in the continental interior for five consecutive years. This was an unusual length of time in the fur trade labor market, where two- or three-year contracts were the norm for winterers. These contracts also contained the caveat that the men could be expected to travel "as well by land, sea or river." While this is probably an indication that expedition leaders had not yet sorted out which of these men would travel by sea on the *Tonquin* to Astoria, it also may have been a precautionary clause suggested by Hunt or Mackenzie to prevent men from reneging on their contracts in case the overlanders had to walk or ride part of the way westward. Although usually illiterate, French Canadian fur trade personnel were very aware of the various clauses, stipulations, and guarantees made in their contracts, and often resisted what they considered to be untoward demands on their time or labor.[16]

These contracts are unusual not only for their five-year duration and their travel mode clauses but also for the generous wages offered. When the PFC began hiring the French Canadian voyageurs in mid-May, it was already offering a lofty 1,000 livres per year with an advance of 60 livres and standard voyageur equipment included.[17] Despite unusually high wages, these sums were obviously insufficient, and by early June McKay was offering lowly middlemen 1,200 livres, or 200 colonial Spanish dollars, per annum, with advances of up to 300 livres and double the standard equipment. This points very clearly to hiring difficulties. For the inland navigation season of 1810, men working for a variety of other companies signed eighty wintering *milieu* contracts in Montreal. The wage rates varied greatly, from a low of 400 livres per year offered by the Michilimackinac Company to a high of 700 livres per year by the NWC for wintering *milieus* heading for its distant Athabasca district. Even multiyear contracts signed in March or April, at the height of the Montreal fur trade hiring season, did not surpass a wage of 600 livres plus standard equipment per year.[18] If one looks at all eighty multiyear middleman contracts signed as early as January 1, 1810, and as late as July, the pattern holds. The PFC agents were providing, on average, 40 percent more, with cash advances twice the size of that normally given upon signing with a Montreal-based company. By June, the Astorians were offering twice the equipment and material goods customarily offered to multiyear signatories.

Despite these various enticements, the overland PFC expedition left Montreal short of its desired complement of men. Expedition leader Hunt pinned his hopes on the Great Lakes fur trade emporium of Michilimackinac, often referred to as Mackinac, to fill out his voyageur numbers before pushing on to St. Louis.[19] Besides recruiting an insufficient number of men, at least 20 percent of those who had signed a contract and pocketed the generous advances deserted prior to the Montreal departure.[20] Interesting examples of this phenomenon are three contracts, all signed on June 6, 1810, in Beek's Montreal office. The three men were Ignace Meyaoscawash, Antoine Tanascaon, and Paul Weaweno, three Nipissing Indians from the Lake of Two Mountains settlement just west of Montreal. They signed the PFC standard five-year contracts at 1,200 livres per year with double equipment provided. All three received a 25 Spanish dollar advance at signing. They were hired in a dual capacity as middlemen and hunters, and negotiated an unusual clause—although half their hunting catch had to be turned over to the company, the other half was theirs to sell to the company at standard post rates. The PFC also had to furnish them with half the ammunition and equipment—*ferraille*—that they needed in order to hunt. But the paper trail ends there. The three native hunters do not show up in the overland expedition ledger books or in any of the narratives about either the land or sea expedition. They simply vanish. The PFC seemed incapable in the hostile NWC-controlled Montreal area to force recalcitrant voyageurs to comply with their signed contracts or to recoup advances provided to deserters.[21]

The peculiarity of the Montreal group hired for the overland expedition is highlighted when the age and experience of the men are analyzed. Jean Baptiste Perrault, the one French Canadian clerk hired for the overland brigade, was an experienced trader forty-nine years of age.[22] Joseph Robillard, the guide to Michilimackinac, also in his midforties, had several previous contracts as a steersman and bowman plying the Great Lakes trade. Both these men, however, left the expedition upon its arrival at Michilimackinac. Pierre Picotte, the canoe steersman, was just twenty-two years old with only one previous contract traced to him. In June 1807, Robert Dickson & Co. hired him out of Michilimackinac, in front of island notary Samuel Abbott, for work along the Mississippi.[23] Perhaps it was this southern experience that prompted McKay to offer him, on May 23, 1810, a five-year contract at 1,400 livres per annum, with a 300 livres advance. Picotte was the third man to either break his engagement or desert upon arrival at Michilimackinac. His last purchase, on August 4 in Mackinac, was four black feathers at a cost of $3.18. After that, he disappeared from the PFC overland ledger books, and no other fur-trading contract out of Montreal or Mackinac with his name can be found.

The balance of the men hired out of Montreal range in age from as young as fifteen (*milieu* André Dufresne) to as old as thirty-four (*milieu* Jean Baptiste Turcotte of the Tanneries de Roland, on the island of Montreal); most voyageurs were in their twenties. What is startling is their clear lack of documented long-haul experience. If the older clerk and guide are removed, the other eleven men had little wintering experience. Only one man hired, Charles Boucher of Berthier, had a previous three-year wintering contract. In 1804, he had signed up with the NWC.[24] Only four others had signed either one-year or "coming and going" seasonal contracts prior to 1810. All these contracts were for Great Lakes destinations. The balance of men hired by the Astorians appear to have had no fur-trading employment experiences, as reflected in formal contractual Montreal engagements.[25]

Yet all these relatively young men came from the heartland of voyageur recruitment country, the parishes situated in the Montreal–to–Trois-Rivières corridor. The farthest eastern parish was Rivière-du-Loup-en-Haut and the farthest west was Vaudreuil, with several voyageurs coming from the island of Montreal itself. These were men whose families and relations were certainly familiar with the voyageur world, even if the individuals hired had only limited documented contacts with fur trade wage employment.

By July 28, 1810, the expedition had reached Michilimackinac in its *canot de maître*.[26] This old trading center was the chief rendezvous of the Michilimackinac Fur Company and a thousand other small associations of trappers and adventurers connected to the fur trade. In the opening years of the nineteenth century, Michilimackinac was still the great outfitting mart of the South, and the center and headquarters of all fur traders who frequented the Mississippi and Missouri waters in search of peltry. Nevertheless, according to Astorian member and chronicler Alexander Ross,[27] Hunt again encountered hiring difficulties, causing vexing delays that stretched into weeks. Alexander Ross and later Washington Irving proposed several explanations for these challenges. Hunt and the PFC were unknown quantities to Mackinac men. According to Ross and Irving, they initially demanded five-year contracts from men who were accustomed to either seasonal deals or, at most, three-year arrangements. The expedition was late in the season, and so most of the interested and capable men had already hired themselves out. According to both Ross and Irving, rumors circulated at Michilimackinac, just as they had in Montreal, that the trek to the Pacific was folly and doomed to fail. Ross argued in his narrative that Hunt, after spending several days recruiting, "could only pick up a few disorderly Canadians, already ruined in mind and in body, whilst the cross-breeds and the Yankees kept aloof," even though he had reduced the length of the contracts from five to three years.[28] Ross added that it was only with the timely arrival of Ramsay Crooks, a Missouri trader who joined the expedition as a partner at Michilimackinac, that the hiring of voyageurs picked up. According to the two chroniclers, a ruse was employed by offering the expedition's voyageurs long feathers to be worn on their hats. These plumes were normally only worn by men who had wintered in the Northwest—the fabled *homme du nord*, as opposed to the lowly seasonal *mangeur de lard*—as a mark of prestige.[29] Because the voyageurs were signing up for a grand adventure to the little-known far western region, Crooks told the men that they were deserving of the honor, which encouraged some to sign up. However, it is hard to believe that men with even nominal fur trade experience were so gullible; more likely, the very generous advances forwarded to these men proved far more enticing.[30] Nevertheless, the newly hired, along with those who had signed on in Montreal, received their feather, but at a price. The quantities, quality, and prices of these items were carefully noted in the ledger books and their cost debited from the hired men's accounts.[31]

For example, "black feathers" and "foxtail feathers" cost the men $.92 each, ostrich feathers $.83 each, and a cock feather a trifling $.67. Still, this was quite a bit of money for men who, at best, were paid 200 colonial Spanish dollars, or 1,200 Lower Canadian livres per annum.

During his sixteen-day stay in Michilimackinac, William Hunt hired seventeen men. Sixteen were French Canadian voyageurs, and one was a clerk of Irish origin, John Reed, who took over the bookkeeping and ledger entries.[32] On paper, at least, Ross's poor assessment of the Mackinac voyageurs seems unfair, for most were men with experience in the Southwest fur trade. Thirteen were based in Mackinac, having hired out from that settlement in previous years with established companies such as the Michilimackinac Company, Robert Dickson, or the Joseph Rolette outfits, and signing multiple contracts in front of resident notary Samuel Abbott.[33] Eleven of these Mackinac voyageurs had an original, traceable Montreal contract. Most of the Mackinac hires were French Canadian men from the traditional St. Lawrence recruitment basin. These men first hired themselves in Montreal, in front of notary Louis Chaboillez or notary Jonathan Grey between 1803 and 1808, to traditional Great Lakes fur-trading concerns such as the Michilimackinac Company; Toussaint Pothier; Todd, McGill & Co.; Forsyth, Richardson & Co.; and Parker, Gerrard, Ogilvy & Co. These men signed one- or two-year contracts with destinations listed as *"dépendences du sud,"* *"dépendances du nord,"* and "Pays d'en Haut." Occasionally, more specific wintering areas such as Michilimackinac, St. Joseph Island, or the vaguer Mississippi were listed. Once in the interior, these voyageurs opted to remain inland, preferring to renew their contracts yearly at Mackinac Island rather than return to Montreal. They were thus professional voyageurs and *engagés* specializing in the Great Lakes and southwestern trade. One could speculate that the fact that they did not return to their hometowns of Maskinongé, Laprairie, or other traditional voyageur parishes at the conclusion of their first inland contracts indicated a lack of economic or affective ties to their childhood homes. It would also explain, in part, their willingness to sign on for the Astorian trek to the other side of the continent.

Further discrepancies with the Ross and Irving narratives emerge when the Mackinac voyageurs' salaries and contract lengths are examined. The contract conditions offered to thirteen of the Mackinac men can be reconstructed from surviving sources.[34] Surprisingly, all of them agreed to five-year terms, contrary to Ross's claim. Their salaries ranged from $150 to $200, which was comparable to the sums offered to the Montreal *engagés*. They were hired between July 30 and August 9 during the first ten days of the expedition's sixteen-day furlough in Mackinac. The first contract came a mere two days after the arrival at Mackinac, when François Landry dit Penotte hired on for five years at $150 per year.[35] He was an experienced voyageur from Maskinongé, having hired on out of Mackinac the previous year for the firm Cadotte & Co, with a Lac Courte Oreille district destination. In 1808, he and his older brother, Joseph Landry dit Penotte, had signed on with the Michilimackinac Company on the same day and for the same salary for a one-year wintering contract in the St. Joseph Island area.[36] In 1809, the Michilimackinac Company had rehired Joseph Landry in Mackinac to go to the Arkansas River. Joseph Landry waited until August 4, 1810, before signing on with the Astorians for the same salary as François.[37]

Presumably, these hirings occurred after the agreement between Ramsay Crooks and the PFC representatives was inked and the experienced Mackinac trader could help with negotiations.[38] Yet nothing tangible seems to have been offered to prospective voyageurs to expedite matters. The cost of the famous feathers with which voyageurs proudly adorned themselves was carefully debited from the men's accounts. One thing that Crooks might have suggested was to buy out or transfer the engagements of desirable men from other fur-trading concerns to the PFC. This recruitment tactic can be traced in at least four cases in the PFC account books. Jean Baptiste Brugiere's July 21, 1810, contract with supplier James Aird to voyage to the Mississippi was transferred on August 2, 1810. Guillaume Leroux Cardinal's contract with Joseph Rolette's outfit was bought out for $50, plus another $32.33 owed the merchant by Cardinal. Jean Baptiste Provost, whose destination had been the Mississippi, was also bought out from Joseph Rolette's trading concern for 200 livres ($33.33). Jean Baptiste Pilon was bought out from a Mr. Berthelotte for 100 livres ($16.67). Hunt was even willing to pay the fines of men who had broken furniture in a tavern brawl, notably Joseph Perrault, a man with experience in the Missouri trade, in exchange for signing up with the overland expedition.[39] Yet as in the case with the contract buyouts and adornments, these amounts were carefully debited from the voyageurs' accounts.[40] Enticements were perhaps not noted directly in the men's entries, but handouts or gifts of money or goods were not noted anywhere beyond the issuing of standard equipment.

These Mackinac voyageurs were given very generous advancements in goods or money. For example, Charles Lussier was hired in Mackinac on August 4, 1810, on a five-year, $150-per-year contract.[41] By August 8, his account was $52.51, as he had spent over a third of his yearly wages in just six days. This was extremely generous on the part of company agents because the danger of desertion was always present.[42] Some of the debits on the Lussier account were for the usual cash advances ($15.00) made at the signing of a contract, along with the ubiquitous black feather ($1.84) and foxtail feathers ($1.84), but other entries included a *capot* (voyageur coat; $8.00), a calico shirt ($3.33), a pair of corduroy trousers ($8.00), a fine hat ($4.00), a silk handkerchief ($2.00), a pair of shoes ($4.00), and a pair of suspenders ($3.00). As with the Montreal hirings, the men signing on at Mackinac were given the same $150- to $200-a-year contract—generous for the times and the job. Remarkably, they were allowed to withdraw from their account up to a third of the yearly income before departure. Lussier was not alone in his desire to be well turned-out. Pierre Brugiere, who had had a previous contract with trader James Aird, also purchased a substantial amount on credit against his PFC $150-a-year account. Articles such as fourteen bread buns ($2.38), a carrot of tobacco ($2.00),[43] a cloth *capot* ($8.00), a fine hat ($5.00), a pair of trousers ($4.00), a shirt ($2.50), and a pair of shoes ($2.30), along with several small sums of cash, meant that this voyageur left Mackinac after having spent close to $42.00 in only four days, or nearly a third of his yearly wages. As noted above, this spending prior to departure was not just a Michilimackinac phenomenon. Some Montreal men had charged up to $70.00 against their company accounts. In fact, by July 6, 1810, the "advances made to the men in money" in Montreal amounted to $845.70.[44]

FROM MICHILIMACKINAC TO ST. LOUIS

The last Mackinac entries in the Reed ledger book are dated August 12, 1810.[45] Presumably the expedition left that day or the day following, for the next entries were made at the Prairie du Chien settlement on August 24, 1810.[46] The expedition crossed Lake Michigan to Green Bay, proceeded up the Fox River, and then down to Prairie du Chien via the Wisconsin River. There, at the junction of the Wisconsin and Mississippi Rivers, they paused for a day to rest and resupply. Some of the voyageurs lined up at the company store for more feathers and foxtails, but the purchases of other items were also noted in the men's accounts.[47] Joseph St-Amand purchased a quart of whiskey for $.75, while Jean Ouvre and Antoine Plante bought tea and sugar.[48] Though basic foodstuff was usually guaranteed in their contracts, "extras" such as tobacco, tea, sugar, and alcohol had to be purchased. From Prairie du Chien, they paddled down the Mississippi to St. Louis, where they landed on September 3, 1810, and stayed until at least October 21, 1810. This was the last large settlement before the true start of the Astorians' trek westward to the Columbia.

While company officials attempted to round out the numbers of voyageurs and other expedition personnel with Canadian or local Frenchmen and American recruits, those hired in Montreal and Michilimackinac enjoyed their last days in a large dynamic center of commerce. The voyageurs spent their future earnings in several ways. Nearly all withdrew varying amounts of cash from their accounts. Others bought goods at the John G. Conegy store in the nearby French settlement of Ste. Geneviève. Some also paid local individuals for services, room and board, or items.[49]

It was during the St. Louis furlough that the differing spending habits emerged between voyageurs hired in Montreal and those hired in Mackinac. Taken as a group, the men hired in Montreal consistently spent less than those hired in Mackinac. For example, in St. Louis, the nine Montreal voyageurs spent a total of $136.54, an average of $15.17 each, although this average was somewhat skewed by the high spending of one Montreal voyageur, Louis Laliberté.[50] In St. Louis, he debited from his account the sum of $68.49. This money went mostly to the purchasing of goods from local merchants. Without his share, the average disbursement for the remaining eight men's account was $8.50.

In fact, Laliberté was exceptional in that his spending habits more closely mirrored those of his Mackinac counterparts rather than his fellow Montreal-contracted voyageurs. Hailing from Faubourg Saint-Laurent (Montreal), he was hired by the PFC in late May 1810 for 1,000 livres ($166.66) per year for five years. He received $49.50 in cash advances prior to the boat leaving Lachine. Louis bought $22.77 worth of feathers and foxtails from the island merchants or at the company store in Michilimackinac, and then spent another $11.58 at Prairie du Chien to purchase a feather and unspecified goods at local merchant James McFarlane's outlet.[51] The St. Louis ledgers reveal a dual pattern of spending and purchasing. Four times between September 3 and October 1, 1810, Laliberté withdrew small amounts of cash, from $.50 to $2.50, for a total of $4.50. He also purchased calico cloth for $2.50 and directed Reed to pay both "G. Bosseron, armourer" and Madame Alvarez a further $2.50 each. From the first, he likely purchased a Bosseron knife, a coveted item that the PFC later sold to its employees for $5 each. What Mme. Alvarez offered is unknown, but other entries in the ledger books mention women as seamstresses, bakers, and boardinghouse managers. Larger cash amounts were debited from Laliberté's account to pay cash to Jos (Buissonnes), Jos (Leblon), and F. (LaBross)—$12.50, $12.50, and $30.00, respectively. Several men owed money to these persons, but the nature of the transactions is unknown. Finally, Louis Laliberté, like several of his fellow French

Canadian voyageurs, bought $5.65 of goods from G. Comegy's & Co. Ste. Geneviève store. In sum, this voyageur spent close to $155.00 of his yearly salary of $166.66 in the first four months of employment for the American concern.[52] Laliberté's spending pattern in those early months was unusual for Astorian French Canadian *engagés* and voyageurs hailing from Montreal, but not for those hired out of Michilimackinac.

The fifteen men hired in Michilimackinac collectively spent $757.31 in St. Louis, an average of $50.48 debited from each man's account. Like their Montreal counterparts, all withdrew small amounts of cash from their accounts, usually between $2.00 and $4.00. This cash could easily have been spent in the city's taverns and brothels, or simply on better food and lodging than those provided by the company. More intriguing, however, was that the bulk of the spending involved buying goods from St. Louis–area merchants. For example, merchant Conegy of Ste. Geneviève sold $34.12 worth of goods to Guillaume Cardinal dit Leroux, $42.25 to Charles Lussier, and a surprising $64.25 to Joseph Gervais.[53] Unfortunately, exactly what these veteran voyageurs purchased from Conegy's and other area merchants was rarely itemized. All the men from Mackinac purchased substantial amounts from the merchants. Of the Montrealers, only the above-discussed Louis Laliberté imitated them. In fact, six of the nine men from Montreal debited only small amounts of cash from their accounts and seemingly made no purchases in St. Louis or Ste. Geneviève stores. Although both groups of men originated from the same cluster of parishes in the Montreal–to–Trois-Rivières corridor, their behavior consistently varied.

FROM ST. LOUIS TO NODAWAY CAMP

The Astorians left St. Louis in the third week of October 1810 and arrived at Fort Osage on October 30, leaving two days later. Prior to their departure from Fort Osage, twenty-one men purchased bison robes from local trader George G. Sibley. Twelve of these men were from the French Canadian core of voyageurs coming down from Montreal and Michilimackinac. All seven of the Mackinac men who purchased robes in Fort Osage had previous experiences with wintering in the Great Lakes, Missouri, and Mississippi regions. Only two of the five hired in Montreal who purchased bison robes had traceable previous voyageur experience. Perhaps they wisely chose to listen to the advice of the more experienced men on the expedition. While bison robes normally sold for $4.00, damaged robes could be obtained for as low as $1.50. This last purchase assured that the men had some protection against cold at the Nodaway wintering camp.[54]

From November 18, 1810, to April 15, 1811, the French Canadian voyageurs remained at the Nodaway camp. This wintering site was situated approximately 750 miles west of St. Louis along the Missouri River, near the mouth of the Nodaway River in present-day Andrew County, Missouri.[55] Again, variations in their purchasing habits at the company store surfaced. According to Reed's ledgers, the nine Montreal voyageurs purchased a total of $265.08 of goods and provisions over those initial five wintering months. This averaged to $29.45 per man, but variations in spending were considerable. André Dufresne from Montreal was rather frugal and bought only $3.00 worth of goods over the course of the winter. Indeed, he bought sparingly throughout the voyage and returned to Montreal in spring 1814 to sue the PFC for owed wages. It seems that he thought that by being frugal he could save most of his earnings for his return to the St. Lawrence valley. During the entire trip, he spent only $27.12, including $20.00 that he had received in advances prior to leaving Montreal. No other contract out of Montreal has been found for this man before or after the Astorian overland trek. At the other extreme was Jean Baptiste Turcotte, an inhabitant of the Tanneries de Roland on Montreal Island, who spent $55.06. This was by far the most money spent by a Montreal-hired voyageur. Many of the items that he purchased, as well as the quantity, indicate that these voyageurs had an interest in bartering and exchange. For example, beyond the ubiquitous purchase of a breech flap, over the five wintering months Turcotte bought six carrots of tobacco for $12.00 and eighteen pipes for $5.50. Although this man had negotiated the handsome salary of $200 a year, it seems unlikely that he would spend well over a month's wages on pipes and tobacco if he did not have exchange or bartering in mind. Because no diary was kept at the wintering camp, however, it is not possible to determine exactly what transpired.

When one looks at the accounts of the Michilimackinac voyageurs, it becomes evident that they also purchased goods for the purpose of exchange. Of the fourteen accounts that were active during those winter months, many charges were made against accounts in exchange for potential trade items.[56] These men collectively spent a total of $450.16 in Reed's little store, an average of $32.15 per man, but, as with the Montreal accounts, variations occurred. The smallest spender was Jean Baptiste Provost of Laprairie, who bought only $10.62 worth of goods. His biggest purchase was three yards of swanskin for $4.50.[57] But this cloth and his other purchases seem quite utilitarian in nature. It is hard to know what his postcontract ambitions were, for he drowned in the final grim weeks of the expedition while cross-ing the Snake River in a makeshift canoe, trying to reach his companions who had food.[58] The most prolific spender was Charles Lussier of Varennes, who expended $63.25 over the twenty or so weeks at Nodaway. Little is known of him except that he was an experienced voyageur who had been initially hired out of Montreal for McGill and Co. on January 17, 1805, on a one-year contract for 500 livres ($83.33).[59] Lussier was later hired out of Michilimackinac—first by Robert Dickson in 1807 and then by the Mich-ilimackinac Company in 1808—to winter at St. Peters River.[60] He finally signed on with the PFC in Michilimackinac in early August 1810, agreeing to a five-year contract worth 900 livres, or $150 per year.[61]

As noted earlier, Lussier was a dandy who outfitted himself before his departure from Michilimackinac, spending over $40.00 on clothes and accessories.[62] Not only was he one of the men who withdrew cash from his account ($12.00) in St. Louis, he also charged unspecified purchases from nearby Ste. Geneviève merchants for an additional $45.25.[63] Other Mich-ilimackinac veterans, such as François Landry dit Penotte of Maskinongé ($54.25), Joseph Gervais of Maskinongé ($43.50), Pierre Bruyère ($31.62), Guillaume Cardinal ($36.62), Antoine Clappin ($35.62), François Mar-tial ($33.00), and Jean Ouvre ($30.62), all spent heavily on trade articles. Although breech flaps ($1.50), red wool caps ($2.00), and packs of playing cards ($2.00) were frequent purchases for all the men, other items, such as brass rings ($.50 per dozen), vermilion ($2.00 a pound), blue beads ($1.50), scalpers[64] ($.50 each), small axes or tomahawks ($1.50 each), silk handker-chiefs ($2.00 each), and the ubiquitous tobacco carrots ($2.00), appear to have been at least partly destined for trade with nearby native populations.[65] The expedition leaders likely tolerated a small amount of trade that profited them because most of what voyageurs possessed were goods, supplies, and items purchased from the company store.[66]

Two realities are confirmed when one looks at the personal items put up for auction after the death of Michilimackinac voyageur Joseph Perrault in December 1810. First, as historian James Ronda notes, voyageurs owned relatively few material goods:

> Joseph Perrault was one of those voyageurs engaged at Mackinac. Sometime in December Perrault died. Nothing is known about the circumstances of his death, and both Ross and Irving are silent on the episode. On December 30 there was an auction of Perrault's goods. Those items suggest how slim an estate a voyageur might amass. Pipes, a tobacco pouch, ragged trousers, tat-tered calico shirts, and worn stockings were among the simple goods put under

the hammer. The proceedings yielded $137.00, which was added to Perrault's wages and brought the estate to $199.50.[67]

More revealing than the net value of the estate was the quantity of exchange goods that Perrault held at the time of his death.[68] Perrault owned one small traveling trunk, referred to as a *cassette*, to carry his goods (sold for $8.00), one worsted sash ($3.00), one blanket *capot* ($9.87), one milled wool cap ($1.12), and one portage collar ($5.75). However, he also had eighteen pipes, ten shirts, four pairs of trousers, plus an assortment of other sundry goods, such as looking glasses (mirrors), silk handkerchiefs, stockings, and swan quills. According to Reed's accounting, the proceeds of the auction netted $131.45. This level of material worth, both in personal possessions and in trade goods, points to a generous yearly salary and strong likelihood that Perrault was trading his goods on the side. This was a common practice in later Rocky Mountain American-based expeditions, but was certainly frowned upon by the large Montreal-based companies and the British-based HBC. The PFC used preprinted contracts like most HBC and NWC voyageur contracts, and added clauses forbidding voyageurs from engaging in trade on their own accounts. The exact words were "*sans pouvoir faire aucune traite particulière*," but this clause may have been in reference to the peltry trade, not other forms of exchange, especially when the PFC profited in selling its employee the needed trade goods. We do not know what the contracts signed in Michilimackinac (or beyond) stipulated, but this tolerance for low-level side-trading would have been an enticement for experienced voyageurs who knew the benefits of having trade items to offer to native populations in the interior. It was also a way for expedition leaders to reduce expedition costs because the sale of items to voyageurs reduced the total cash amount that would eventually have to be paid out at the end of their contracts.

FROM NODAWAY CAMP TO FORT HENRY

The expedition departed from its winter camp in mid-April. John Bradbury reported in his travel journal that the expedition was comprised of nearly sixty men, forty of whom were French Canadian voyageurs.[69] A total of twenty-three came from Montreal and Michilimackinac (nine and fourteen, respectively), with the remainder hired in St. Louis during the previous autumn and winter. While traveling up the Missouri toward the Arikara villages, voyageur purchases were predictably sparse. The expedition stopped for a few days in May in the Mahas village. Five of the nine voyageurs from Montreal purchased either vermilion (one-quarter pound for $1.00) or carrots of tobacco ($1.00 each) from Reed's provisions. Twelve of the fourteen Mackinac voyageurs also secured trade goods from Reed. Again, differing patterns emerged between the two groups. Only one of the Montreal men, Jean Baptiste Turcotte, purchased more than one item and spent more than $1.00 during their stay. Mackinac men spent, on average, $1.80 each on trade items at the Mahas village. Five of the twelve Mackinac men who purchased items from Reed's supplies made multiple purchases. Four of these five had Great Lakes and upper Missouri wintering experience, and were perhaps more cognizant of what the Mahas coveted. Mackinac men bought scalpers ($1.00 each), brass rings (three for $.10), and calico cloth at $2.25 a yard.[70] Bradbury noted in his account book that these trade goods were exchanged for a number of items, including meat, tallow, corn, and marrow.[71] The expedition departed the Mahas village under a cloud of worry on May 14, 1811. Villagers had warned expedition leaders of the threat of Sioux hostility. The Sioux were particularly wary of losing their position as middlemen traders between nations such as the Arikaras and Mahas and those farther inland. European intrusions into Sioux trade territory created a potentially explosive situation.

The expedition's next important stop was in the Arikara (Sanish) villages near the present-day North and South Dakota border on the banks of the Missouri. It was here that expedition leader William Hunt decided to abandon their four boats, resolving instead to cut across the prairie on horseback and on foot. After spending over a month with the Arikaras, attempting to procure a sufficient number of horses, he was reduced at one point to bartering with his competitor, Manuel Lisa of the Missouri Fur Company (MFC), for horses held at a nearby MFC post. There is no record of how the veteran voyageurs, used to a life on waterways except for the unavoidable portages, felt about setting out on foot or horseback. However, Reed's account recorded the purchase of a great many moccasins at $.25 a pair in the days just prior and just following their mid-July departure from the Arikaras.

In the course of this monthlong sojourn, a majority of the expedition's hired men spent heavily at the company store on goods mainly destined for bargaining with the native population.[72] Again, variations in quantity of items purchased and the size of the debt incurred differed from man to man, but also from group to group. Taken as a group, the Montreal men spent $86.82 on trade items, an average of $9.64 per man. This included Jean Baptiste Turcotte, who bought $22.00 of goods, and the parsimonious

André Dufresne, who bought only one moccasin awl for $0.12½. The fourteen voyageurs hired in Mackinac collectively spent $183.50, an average of $13.11 per man, with totals varying from $6.50 for Jean Ouvre to $28.25 for François Landry dit Penotte. A number of items were exchanged between the voyageurs and their Arikara hosts, but the three staples were vermilion and blue beads at $4.00 per pound each and scalpers at $.50 per unit. Thirteen Mackinac men bought five-and-a-half pounds of vermilion for a total of $22.00, meaning an average of three-eighths of a pound and $1.50 per man. Four Montreal men bought a total of one-and-three-quarter pounds of vermilion worth $7.00, an average of slightly more than three-eighths of a pound and $1.75 per man. Again, internal discrepancies within these groups surfaced, as only one Mackinac man bought no vermilion, while five Montreal men abstained. Of the four Montrealers who made purchases, three spent $1.00 each for their quarter pound of vermilion, while the fourth, François Trépanier, acquired three-quarter pounds of the powder. Four of the twelve Mackinac men bought only $1.00 worth of goods each, while the others bought larger quantities, such as François Landry, who purchased $3.00 worth.

Seven Montreal men purchased three-and-three-quarter pounds worth of blue beads, a highly prized trade item, for $15.00. André Dufresne and Louis Laliberté, who had both foregone purchasing vermilion, also abstained from beads. Jean Baptiste Dufresne, the Montrealers' most prolific Arikaras spender, bought $5.00 worth of beads. The others spent between $2.00 and $2.50 each on the trade beads. Twelve Mackinac men bought nine-and-three-quarter pounds of the blue beads, for a total of $39.00. Jean Baptiste Provost and Étienne Lussier purchased no beads, while Joseph St-Amant ($5.50) and Joseph Landry ($4.50) invested heavily in these items. The ten other Mackinac men spent between $2.00 and $4.00 on the beads. Finally, scalpers or scalping knives were a significant trade item between the voyageur men and their Arikara hosts. The company charged $.50 for each scalper, and four Montreal men bought between them a total of ten scalpers. In contrast, thirteen Mackinac men bought fifty-six scalpers. Individual scalper purchases varied from one, purchased by Joseph St-Amant, to a total of eight, acquired by Jean Baptiste Pilon.[73]

As a group, the Michilimackinac men spent more of their wages during their stay in the Arikara village on items for trade with local populations. More of them bought greater amounts of the three basic staples of exchange: vermilion, blue beads, and scalpers. Mackinac men also purchased from company stores a greater variety of exchange goods compared to their Montreal cousins. Silk handkerchiefs ($2.50), cartouche knives ($.75), paper looking glasses ($.50),[74] shrouding cloth ($4.00 per yard), carrots of Albany Tobacco ($3.00), and spotted swanskin cloth ($1.00 per yard) were all carefully itemized in Reed's ledgers as debits against the Michilimackinac men's accounts. The men from Mackinac consistently outspent the men from Montreal. Notwithstanding variations within the two groups, the overall tendency is apparent.

The purchase of all these trade items begs the question of what these men were acquiring from the Arikaras. Historically, the tribe was known for its corn and bean crops and horse herds, goods that attracted Sioux and Cheyenne purchasers.[75] Some of the expedition's journals point to items coveted by the French Canadian voyageurs. Bradbury wrote:

> Travellers who have been acquainted with savages have remarked that they are either very liberal of their women to Strangers or extremely jealous. In this species of liberality no nation can be exceeded by the Aricaras who flocked down every evening with their wives, sisters, and daughters, each anxious to meet with a market for them. The Canadians are very good customers, and Mr Hunt was kept in full employ during the evening, in delivering out to them blue beads and vermilion the articles in use for this kind of traffic. This evening I judged that there were not fewer than eighty squaws, and I observed several instances wherein the squaw was consulted by her husband as to the quantum sufficit of price.[76]

Brackenridge agreed:

> It appeared to me while we remained at the village, that their female have become mere articles of traffic: I have seen fathers bring their daughters, brothers their sisters; and husbands their wives to be disposed of for a short time to the highest bidder. I was unable to account for this strange difference from all other people I have ever read of, unless from the inordinate passion which seized them for our merchandise. . . . Seeing the chief one day in a thoughtful mood, I asked him what was the matter—"I was wondering" said he "whether white people have any women amongst you." I assured him in the affirmative. "[T]hen" said he "why is it you people are so found of our women, one might suppose they had never seen any before."[77]

The Canadians paid a nonmonetary price for these dalliances—several came down with syphilis. The disease, however, did not appear to worry them overly. Although expedition partners had thoughtfully purchased quicksilver vials, mercury pills, and mercury ointment in Montreal for such an event, the men preferred their own cures.[78] As Bradbury commented in a bemused tone:

> I was not less surprised on learning that at least two thirds of our Canadians had experienced unpleasant consequences from their intercourse with squaws, not standing which traffic, mentioned before, continued. I had been informed by Jones and Cason of the existence of this evil, but found it was the mildest description . . . they do not fear it. I found some of the Canadians digging up roots which I understood they made a decoction, and used it as a drink. They mostly preferred the roots of Rudbeckia purpurea [purple coneflower, purple echinacea] and sometimes they used those of Houstonia Longifolia [long-leaf summer bluet].[79]

On a superficial level, and certainly to the journal keepers, the motives behind the exchanges were obvious. The French Canadians were in search of sexual comforts, and the Arikaras coveted the trade goods. Though true at some level, the actors involved may have had ulterior motives that escaped the attention of the leaders and chroniclers of the expedition. Possible additional reasons motivating the French Canadian voyageurs and especially those from Michilimackinac will be discussed below. Added incentives motivating the native men and women involved in the exchange are perhaps harder to grasp. Obviously the Arikaras were familiar with and desired the trade goods offered by these voyageurs. From the description, it is also obvious that sex, among other things, as a possible medium of exchange was also understood. The fact that couples, fathers with their daughters, and brothers with their sisters came to traders' camp and all, including the women, openly discussed the going rates indicates that this was a familiar and accepted transaction. One can only speculate if perhaps more than sex for beads and vermilion was being exchanged. Certainly authors such as Alice Kehoe have argued there was a tradition of transfer of powers through sexual intercourse among some of the northern plains tribes.[80] These flamboyant, pomaded, and feathered voyageurs bearing coveted goods were perhaps perceived as holders of power. Husbands, brothers, or fathers might perhaps have sought to benefit spiritually if their women kin were intimate with these French Canadians. On a more prosaic level, these Indians, familiar with the fur trade world, perhaps saw these voyageurs not as lowly salaried employees of large trading concerns but as traders themselves. The Arikaras may have been trying to integrate them into their kinship networks for their own advantage. They were setting up a system of mutual obligations and benefits, thus replicating a system that had existed in the Great Lakes region for generations.[81]

In the days just before the expedition's departure from the Arikara village and in those following, voyageurs purchased several more pairs of moccasins. Montreal voyageurs, perhaps for the first time, truly understood the clause inserted in their contracts: "*aller dans les pays sauvages tant par mer, rivière ou par terre*" ("to go into the wild countries either by sea, river or by land"). Nothing in the voyageur culture or ethos prepared the men for endless days of walking over broken prairie as they suffered from thirst and heat. Little grumbling was reported, but an increase in footwear purchase was recorded in the ledgers. Montrealers bought sixteen pairs of moccasins, ten of which were purchased by Jean Baptiste Turcotte, possibly for resale. The Mackinac men bought forty-one pairs of moccasins. Four of these men, perhaps having greater walking experience or a clearer idea of the terrain ahead, bought seven or more pairs of moccasins. Hunt opened his journal by noting the departure of the expedition:

> Messrs Hunt, Mackenzie, Crooks, Miller, McClelland and Reed who were accompanied by fifty-six men, one woman and two children and had gone by water from Saint-Louis to the Aricaras village on the Missouri, left there with eighty-two horses laden with merchandise, equipment, food and animal-traps. All travelled on foot except for the company's partner and the woman or squaw.[82]

They left their Arikara hosts on July 18, 1811, arriving in early October at Fort Henry, just west of the Continental Divide in the Grand Teton Mountain Range on the banks of the Snake River. Fort Henry was the last stop for the expedition as a coherent whole. The attempt to navigate the Snake River ended in several disasters. The men struggled to reach the headway of the Columbia in an unforgiving terrain as winter conditions worsened, and so the expedition was forced to split up and provisions and goods cached as the river proved unnavigable. It was no longer a functioning expedition, but rather a grim struggle to survive and reach Fort Astoria. Ledger entries that began to taper off reflected dire circumstances. The Montreal and Mackinac men could not have known the hardships that they would face by attempting to cross the Continental Divide to reach the mouth of the Columbia River.

In the three months between the departure from the Arikara village and the expedition's arrival at Fort Henry, the French Canadian voyageurs continued to purchase goods from Reed's company store, and their accounts continued to be carefully annotated and debited. As had been the case since departing from Michilimackinac, variations in purchasing patterns between the two groups persisted. Eight out of the nine Montreal voyageurs purchased items worth a total of $73.30 during the pedestrian and equine phase of their trek. The holdout was the ever-parsimonious André Dufresne. On average, these eight spent $9.13 each during the expedition's final days as a cohesive unit. There was a range again among individual Montrealers. Charles Boucher purchased only $2.50 worth of items, while the profligate Jean Baptiste Turcotte secured goods totaling $26.24. As noted previously, Turcotte's behavior consistently resembled that of the men from Mackinaw. Of the total spent by the Montrealers, $30.00 went to securing carrots of Albany Tobacco ($3.00 each), mostly purchased as half-carrots. Cartouche knives ($.75), moccasins ($.25), and buffalo robes ($1.00) were also popular items as winter approached.[83]

All fourteen remaining Mackinac voyageurs purchased company goods, according to Reed's ledger books. The men debited their accounts for a total of $252.30. As expected, they spent on average nearly twice as much ($17.38) as their Montreal brethren. The purchases ranged from a low of $7.52 for Étienne Lussier to a high of $39.44 for Joseph Gervais. They spent $78.80 on tobacco carrots alone ($5.62 each on average). As with the Montrealers' accounts, bison robes, moccasins, and Cartouche knives figured prominently in their purchases. However, other items in greater quantity and more diversity also figured in the Mackinac men's ledgers. Nine distinct purchases of half-yards of scarlet cloth for $3.00 per half-yard were carefully noted in the accounts. By comparison, only Montrealer Turcotte purchased scarlet cloth. Cotton shirts of $4.00 each were purchased by five Mackinac men, while silk handkerchiefs ($1.50) caught the fancy of a further four men. Other popular items were Bosseron knives ($5.00) and blue baize (felt-like cloth) at $2.00 per yard. Whether these purchases were for personal use or trade with Crows, Shoshones, or Flatheads is uncertain.[84]

BEYOND THE ASTORIAN OVERLAND EXPEDITION

Members of the Hunt overland expedition straggled into Fort Astoria in the early months of 1812. An initial group of eleven men, including John Reed, arrived at Fort Astoria on January 18, 1812. Post manager Duncan McDougall noted in his diary that day:

> About 5 P.M. We were agreeably surprized by the arrival of Messrs. Donald McKenzie, Robert McLellan & John Reed (clerk), with 8 hands, viz: William Cannon, Joseph L'Andrie, Andrez Dufresne, Etienne Leucier, Michel Samson, Andrez Valle, Prisque Felax, Guillaume Le Roux, dit Cardinal, in two Canoes,

they having left Messrs Hunt & Crooks with 36 men on 2nd November last, on this side of the R Mountains, among the Snake nation. [They separated from the party to search for horses, but being unable to bring them any assistance they continued on their way here.] They encountered considerable hardships.[85]

And again when a second, larger group made it on February 15, McDougall carefully wrote:

About 2 pm we were agreeably surprised by the arrival of Mr Hunt with 30 men, a Woman & 2 children in 6 canoes. They met with Mr Crooks, but were obliged to leave him & 5 men with the Snake Nation, they being too weak to proceed. Mr Hunt thinks they will winter thereabout.[86]

The eighteen-month trek across the continent was now over for the Montreal and Michilimackinac voyageurs. And yet differences in behavior persisted between the two groups. Of the nine Montreal voyageurs who made it to Astoria in 1812, six are known to have left on the 1814 return trip to Montreal. A seventh, Louis Laliberté, also returned to Montreal at some point after wintering at the Flathead post in 1813–1814. Bazil Brousseau and André Dufresne headed home with the specific intent to sue the PFC for unpaid wages. Most of the nine Montreal men disappeared from fur-trading documents after the end of the expedition. Some, like Jean Baptiste Delorme and Jean Baptiste Turcotte, perished in the interior. Another, Louis Laliberté, went back and forth between Montreal and the Indian country as a professional voyageur. The 1821 merger found him listed as working at Fort des Prairies for 1,000 livres per annum. And others, like Charles Boucher, simply vanished without a trace from the accounts and ledgers. None of the group apparently chose to remain for any length of time in the Columbia district. Perhaps Turcotte, whose spending habits so resembled those of the Mackinac men, decided to remain in the far Northwest, but he died of scrofula (tuberculosis) in 1813. Seemingly only one of the Montreal men, Jean Baptiste Delorme, engaged in another westward fur-trading brigade, returning west of the divide by 1819, when he died near Fort Nez Percés.[87]

The fourteen men hired in Michilimackinac continued to distance themselves from the St. Lawrence valley. Five chose to remain in the Far West until at least the 1821 NWC and HBC merger. Joseph Gervais and Étienne Lussier settled and farmed in the Willamette valley or the French Prairie. The other three, Guillaume Cardinal, François Martial, and Jean Baptiste Ouvre, remained in the Columbia district until at least 1821 (and perhaps beyond) as fur trade employees or freeman trappers. A sixth man, Joseph St-Amant, left on the Fort William express on May 1, 1814, but was back with the Snake River brigades by 1822, when he deserted the HBC to work for Missouri traders. Two men drowned prior to arriving at Astoria, and a third, François Landry, died after falling from a horse in 1814. The remaining five voyageurs disappeared from the records after 1814. They may have returned east, but none appear to have signed new fur trade contracts out of Montreal or worked for the larger trading concerns.[88] It is possible that they returned to their old Michilimackinac home base and remained active in the Southwest trade. Six of the eleven Mackinac men who survived past 1814 remained or returned west of the Continental Divide. Their commitment to making a life for themselves in the interior continued well after their arrival at Astoria in 1812, just as the desire to return to Montreal, at least for a time, prevailed among the Montreal hired men.[89]

By 1810, Michilimackinac and the Great Lakes basin were very much part of the "old Northwest." At the same time, the area was well within Montreal's sphere of influence and easily reached by that city's seasonal summer voyageurs. Yet differences in behavior and lifestyle emerged and persisted between the men based in Montreal and those who furloughed in Mackinac. The differences in socioeconomic behavior between the two groups become readily apparent through an analysis of the account books. But the reasons behind the differences remain elusive. It appears that most of the men hired in Montreal wanted to work for a specific period of time—in this case, five years—for the most money possible. They were *habitants*, engaging in fur trade employment to help fund agrarian pursuits in their home parishes or artisanal work in Montreal. Although they occasionally indulged in purchases for trade or personal use, they were, by and large, parsimonious. These men were attempting to save money because, at the end of the journey, they wanted to go home.

At first glance, the Mackinac men were typical short-haul voyageurs who had signed their first contracts in Montreal only a handful of years prior to signing on with the 1810 PFC expedition. The pivotal decision for the Mackinac men was in opting to renew their contracts in front of the island notary Samuel Abbot rather than return to Montreal. Their pre-1810 employment destinations were posts in the Great Lakes basin and upper Missouri or Mississippi watersheds, and usually involved one wintering season. However, there was an obvious mental and physical break with Montreal and the St. Lawrence valley settlements. Their *pied à terre* was now Mackinac. This is where they relaxed, spent their money, and renewed their contracts in the fur trade in-between voyages to nearby wintering sites.

While they may not have worn the feather of the legendary *hivernants* of the far Northwest and the fabled Athabasca men, they behaved like them. They were not trying to save money for a triumphant return to their home villages to purchase land, marry, and settle as *habitants* near family and church. They had become professional wage laborers committed to a career in the fur trade, with no apparent desire to return to the agrarian life in the Montreal–to–Trois-Rivières corridor. Although they may have returned for visits to Montreal and nearby family and villages, the basis of their existence was the Pays d'en Haut.

Yet these Mackinac men were not people who had, by and large, signed on with the larger fur-trading concerns, such as the North West or XY Companies, with destinations northwest of Fort William. These men came from families with deep links to the Great Lakes and Southwest trade—what historians have called the "French River World."[90] When circumstances or preferences made them leave their St. Lawrence homes, they hired themselves out to smaller outfits, such as the Michilimackinac Company or individual traders in the Great Lakes basin or Illinois Country. None appear to have signed up with large trading concerns to winter in the far Northwest. Although they were distancing themselves from their home parishes, they were also staying within a generations-old tradition of making a life in the Southwest fur trade network. This was an extended French world where kin and parish neighbors could be found with relative ease along with familiar and often friendly Great Lakes aboriginal nations.

Yet one should not dismiss these Mackinac men as simply spendthrift laborers living day by day, squandering their wages without thought to the future. That is how the amused chroniclers described these men's behavior among the Mahas, Arikaras, and other western tribes. While the attraction of sexual and other favors by native women is not to be discounted, and was likely a significant contributing factor to the Mackinac voyageurs' behaviors, other factors were at play. The distinct possibility of acquiring syphilis did not deter the need for immediate physical gratification nor did it prevent the creation of exchange networks, reciprocal ties, or fictive kinship networks. These were voyageurs who had, by and large, turned their backs on the St. Lawrence valley and made a bold move out of the safe and familiar Great Lakes fur trade world to travel into the Far West. The real curiosity about these Mackinac men was their decision to sign five-year contracts, taking them out to the very edge of the known French River World. Perhaps these men were simply part of an expected percentage of bolder and more ambitious Mackinac men who, after a few years' apprenticeship in the Great Lakes fur trade world, ventured farther inland via the Mississippi and the

Missouri. These men were turning their backs not only on Montreal but also on Mackinac. They realized a need to (re-)create support networks in regions farther west. They may have harbored ambitions to become *hommes libres* or petty traders at the end of their PFC contract, thus reducing their dependency on the big fur-trading concerns that had financed their westward move. If so, heading west into lands not directly under the control of the large companies made sense. It also made sense for them to join endeavors to establish contacts and relations with interior tribes. This would explain their desire to spend money prior to their departure from Mackinac and to be impressively dressed and bedecked with plumes and silk handkerchiefs, so as to impress the peoples whom they would encounter on the journey. It would also explain their large purchases in St. Louis and from the PFC stores during visits to tribal settlements. Because they were not trading for furs, the company officials tolerated the exchanges. The relatively inexperienced traders heading the expedition may not have discerned the longer-term ambitions of these men to become free traders. The traders would have only seen the decreasing financial obligations at the end of the voyageurs' contracts and the reinforcement of ethnic stereotypes with each apparently frivolous purchase.

As noted earlier, the voyageurs' socioeconomic behavior on this harrowing westward trip may have been more calculated than immediate sexual gratification, vanity, or impressing fellow travelers and encountered peoples. In his memoirs, HBC postman and trader Isaac Cowie described a métis voyageur and petty trader called Olivier Flammand as a "walking advertisement." Flammand, however, explained to the novice Cowie that he dressed flamboyantly and was overtly generous not only to win the smiles of the fair sex but also to put to shame the American traders in their shoddy clothes. Cowie went on to note:

> the end had amply justified the means, for these hunters, envious of him and desirous to eclipse him, one after another began to give up furs and robes which they had previously refused to trade with him, for fine blue cloth capotes with brass buttons, fine cloth trousers, broad l'Assomption belts, fine colored flannel shirts, black silk neckerchiefs, and foxtail plumes, anointments of pomatum and scented hair oil, besides silver finger rings and gilt earrings.[91]

Simply put, beyond immediate gratification, these men were establishing not only contacts but a presence. They were branding themselves. An aspiring free trader had to cultivate links among the tribes, to both dress and act the part of a successful free trader. These men, with their deep roots in the fur trade world, would have known that becoming a voyageur could be the first step to becoming a free trader.

CONCLUSION

The differences in overall behavior between these two groups of men allows us to ascertain that the decision to commit to the life of a voyageur was made early in a man's career. The Mackinac men, by and large, remained in the interior after their first contract out of Montreal. Whatever motives they had for signing up also led them to stay in the interior. This study points to a need to examine the social and economic backgrounds of those who engaged in the fur trade and never returned to the places of their birth. While many have studied the social and economic background and subsequent behavior of those voyageurs who intended to return to their home parishes to invest in agriculture, no detailed research has yet been conducted on those who never returned.[92] Glamour, glory, and adventure, along with innate restlessness, may have spurred the departure for some nascent voyageurs, but other "push" factors may provide more tangible explanations.

The first decades of the nineteenth century saw a profound restructuring of the St. Lawrence valley agrarian economy.[93] Although labeling this process an "agrarian crisis" has been disputed by some researchers, there is no avoiding the fact that the changes benefited some, but not all.[94] All researchers agree that a growing landless rural proletariat was emerging in the seigniorial lands of Lower Canada.[95] Background research on these Mackinac men indicates that they were either younger sons with dim prospects of inheriting land or the children of landless parents. For people without the possibility of apprenticeship in an artisanal trade, becoming a voyageur might have seemed an obvious choice. They would have known that becoming a voyageur could be the first step to becoming a free trader. It should not be forgotten that these men hailed from old voyageur villages. They and their families were familiar with the Southwest French River World. Family and business links to settlements such as Kaskaskia, Cahokia, and Ste. Geneviève on the banks of the Mississippi were generations-old. They were following well-paddled routes into the South and West, and by signing up with the PFC overland expedition to the West, they were testing the edges of the French River World, a vast space where they knew what the possibilities were and how the game was played.

NOTES

1. Bryan D. Murphy, "The Size of the Labour Force in the Montreal Fur Trade, 1675–1790: A Critical Evaluation" (M.A. thesis, University of Ottawa, 1986).
2. Carolyn Podruchny, *Making the Voyageur World: Travelers and Traders in the North American Fur Trade* (Toronto: University of Toronto Press, 2006), 5.
3. To these must be added about 2,000 Iroquois and other native voyageurs from the region of Montreal and, certainly after 1821, a growing in situ métis population in the interior.
4. Podruchny, *Making the Voyageur World*; Tanis C. Thorne, *The Many Hands of My Relations: French and Indians on the Lower Missouri* (Columbia: University of Missouri Press, 1996); Heather Devine, *The People Who Own Themselves: Aboriginal Ethnogenesis in a Canadian Family 1660–1900* (Calgary: University of Calgary Press, 2004).
5. The American Fur Company was chartered by John Jacob Astor (1763–1848) in 1808 to compete with the great fur-trading companies in Canada—the NWC and the HBC. Astor's most ambitious venture—to control the Columbia River valley fur trade via the establishment of a post at Astoria, Oregon, at the mouth of the Columbia River—was made under a subsidiary, the PFC. His early operations around the Great Lakes were under another subsidiary, the South West Company, in which Canadian merchants played a part. The War of 1812 destroyed both subsidiaries. The American Fur Company reorganized and resumed operations by 1817 and remained the most dominant fur company on American soil until the late 1830s.
6. Astor sent two expeditions to establish Fort Astoria. The first was a sea expedition using the ship *Tonquin*. The *Tonquin* left New York on September 8, 1810, and arrived at the Columbia River on April 12, 1811, establishing the first American-owned outpost on the Pacific Coast. The second expedition, the focus of this essay, was an overland expedition, often called the Astor Expedition or the Hunt Party (named for Wilson Price Hunt, who led it). The party ascended the Missouri River by boat as far as the Arikara villages near present-day Mobridge, South Dakota, and then went west overland on horseback and on foot.
7. John Reed 1810–1812 Journal, 2 vols., Harvard Business School, Baker Library, John Jacob Astor Collection.
8. Henry Marie Brackenridge, *Views of Louisiana Together with a Journal of a Voyage Up the Missouri River, in 1811* (Pittsburgh: 1814; repr., Ann Arbor, Mich.: University Microfilms, 1966); John Bradbury, *Travels in the Interior of America in the Years 1809, 1810 and 1811* (Liverpool: 1817; repr., Ann

Arbor, Mich.: University Microfilms, 1966); Wilson Price Hunt, "Voyage de M. Hunt et de ses compagnons de Saint-Louis à l'embouchure de la Columbia par une nouvelle Route à travers les Rocky-Mountains," *Nouvelles annales des voyages, de la géographie et de l'histoire* 10 (1821): 31–88; Wilson Price Hunt, "Journey of Mr. Hunt and His Companions from Saint Louis to the Mouth of the Columbia by a New Route across the Rocky Mountains," in *The Discovery of the Oregon Trail: Robert Stuart's Narratives and Additions*, ed. Philip Ashton Rollins (New York: Charles Scribner's Sons, 1935); Henry Marie Brackenridge, "Journal of a Voyage up the River Missouri; Performed in Eighteen Hundred and Eleven," in *Early Western Travels 1748–1846*, ed. Reuben Gold Thwaites (Cleveland: Arthur H. Clark, 1904), 6:19–166.

9. Jeannette E. Graustein, "Nuttall's Travels into the Old Northwest: An Unpublished 1810 Diary," *Chronica Botanica* 14 (1951): 3–88; Jeannette E. Graustein, *Thomas Nuttall Naturalist: Explorations in America 1808–1841* (Cambridge, Mass.: Harvard University Press, 1967).

10. Alexander Ross, *Adventures of the First Settlers on the Oregon or Columbia River* (London: 1849; repr., Lincoln: University of Nebraska Press, 1986); Gabriel Franchère, *Journal of a Voyage on the North West Coast of North America during the Years 1811, 1812, 1813, and 1814*, trans. Wessie Tipping Lamb, ed. W. Kaye Lamb (Toronto: Champlain Society, 1969).

11. Washington Irving, *Astoria: Or, Anecdotes of an Enterprise beyond the Rocky Mountains, 1836*, ed. Edgeley W. Todd (Norman: University of Oklahoma, 1964).

12. Bertrand Desjardins, Jacques Légaré, and Hubert Charbonneau, "Projet de recherche en démographie historique/The Research Program in Historical Demography," http://www.genealogy.umontreal.ca/en/acces.htm; Nicole St-Onge, "Voyageur Contracts Database Project" (University of Ottawa and Société historique de Saint-Boniface), http://shsb.mb.ca/en/Voyageurs_database.

13. Early departures were necessary for two reasons. The canoes bound for distant inland posts had to have sufficient time to reach them before the winter freeze of navigable waterways. Also, the early departure dates were to ensure that returning season brigades would be back in time to ship the furs from Montreal and Quebec City before those seaports became ice bound.

14. John Beek, Louis Chaboillez, Jonathan Grey, and Henri Griffin were four important notaries in Montreal who specialized in working for the fur trade companies, especially concerning the signing of contracts at the end of the eighteenth and beginning of the nineteenth centuries.

15. A total of thirty-nine contracts were located in Beek's papers. It is suspected that the contracts for the balance of the men were signed in front of a rural

notary and have yet to be located. Archives nationales du Québec, Centre de Montréal (ANQ-M), John Gerbrand Beek, 1781–1822, cote CN601, S29.

16. Podruchny, *Making the Voyageur World*.

17. The standard equipment offered to these men was one three-point blanket, a portage collar, a pair of shoes, six lengths (*aunes*) of cotton cloth, and three carrots of tobacco.

18. See, for example, the contract of André Dufresne of Montreal, signed in front of notary John Beek on May 16, 1810, as a middleman for the PFC for a period of five years. ANQ-M, John Gerbrand Beek, 1781–1822, cote CN601, S29.

19. Jacqueline Peterson notes that "Michilimackinac ranked as the most important of all the advance posts of Canada. The name later shortened to Mackinac, which the French used to designate the shore on both sides of the straits between Lakes Michigan and Huron as well as the island itself." Jacqueline Peterson, "Many Roads to Red River: Metis Genesis in the Great Lakes Region, 1680–1815," in *The New Peoples: Being and Becoming Métis in North America*, ed. Jennifer S. H. Brown and Jacqueline Peterson (Winnipeg: University of Manitoba Press, 1985), 45.

20. Robert Englebert, "Diverging Identities and Converging Interests: Corporate Competition, Desertion, and Voyageur Agency, 1815–1818," *Manitoba History* 55 (2007): 18–24. Englebert documents a period of high desertion in fur trade personnel from 1815 to 1818, when the HBC and rival NWC were in a state of near-open warfare trying to secure the peltry trade in the lucrative Athabasca district. Voyageurs may have perceived the 1810 PFC hiring efforts as another form of competition by a new fur interest against older, more established concerns. They suspected, rightly, that the PFC would not be in a strong enough position that year to track down and prosecute miscreants. As in the later period studied by Englebert, deserters could sign a second contract with another company, seemingly without any consequence.

21. High desertion rates appear to have been chronic problems for companies trying to break into the Montreal fur trade labor market. Fur trade personnel realized that in times of intense competition, prosecution of deserters was a difficult undertaking for employees with few or no local ties. The HBC later faced a similar problem from 1815 to 1818 when it attempted to recruit French Canadians in Montreal to defy the NWC in the interior. The American Fur Company faced a 40 percent rate of desertion on the first expedition out of Montreal in 1817. Both companies were defying the NWC on its home base and incurring its wrath. Voyageurs knew this and took advantage, playing one against the other. See Englebert, "Diverging Identities and Converging Interests"; David Lavender, *The Fist in the Wilderness* (New York: Doubleday, 1964), 259.

22. Jean-Baptiste Perrault, *Jean-Baptiste Perrault, marchand voyageur parti de Montréal le 28e de Mai 1783* (Montreal: Boréal Express, 1978).

23. Samuel Abbott, *Michigan Voyageurs: From the Notary Book of Samuel Abbott, Mackinac Island 1807–1817*, ed. Donna Valley Russell (Detroit: Detroit Society for Genealogical Research, 1982), 8.

24. Boucher signed a three-year contract with McTavish Frobisher & Co. on February 2, 1804, in front of notary Louis Chaboillez, to go to Fort Kaministiquia and the Northwest. He was paid 700 livres per year. ANQ-M, Louis Chaboillez, 1787–1813, cote CN601, S74.

25. The statements above are based on an analysis of the 32,000 voyageur contracts inventoried in St-Onge, *Tracing the Voyageurs.*

26. John Reed 1810–1812 Journal, 1:10.

27. Ross, *Adventures of the First Settlers*, 176.

28. Ibid., 177.

29. Podruchny, *Making the Voyageur World.*

30. David Lavender's biography of Ramsay Crooks offers a more nuanced explanation for the hired hands' seeming reluctance than the facile and somewhat derogatory explanations advanced by Ross or Irving: "Voyageurs could not be gathered at will however. The only ones who were free were those who had just completed a long tour of duty in the wilderness. They had no intentions of going back to the *pays sauvages,* without the regale they considered an almost inalienable right. . . . Irving adds that the voyageurs were reluctant to face the unknown dangers of the distant land, a timidity characteristic enough of the French Canadians. But then he says that Hunt overcame the reluctance by giving out colored feathers which anyone who signed could wear in his hat as a childish symbol of his hardiness. Perhaps, but dates are also suggestive. The party left the island on August 12. This was the normal time for Missouri River boats to start out." Lavender, *Fist in the Wilderness,* 130–133.

31. John Reed 1810–1812 Journal, 1:14–41.

32. Jean Baptiste Breaux (Bro) seemingly deserted the expedition prior to its departure from Michilimackinac.

33. See, for example, entries for Étienne Lussier (Michilimackinac Company, July 6, 1808, St. Joseph Island; and J Bte Caron and Co., June 25, 1807, Wisconsin River); François Martial (Robert Dickson, June 16, 1807, Mississippi River); and Jean Baptiste Provost (Joseph Rolette, July 21, 1810, Mississippi River), in Abbott, *Michigan Voyageurs.*

34. In the Baker Library's Astor Papers collection, there exists a document titled "Astoria Accounts 1811–1813." It is a "Statement showing the number of clerks, men in the employ of the Pacific fur Co., when free, the amount of their wages

annually and the recapitulation of the total amount of their wages at the expiration of their contracts." Surviving contracts for Montreal men were examined for consistency regarding date of hiring, duration of contract, and salaries negotiated. The biggest worry was that either party along the way would renegotiate salaries or contract length. This, however, was not the case. For example, in the 1813 Astoria document, Antoine Papin of Montreal was listed as having a five-year contract that paid him $166.66 per year and expired on June 15, 1815. The original Montreal contract signed in front of notary John Beek had him signing up on June 16, 1810, for a five-year stint at 1,000 Lower Canadian livres per year (equivalent to $166.66). This information is consistent for the eleven Montreal voyageurs whose names appear on both documents. It can therefore be safely assumed that the information found on the 1813 document for the Mackinac voyageurs who had not deserted or died before reaching Astoria is consistent with the terms negotiated for these men in 1810. Astoria Accounts 1811–1813, Harvard Business School, Baker Library, John Jacob Astor Collection.

35. James P. Ronda repeats the earlier writers' statement that Hunt reduced the length of the contracts from five to three years, and that Landry was the first to sign up under the new regime. This does not appear correct, given the consulted archives. James P. Ronda, *Astoria and Empire* (Lincoln: University of Nebraska Press, 1990), 119–120.

36. On February 2, 1808, Joseph Landry dit Penotte and François Landry dit Penotte, both residents of Maskinongé, signed identical one-year contracts with the Michilimackinac Company to winter in the dependencies of St. Joseph Island for 400 livres. The contracts were written up by notary Louis Chaboillez and the merchant representative in Montreal for the Mackinac Company, Toussaint Pothier. Joseph and François were the sons of Joseph Landry, an Acadian from Port Royal who first resided in Riviere-du-Loup-en-Haut (Louiseville), where he married Marie Antoinette Lacharite. Their first children, including Joseph, were born in Riviere-du-Loup-en-Haut, but the family eventually settled in Maskinongé. They had eleven known children, of whom nine lived past childhood. Joseph and François were among the older children. ANQ-M, Louis Chaboillez, 1787–1813, cote CN601, S74.

37. Astoria Accounts 1811–1813, Harvard Business School, Baker Library, John Jacob Astor Collection.

38. This is conjecture given that the first entry for Ramsay Crooks is dated August 10, 1810, when his account was debited for the sum of $1.00. John Reed 1810–1812 Journal, 1:39.

39. Joseph Perrault signed a contract with Robert Dickson and Co. on July 31, 1807, to work on the Missouri. Abbott, *Michigan Voyageurs*, 15.

40. John Reed 1810–1812 Journal, 1:14–41.

41. Astoria Accounts 1811–1813, Harvard Business School, Baker Library, John Jacob Astor Collection.

42. One probable case is Jean Baptiste Breaux (Bro), who was hired before August 1, 1810, at Mackinac. Debits to his account totaled $122.43 between August 1 and 9, mostly on cash advances but also for feathers and a rifle. No other entries for him appear except for one on November 18, 1810, in Nodaway, where a further $115.75 was debited for purchases made "some time ago." He then disappeared from all expedition documents, and there was no entry in the ledger books, suggesting that his contract was sold or transferred to another concern.

43. One method of packing trading tobacco in the eighteenth and nineteenth centuries was to make leaves into a compact package wrapped in linen and wound with cord to make a "carrot" weighing about one pound (400 grams).

44. John Reed 1810–1812 Journal, 1:13.

45. Ibid., 1:41.

46. The Reed accounts note that more canoes were purchased or exchanged for on July 31, 1810, at Michilimackinac. This entry and the other expedition supplies purchased during the Mackinac stopover were carefully itemized by Reed during the month of December in their wintering camp at Nodaway. Ibid., 1:107.

47. "Company store" is used in this essay to refer to the goods, merchandise, and trade items the expedition brought with it into the interior. Voyageurs and other employees could purchase these goods on account. They were usually sold to the men at a rate roughly four times what they had cost the company. For example, vermilion purchased in Montreal at $0.97 a pound was resold to the men for $4.00 a pound.

48. John Reed 1810–1812 Journal, 1:41–44.

49. Ibid., 1:45–74, 90–169.

50. Ibid., 1:45–74.

51. Ibid., 1:44.

52. Ibid., 1:1–74.

53. Ibid., 1:101, 102, 105.

54. Ibid., 1:75–77.

55. Ronda, *Astoria and Empire*, 135.

56. One of the Mackinac men, Joseph Perrault, died of unknown causes at the wintering camp in December 1810.

57. Swanskin was any of several flannel or cotton fabrics with a soft nap.

58. Hunt, "Journey of Mr. Hunt," 298.

59. ANQ-M, Louis Chaboillez, 1787–1813, cote CN601, S74.

60. Abbott, *Michigan Voyageurs*, 8, 16.

61. Astoria Accounts 1811–1813, Harvard Business School, Baker Library, John Jacob Astor Collection.

62. John Reed 1810–1812 Journal, 1:31.

63. Ibid., 1:101.

64. Scalpers were single-edged knives with an eight-inch-long blade and a wooden handle. They were ubiquitous in the fur trade.

65. Ibid., 1:90–169. Some indications of what was being purchased from the native population can be gleaned from the expedition journals. Bradbury noted that when he arrived at Fort Osage from St. Louis with Hunt and some men hired over the winter, they met up with Crooks, who had come down from the wintering camp with ten men. Bradbury wrote in his journal entry of April 8, 1811, "He [Dr. Murray of Fort Osage] walked with me down to the boats, where we found a number of squaws assembled, as Dr Murray assured me, for the same purpose of females of a certain class in the Maritime towns of Europe, crowd around vessels lately arrived from a long journey, and it must be admitted with the same success." Bradbury, *Travels in the Interior of America*, 27.

66. For example, in early July Alexander McKay purchased twenty pounds of vermilion in Montreal for $19.40, or $.97 a pound. Voyageurs purchasing this popular trade item over the course of the inland expedition were charged up to $4.00 a pound at the company store. John Reed 1810–1812 Journal, 1:9.

67. Ronda, *Astoria and Empire*, 136.

68. Personal communications with Carolyn Podruchny, Robert Englebert, and Heather Devine.

69. Bradbury, *Travels in the Interior of America*, 47. John Bradbury (1768–1823) was a Scottish botanist noted for his travels in the U.S. Midwest and West in the early nineteenth century and his eyewitness account of the December 1811 New Madrid earthquake. In 1811, he and naturalist Thomas Nuttall joined the overland expedition to Fort Astoria for a portion of its travels.

70. John Reed 1810–1812 Journal, 2:20–27.

71. Bradbury, *Travels in the Interior of America*, 65.

72. John Reed 1810–1812 Journal, 2:35–114.

73. Ibid.

74. These referred to trade mirrors.

75. Ronda, *Astoria and Empire*, 158.

76. Bradbury, *Travels in the Interior of America*, 124.

77. Brackenridge, *Views of Louisiana Together*, 257–258.

78. John Reed 1810–1812 Journal, 1:8.

79. These immune system-boosting decoctions alleviated symptoms, but did not cure. Bradbury, *Travels in the Interior of America*, 170.

80. Alice B. Kehoe, "The Function of Ceremonial Sexual Intercourse among Northern Plains Indians," *Plains Anthropologist* 15, no. 48 (May 1970): 99–103.

81. Susan Sleeper-Smith, *Indian Women and French Men: Rethinking Cultural Encounter in the Western Great Lakes* (Amherst: University of Massachusetts Press, 2001).

82. Hunt, "Journey of Mr. Hunt," 281.

83. John Reed 1810–1812 Journal, 2:114–150.

84. Ibid.; Hunt, "Journey of Mr. Hunt," *passim*.

85. Duncan McDougall and Robert F. Jones, eds., *Annals of Astoria: The Headquarters Log of the Pacific Fur Company on the Columbia River, 1811–1813* (New York: Fordham University Press, 1999), 68.

86. Ibid., 72. Crooks and a hired man, John Day, arrived on May 12, 1812.

87. Bruce McIntyre Watson, *Lives Lived West of the Divide: A Biographical Dictionary of Fur Traders Working West of the Rockies 1793–1858* (Kelowna, B.C.: Centre for Social, Spatial, and Economic Justice; University of British Columbia-Okanagan, 2009).

88. St-Onge, *Tracing the Voyageurs.*

89. Watson, *Lives Lived West of the Divide.*

90. Robert Englebert, "Merchant Representatives and the French River World, 1763–1803," *Michigan Historical Review* 34 (Spring 2008): 63–82.

91. Isaac Cowie, *A Company of Adventurers: A Narrative of Seven Years in the Service of the Hudson's Bay Company during 1867–1874, on the Great Buffalo Plains, with Historical and Biographical Notes and Comments* (Toronto: W. Briggs, 1913), 352.

92. Thomas Wien, "Familles paysannes et marché de l'engagement pour le commerce des fourrures au Canada au XVIIIᵉ siècle," in *Famille et marché XVIe–XXe siècles*, ed. Christian Dessureault, John A. Dickinson, and Joseph Goy (Sillery, Q.C.: Éditions du Septentrion, 2003), 167–180.

93. Fernand Ouellet, *Le Bas Canada 1791–1849: changements structuraux et crise* (Ottawa: Éditions de l'Université d'Ottawa, 1980).

94. Jean Pierre Wallot and Gilles Paquet, *Un Québec moderne, 1760–1840: essai d'histoire économique et sociale* (Montreal: Hurtubise, 2007).

95. Jean Lafleur, Gilles Paquet, and Jean-Pierre Wallot, "Le coût du sol dans la région de l'Assomption, 1792–1825: enrichissement, enchérissement et liens au marché," in Dessureault, Dickinson, and Goy, *Famille et marché XVIe–XXe siècles*, 95–114.

Contributors

Arnaud Balvay is an independent scholar. He received his PhD in history from Université Paris 1—Pantéon-Sorbonne and Université Laval in 2004. He published *La Révolte des Natchez* (2008) and *L'épée et la plume: Amérindiens et soldats des troupes de la Marine en Louisiane et au Pays d'en Haut, 1683–1763* (2006). His current research project focuses on the history of eighteenth-century France and, more specifically, the spies of Louis XV.

Robert Englebert is an assistant professor of history at the University of Saskatchewan, Canada. He received his PhD in history from the University of Ottawa in 2010. He has published on the fur trade and the Illinois Country, including "Diverging Identities and Converging Interests: Corporate Competition, Desertion, and Voyageur Agency, 1815–1818," *Manitoba History* (2007); "Merchant Representatives and the French River World in North America, 1763–1803," *Michigan Historical Review* (2008). His current research project focuses on French transcolonial and early transnational linkages from Quebec City to New Orleans from the 1730s to 1805.

Gilles Havard is a researcher at the Centre national de la recherche scientifique (CNRS) and a member of the Centre d'études nord-américaines (CENA) at L'École des hautes études en sciences sociales in Paris. He received his PhD from Université Paris-Diderot—Paris 7. He has published several books, including *Empire et métissages: Indiens et Français dans le Pays d'en Haut, 1660–1715* (2003) and *The Great Peace of Montreal: French-Native Diplomacy in the Seventeenth Century,* trans. Phyllis Aronoff and Howard Scott (2001). He is also the coauthor of *Histoire de l'Amérique française,* 3rd ed. (2008). His upcoming book examines the history of the early French fur traders in the Great Lakes region and is entitled *Histoire des coureurs de bois.*

Kathryn Magee Labelle received her PhD in history at The Ohio State University in 2011. She held a Social Sciences and Humanities Research Council of Canada Postdoctoral Fellowship at York University (2011–2012) and is currently an assistant professor at the History Department, University of Saskatchewan, Canada.

Her publications include "'They Are the Life of the Nation': Women and War in Nadouek Society," *Canadian Journal of Native Studies* (2008); "History Repeats Itself: Huron Childrearing Attitudes, Eurocentricity, and the Importance of Indigenous Worldview," *Canadian Journal for Native Education* (2008); and "They Spoke Only in Sighs: The Loss of Leaders and Life in Wendake, 1632–1640," *Journal of Historical Biography* (2010). Her manuscript "Dispersed, But Not Destroyed: A History of the Seventeenth-Century Wendat Diaspora" is currently under review with the University of British Columbia Press. Her academic areas of research include Native North America, indigenous systems of power and leadership, gender relations, and the Wendat diaspora.

Robert Michael Morrissey is an assistant professor of history at the University of Illinois in Urbana-Champaign. He received his PhD from Yale University in 2006. His book *Empires, Identities and Communities in Illinois Country, 1673–1785* will be published by the University of Pennsylvania Press. He has written several articles and book chapters, including "I Speak It Well: Language, Communication, and the End of a Missionary Middle Ground in Illinois Country, 1673–1712," *Early American Studies: An Interdisciplinary Journal* (2011).

Christopher M. Parsons is a Barra Postdoctoral Fellow at the McNeil Center for Early American Studies, University of Pennsylvania. He received his PhD from the University of Toronto in 2011. He has published work on the circulation of medical knowledge in Jesuit missions in New France, and has a forthcoming article, "Ecosystems under Sail: Specimen Transport in the Eighteenth-Century French and British Atlantics," in *Early American Studies: An Interdisciplinary Journal*. His interests include connecting histories of science and the environment in colonial North America and the Atlantic world, as well as the role of indigenous cultures and knowledge in the history of French enlightenment science.

John Reda is an assistant professor of history at Illinois State University. He received his PhD from the University of Illinois at Chicago in 2009. He is currently in the process of completing a book, *From Furs to Farms: Land, Race, and Sovereignty in the Mississippi Valley, 1762–1825*, for Northern Illinois University Press's Early American Places series. His research interests include colonial, early national American history, and the French in North America.

Nicole St-Onge is a full professor of history at the University of Ottawa. She received her PhD from the University of Manitoba in 1990. She has published numerous articles, including "'Trade, Travel and Tradition: St. Lawrence Valley Engagés to the American Fur Company, 1818–1840," *Michigan Historical Review*

(2008), and "Plain Métis: Contours of an Identity," *Australasian Canadian Studies* (2009). She is also the author of *Saint-Laurent, Manitoba: Evolving Métis Identities, 1850–1914* (2004), and is a contributing editor for the forthcoming collection, *Contours of Métis Landscapes: Family, Mobility and History in Northwestern North America* (University of Oklahoma Press). Her research interests include fur trade and métis history, as well as microhistory.

Guillaume Teasdale teaches in the Department of History at the University of Windsor, Ontario. He received his PhD from Toronto's York University in 2010. In 2011–2012, he held a Social Sciences and Humanities Research Council of Canada Post-Doctoral Fellowship in the Centre for Research on French Canadian Culture at the University of Ottawa, Ontario. His publications include "Old Friends and New Foes: French Settlers and Indians in the Detroit River Border Region," *Michigan Historical Review* (2012) and "Les débuts de l'Église catholique américaine et le monde atlantique français: le cas de l'ancienne colonie française de Détroit," *Histoire & Missions chrétiennes* (2011). He is currently working on his first book manuscript, which focuses on the French of the Detroit River region in the 1730s–1810s. His research projects focus on the history of the colonial Great Lakes region, with an emphasis on French-Indian relations.

Richard Weyhing is an assistant professor of early American history at the State University of New York, Oswego. He received his PhD from the University of Chicago in 2012. His research interests span the Atlantic and cover various aspects of the economic, political, and cultural histories of European empires in the Americas during the early modern period.